SPEND YOUR WAY TO WEALTH

Kathleen L. Cotton, CFP

BOSTON · B · BOOKS

While a great deal of care has been taken to provide accurate information, the ideas, suggestions, general principals and conclusions presented in this book are subject to local, state, and federal laws and regulations, court cases and any revisions of same. This publication is sold with the understanding that the publisher and the author are not engaged in rendering legal, accounting, or other professional services. The reader is thus urged to consult legal or financial counsel regarding any points of law. For information on the author's other publications, please write Wealth Books, 300 Lenora, #B258, Seattle, WA 98121.

Published by: Boston Books
Cover Design: Boston Books
Interior Design: Boston Books
Executive Editor: Beth Tibbetts
Typesetting: Laser Services

Printed in the United States of America

Publisher's Cataloging in Publication Data
(prepared by Quality Books, Inc.)

Cotton, Kathleen L.
Spend your way to wealth: a complete new approach to retirement and investment planning that really works/ Kathleen Laura Cotton

p. cm.
Includes bibliographical references and titles
ISBN 0-9616683-8-5
1. Finance, Personal. 2. Retirement — Planning. 3. Investment.
I. Title
HG179.C6 1992 332.024 LC 91-077335

CREDITS AND ACCOLADES

Acknowledgment pages are seldom read with great enthusiasm, yet without the individuals cited on pages such as these, good books would not be. Readers, editors, and others play important parts in helping shape ideas into cohesive thoughts, sentences into paragraphs, paragraphs into chapters, and chapters into books.

This book has been no exception.

My editor, Beth Tibbetts, has kept me on the right track with her swift deletions of words I once thought were brilliant, and organization and condensation of the remaining material into informative yet still readable chapters.

Thanks are in order to my many technical readers: Tim Pinkney, CFP, Harriet Kane, CFP, Tracy Heffelfinger, CFP, Brenda Hammer, CPA, Rachel Paysse, CFP, Geri Littlewood, CFP, Larry Fowler, CPA, Paul Bishop, Attorney at Law.

And, to my husband, who has given new meaning to the word patient.

Other Books
By Kathleen Cotton

Financial Planning for the Not Yet Wealthy
FinPlan Publishing, 1987

Keys to Controlling Your Financial Destiny:
Financial "Insider" Tips Every Woman Needs to Know
FinPlan Publishing, 1990.

ABOUT THE AUTHOR

Kathleen Cotton, CFP, is a Washington State native, circa 1940s, and currently resides in Mukilteo, Washington with her husband and children. In 1981, she received a B.S. in Business/finance from City University and the CFP certification in 1984. She is a fee-based financial advisor, Registered Investment Advisor, and partner in Cotton & Heffelfinger. Her practice is centered around investment management and retirement planning for those near or entering retirement years with an emphasis on client education.

She is an adjunct faculty member at City University, and has taught financial planning workshops for numerous community colleges in Western Washington; corporate clients, such as GTE, Paccar Financial, Washington Natural Gas, Boeing, Washington Hospital Association, West Seattle and Everett General Hospitals, Seattle Community College faculty, Seattle Steel, Seattle City Council, AARP; and at numerous association conventions.

Kathleen is listed in ***"Who's Who in Finance and Industry," "Who's Who in the West,"*** and ***"The World's Who's Who of Women."*** She has been active in industry leadership, serving as 1987-88 president of the Washington Chapter of the International Association for Financial Planning, and is a member of the International Society of Retirement Planners and the Institute for Certified Financial Planners.

Table of Contents

INTRODUCTION

"I take the view, and always have done, that if you cannot say what you have to say in 20 minutes, you should go away and write a book about it."

Lord Brabazon

Long ago I found I could not say what I wanted in 20 minutes or less, so I wrote a book. As one book can lead to another, my first book, ***Financial Planning for the Not Yet Wealthy*** was followed by ***Keys to Controlling Your Financial Destiny*** and now, ***Spend Your Way to Wealth.***

The material in this book reflects a significant part of my life. Over the past decade, financial planning has been not only my profession, but my avocation. I've seen first hand the havoc that inadequate planning can create and I've tried to find the best ways to help people deal with financial problems.

The idea of personal financial planning has been around for a long time, but it has only been formalized in the last 15-20 years. Your parents or grandparents may not have been able to define their long term financial needs with any clarity. They may have simply coped with the results of their financial habits — reaching whatever destinations life held for them. For many, luck was with them and the results were adequate; for many others, however, the results were less than enviable.

Today, financial opportunities abound and there is no shortage of excellent books on personal finance which can help you take advantage of these opportunities. These books range in format from general to very specific topics. In addition, radio and television talk shows frequently cover financial issues. Popular magazines, such as ***Money*** or ***Changing Times,*** devote entire issues to personal finance. Yet failure to make good financial decisions is still a common malady among the general population. Whether this failure is due to lack of knowledge, lack of time, or apathy — the results are the same: PROCRASTINATION! One of my favorite quips in the past has been and still is true, "Procrastination is the enemy of success and a great friend of the IRS."

IS A FINANCIAL PLAN NECESSARY?

Planning is an essential element of success for many of life's endeavors. Without plans, diagrams, road maps, blueprints, directions, recipes, instructions, guidance, and so forth, successful results cannot be assured. An analogy often used is to compare financial planning to taking a road trip to a desirable vacation spot. Before you embark on this trip, you check your equipment, estimate the time of arrival, and how much the trip will cost as well as the vacation time. There are many ways you can reach this destination. You can take the direct route with a single-minded focus, or you can take side excursions which may delay your arrival but eventually lead to the destination. In either case, you might encounter surprise obstacles or detours which require you to make slight adjustments to your direction and time of arrival. Financial planning works just like that.

Your financial planning destination can be retirement or financial independence, with side trips for education funding or other interim goals, income and asset protection, and financial housekeeping. The process starts with clarifying your value systems and financial goals. The end result will be financial security: knowing you are making the most of your financial resources both today and for the future.

HOW TO USE THIS BOOK

Spend Your Way to Wealth has been developed to be a practical and informative tool to aid readers in gaining control over their finances. The book's concepts and philosophies were developed over years of teaching personal finance to employees of corporations and colleges. The idea of spending your way to wealth is novel. Yet it is possible — and will be easier — for those who possess the motivation to evaluate where they are today and what actions are necessary to make a positive change in their financial life. By fully utilizing each set of worksheets, the reader, whether novice or knowledgeable, will find this book to be a practical guide to managing money and creating wealth.

Many readers will be tempted to skip around, reading the chapters which are of the most interest first. It is better to read the chapters in order. Each chapter covers fundamental concepts which form a growing base for the chapters that follow.

Chapters 1 through 4 build a foundation of information relating to money and its uses: common obstacles are explored and defused in Chapter 2, financial organization is made easy in Chapter 3, and Chapter 4 lays the groundwork for the procedure and process of improving your financial potential.

Setting goals is the starting point for all plans. Chapter 5 provides a framework for clarifying your goals and evaluating your ability to achieve those goals based on a priority system. It is at this point that you start encountering worksheets. Completing the worksheets will help you attain the maximum value from this book.

The next two chapters help you evaluate the here and now. Understanding the elements of your net worth and the importance of periodically updating the net worth statement is the subject of Chapter 6. Worksheets are provided to examine your net worth as well as tips on how to increase it which brings me to Chapter 7. This chapter may be the most valuable in the book for it is here that you learn how to create spending solutions.

Chapter 8 discusses cost-effective wealth protection through the use of appropriate insurances. If you've built or want to build a base of assets, it is critical that you understand and make informed decisions about protection. Some of the smartest spending decisions you can make will involve this area.

In Chapter 9, eight compelling reasons for home ownership are outlined, followed by how to evaluate mortgage qualifications, amortize loans, and evaluate the economics of owning and managing rentals. Be sure to review the eight most common mistakes of real estate investors.

Designing a plan for wealth is less daunting for those who have a solid foundation in both the art and science of portfolio design. Chapter 10, one of the most important chapters, takes the reader from the basic elements of categorizing assets through quantifying a portfolio for optimum risk and return. Investment risks are explained, performance records are compared, and conservative through aggressive postures are evaluated. Also the reader will learn to allocate assets and evaluate economic indicators as well as discover eight fail-safe investment rules.

Chapters 11, 12, and 13 educate the reader on practical investment choices. Cash, stocks, bonds, tax deferred annuities, mutual funds, and other investment areas are explained in detail. Readers can match objectives with mutual funds, understand the theory behind successful stock market selections, put taxes in their place, and build profit into bond investing. Chapter exercises involve the reader in concept as well as theory.

Chapters 14 and 15 focus on reducing taxes — a worthy goal for every American. The challenge is two fold: reducing current federal income tax and arranging the disposition of one's wealth to try and reduce or eliminate estate taxation. Basic estate planning tools, such as wills, trusts, durable power of attorneys, are explained in non-technical terms.

The next four chapters provide financial insight into the amount of effort required to achieve the two most common objectives of the American public — retirement and education funding.

Will you be able send your child to college? Chapter 16 enumerates college funding strategies, such as tax deductible college funding, gifting strategies to maintain control, six borrowing sources, financial aid, and specialized investment choices. Four common myths are exposed and realistic solutions suggested.

Chapters 17, 18, and 19 are devoted to pre-retirement or "financial independence" planning, retirement program choices for deferred spending options, and distribution planning for those knocking on retirement's door. These chapters present important elements of financial planning for the retirement years and illuminate the importance of early self-funding actions. The reader is provided with necessary information and tools for evaluating the amount of effort required to complete retirement goals on time.

Readers who have filled out the appropriate worksheets and analyzed their situation will be aware of financial strengths, weaknesses, and constraints. At the conclusion of this undertaking they will have two choices: forge ahead on their own or consult with a professional advisor.

Those seeking to self-analyze will appreciate Chapter 20. Lifetime financial stages are covered by age and family structure starting with single adults and concluding with retirees. In this section, necessary actions are outlined and general recommendations are made for the various stages of adulthood.

Those who realize their financial situation may be too complex to adequately self-evaluate will embrace Chapter 21. Here the reader will find an explanation of the "who's who" in finance, and 20 questions for better advice.

The final chapter is concerned with motivating the reader to act upon the information in this book and thus avoid saying someday, "I wish I had done this when I was ____" (you fill in the blank).

If motivation motors are running, seize the moment. Read through the resource listings in the Appendix and check applicable resource items to expand your knowledge base. Start now — knowledge, money, and time are powerful allies in the quest for financial success.

Informative and inspiring, ***Spend Your Way to Wealth*** can be a springboard to help catapult **YOU** on the road to riches.

Good wealth...

CHAPTER 1

RETHINKING THE MONEY GAME

"Money is always on the brain as long as there is a brain in reasonable order."

Samuel Butler

Are you wealthy? If you answered that question yes, you probably wouldn't be reading this book. The chances are you're aspiring to wealth, and perhaps by the last passage in this book, you'll also be inspired to strengthen the link between your spending and your wealth.

Wealth is a very personal issue. One person's wealth could be peanuts to another. It all depends on your point of view: on where you are, financially speaking, and where you hope to be. A streetperson could feel as though he or she had won the lottery if handed a $500 bill, but the same $500 wouldn't go very far in a typical middle-class family of four — it might not even cover their food bill. As you can see, relative circumstances have much to do with financial satisfaction and whether or not one feels wealthy.

A better question is: what would it take to make you FEEL wealthy? For many people, it wouldn't be winning the lottery or even inheriting money; it could be just an improvement over their present financial situation. Having money today and money tomorrow is the objective.

A "SPENDSIBLE" APPROACH

Remember the old sayings, "The love of money is the root of all evil," and "It's harder for a rich man to get to heaven than for a camel to pass through the eye of a needle."

You've heard these and many more in your adult life and even during childhood. These types of sayings must have been either invented by the rich to keep the competition in place or forecast by the prophets. Regardless of their origin, money myths have had an impact on our values and our subsequent behavior with money.

To be more positive, put these thoughts in your subconscious: "Money isn't everything, but it's right up there with oxygen." Or how about, "Money can't buy happiness, but it can buy some perfectly acceptable substitutes."

None of these sayings are one hundred percent accurate, but the idea is to make the accumulation of money an enriching experience. In order to do this, you must rethink how you handle money. Are you satisfied with the money in your life? Is your glass half-empty or half-full? No one ever has enough money in their life, unless they are "filthy" rich. Otherwise, money comes in and gets absorbed or as I like to say, "we rise to meet the occasion." It is up to you, therefore, to make your experience with money positive.

Money is nothing more than a vehicle for putting life values to work. If you consider that the basic purpose of money is to help you to have a better life, then money starts to feel good — and it should. I have coined a word — "spendsible" to help you accentuate the positive and sensibly spend your way to wealth. And, enjoy every minute.

In this country, many people have been psychologically conditioned to think that saving money is equivalent to scrimping and denying ourselves of pleasure — punishment in fact. The word "budget" evokes feelings similar to those experienced when contemplating a visit to a dentist. Spending then becomes an exercise in guilt production reinforcing the assumption that this is a negative activity. It is a vicious cycle — spend, guilt, negative feedback and, instead of putting money aside for the future, these people continue to seek love and comfort in the here and now through current gratification. For hundreds of years, money has been substituted for love. Frequently when feeling the most unloved, the urge to buy a new pair of shoes, tools, gadgets for the car, new drapes or a trip around the world can be overwhelming. This type of spending is referred to as discretionary and may result in the ownership of large collections of material items all having one common characteristic — fleeting values which depreciate, disintegrate, decline, or disappear.

A negative psychological response to the activity of savings short circuits even the best intentions with the result that money is never "spendsibly" distributed until the future arrives. There are two truisms about life to keep in mind: 1) when you are in your 20s and 30s, your internal clock is set to slow due to the abundance of time and 2) after you hit the half century mark, the clock switches to double time.

Every spending decision you make has a current and future impact on your quality of life. In order to derive emotional pleasure from making "spendsible" decisions, myopic vision must be corrected. You have to be able to see the future in living color. What is it you want to be doing and when? Take a moment to fantasize about this. Close your eyes, visualize your future retirement. Where are you? What are you doing: lying on a sunny beach, exploring a new continent, working for the love of it, or simply enjoying financial independence? The future must be so real, you can smell it. The easiest way to make that happen is to describe, in great written detail, those visions. Now which ones dredge up lust and longing from you and go so far as to make you wish you were older today? You've got it! Those are the goals for which you'll be glad to exchange negative for more positive behavior.

LINKS TO WEALTH

The first and most important resource you have within your grasp is your ability to earn income. It takes skill to do this well — just as it takes skill to spend it well to build or increase your net worth. The pie chart illustrates this concept:

The three elements of the pie — life-style expenditures, taxes, and investments — can be spending choices. Your life-style spending includes all the needs or wants you've

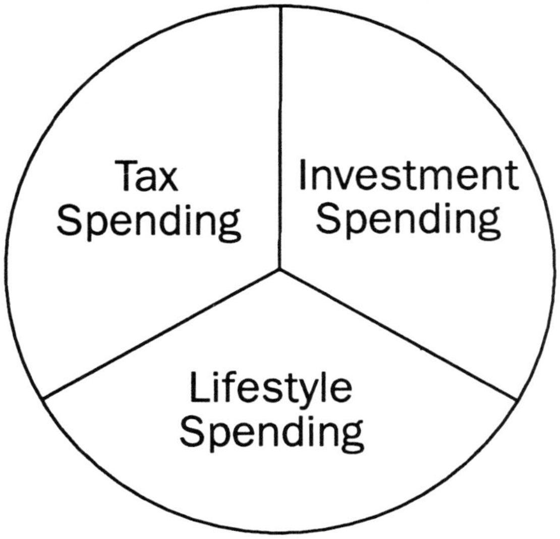

identified as important to you. The tax area includes federal, state, sales, excise, and Social Security taxes. The last slice, investments, can be a multitude of assets from cash to stocks and bonds. It is also the link to your wealth. To repeat myself, get excited about it. In fact, hunger after it. Your degree of hunger for growing personal wealth will be determined by how well you identified and described your future life-style. It is obvious that the investment slice can be bigger when taxes and spending are reduced, or held flat while income rises. If you don't "spendsibly" cut the investment slice of the pie, wealth will continue to be an elusive dream rather than a reality.

The next illustration, the factory concept, compares your asset structure to that of a factory or some facility that produces wealth. This plant consists of all the financial resources that work together to yield a desired amount of money each year.

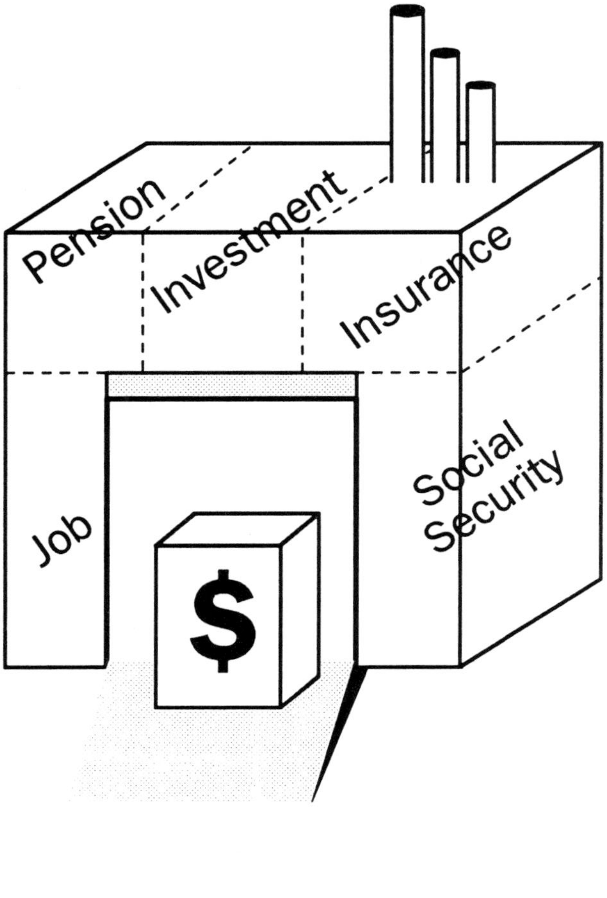

Each person's factory consists of several departments which must receive an investment to continue production. For most people, these departments include job, investments, Social Security, pensions, and insurance. It doesn't matter which department of the capital factory produces the output, as long as you can pick up sufficient cash from the loading ramp each year to take care of your current cash needs. You will spend your cash differently depending on which life stage you are in. When cash from one department ceases, the others must increase their cash production to keep filling the cash box shown on the ramp. When you retire, for instance, the job department closes down and the pension, Social Security, and investment departments take over. Similarly, if you die or become disabled, the insurance department joins the remaining departments to replace the lost earnings for your partner.

Personal assets are not mingled with other factory assets. These assets are not usually responsible for producing cash flow but are held for pleasure or consumption.

The relationship between the pie and the factory is critical to your financial success. The factory is built, strengthened, and enlarged as "spendsible" money management occurs.

MONEY MYSTERIES

Despite money's obvious real-world value, it is still surrounded by mystery:

- Money is a paradox. It's exciting to watch it grow, but tedious to track monthly expenditures and plan investment spending. Money has often been compared to love. When we have it, we don't think about it, but when we don't have it, it is all we think about.
- Like sex, money is something we usually don't learn enough about soon enough. Even in the 1990s, classes in money management are not standard in high school curriculums. Progress is being made, but there are still two or three generations which have had to make up their own rules. Parents often do not feel comfortable discussing the family finances with their children. Married couples may not share feelings involving money with each other. And in general, discussing personal finances with friends and acquaintances is almost taboo.

By the way, when was the last time you shared anything significant about your finances with a friend or relative — how you reduced your taxes last year, lost your shirt on that bad investment, or managed to spend your entire annual salary without "spendsible" wealth accumulation?

- Money is a symbol of an individual's accomplishments, security, and personal power — it's a subject everyone, from spendthrift to miser, has strong feelings about.

MONEY HARMONY

Money is also a burr in the side of many marriages. Statistics reveal that a majority of marriages suffer discord over the subject of money. There is a wealth of information written about money and couples. One comprehensive book on the subject is ***American Couples — Money, Work and Sex***, coauthored by Pepper Schwartz, Ph.D. and Philip Blumstein, Ph.D. Another, ***Rich is Better***, by Tessa Warschaw, Ph.D., offers insights into poverty games played by couples. Two more recent books, ***Couples and Money***, by Victoria Felton-Collins, and ***How to Stop Fighting About Money and Make Some***, by Kaycee Krysty and Kristianne Blake, discuss constructive steps for solving marital money disagreements.

The triangle of men, women, and money can be destructive to the most stable of marriages. Conflicts arise over who makes the decisions, how the income is split, which items get purchased and what bills are paid. More arguments take place over how money is managed rather than over how much is earned. The delegating of responsibility for the household spending often enables the delegator to sit as judge and jury when value systems create conflict over purchases. I remember one couple who had a unique way of dealing with money management. He gave her cash allowances at the beginning of each month which were placed in envelopes identified for particular expenses (food, gas and oil, clothing, and so forth). During the month if one envelope dried up, she would move on to the next envelope to cope with spending needs during the month. At the end of the month, the husband would demand justification from his wife on her methods of managing the money. If they didn't meet his standards (the jury), he would chastise her (the judge). Neither of them enjoyed a very productive relationship with money.

Cohabitating couples or couples that have remarried usually keep their finances separate in an effort to maintain control and equality. This may be one of the last remaining vestiges of their independence. But separating finances into his and hers can also be a deterrent to making long-term commitments to relationships.

Having a family can also substantially increase financial anxieties. If you want to reduce the anxieties — both yours and your children's — which come with money management, according to noted financial columnist, William Donoghue, you should:

- Teach them to manage their finances.
- Give them some money to spend on investments.

They'll grow up appreciating the value of money and be a step ahead of the crowd in understanding the investment markets. Parents play a big role in helping shape their child's responses to money. Think about how you were raised, how your parents treated money, how much was available when you were growing up, and your experiences as an adult. All those experiences contributed to your attitude about money. This doesn't mean you are stuck with the same financial biases your parents had, rather it means every opportunity available should be used to further examine money attitudes and, if necessary, rethink your money game.

DEVELOPING YOUR FINANCIAL POTENTIAL

Whatever your attitudes toward and definition of wealth and happiness, you no doubt want to move forward. Within these pages are quips, quotes, cartoons, analogies, and tools for everyday living which will help you attain your financial potential. I've endeavored to open the door of information wide enough so that you can glimpse opportunity and grasp the moment. Each chapter plays an essential part in the process of financial planning. Some will be quite exciting to you and others may bring a yawn or two, but each is vitally important to building a fail-safe financial plan. This information along with a positive mental attitude and eagerness to "spendsibly" use your money can hasten your trip to the goal of your dreams.

CHAPTER 2
ROADBLOCKS TO SUCCESS

"We have to understand the word can only be grasped by action, not by contemplation. The hand is more important than the eye. The hand is the cutting edge of the mind."

Jacob Bronowski

Before moving further along the road to wealth accumulation and money management, it is necessary to identify roadblocks that might keep you from achieving your financial goals.

Potential roadblocks are everywhere: overspending in the wrong areas, expensive insurance coverage (or none at all), disorganization, unsuitable investments, poor employee benefits, and inadequate knowledge.

These obstacles can all be managed if you are willing to devote some time to your financial affairs. In fact, you will see how to overcome all of them, and more, in this book. First, let's talk about two more subtle roadblocks: one is imposed upon you by the economy — inflation; the other is a personal trait just about everybody has in common — procrastination.

INFLATION — THE REAL STORY

Along with death and taxes, inflation is an unpleasant fact of life. You must plan for the fact that money spent in the future will be worth less than money spent now (i.e., a dollar in the future will buy less than it does today). If you want to maintain your standard of living (and who doesn't?), you must face the fact that more money will be needed in the future as our society experiences varying degrees of inflation.

To fully appreciate the impact of inflation, let's look into the future of two couples. First, Larry and Susan Young, a couple in their mid-30s, have a household income of $50,000 from which they net $3,000 a month to meet their lifestyle needs. They expect inflation to average five percent between now and their retirement years:

Current expense need:	$3,000
Annual Inflation Increase:	5%

Based on these figures and using the Rule of 72 (follows) — in fourteen years, they would require twice as much income to satisfy the same lifestyle as they currently enjoy.

Solutions for this dilemma are limited. Either their income increases in response to inflationary pressures, or they have to suppress their lifestyle. Since Larry is employed by a major corporation, it is probable his salary will keep pace with inflation.

But what about those individuals who have retired on fixed incomes, such as a second couple, John and Clara Elden. Inflation can be deadly to their financial security. John and Clara are anticipating retirement this year when both are 62. At the onset of their retirement journey, they plan to trim their expenses by 20% to $2,500 a month. Their income needs will be provided by John's pension of $1,200 a month and their combined Social Security payments of $1,300.

Current Expense Need	$2,500
Annual Inflation Increase	5%

John's pension is fixed, but not his Social Security. The government professes it will increase Social Security benefits each year by the percent change in the Consumer Price Index (CPI). This is how inflation impacts John and Clara in 14 years:

Total Income Need	$5,000
Pension ($1,200) plus his Social Security ($1,300) increases to $2,600 with cost of living adjustments	$3,800
Shortfall	$1,200

Again solutions are limited. John and Clara must have investment funds available to supplement their future inflated needs in order to maintain the same purchasing power yearly, or they must reduce their standard of living. It takes $5,000 to maintain John and Clara's purchasing power, but with their fixed income resources totalling only $3,800, they must reduce their spending by 24% — a solution unpalatable to many individuals.

THE INCREDIBLE SHRINKING DOLLAR

Estimating Inflation

A quick way to estimate how long it will take for your spending needs to double is to use the Rule of 72. Divide the average rate of inflation, 5%, into the number 72 to estimate how many years it will be before your spending power is cut in half, that is, when you require twice as much income to maintain your present level of spending. What if inflation is higher?

72	÷	5	=	14.4 years
72	÷	6	=	12.0 years
72	÷	7	=	10.2 years

During the ten year period between 1974 and 1983 inflation was high — 8.3% — the highest ten years in history. In 1982, inflation started edging down and, by 1986, fell to 1.1%. Where is inflation today? The early 90s started out with a bang — annualized inflation was over 6%. But if you average it back to 1939, inflation has averaged about 4.5%. For 1990, it was 6.1%; 1991 finished up at 3.1%. This illustrates how quickly the CPI can change. How high will the next decade of inflation be? What will the average be for the rest of your lifespan? Will it go up? Will it go down? The table below shows the yearly inflation rate during the decade of the 70s and 80s.

CONSUMER PRICE INDEX
DECADE OF THE 70'S AND 80'S

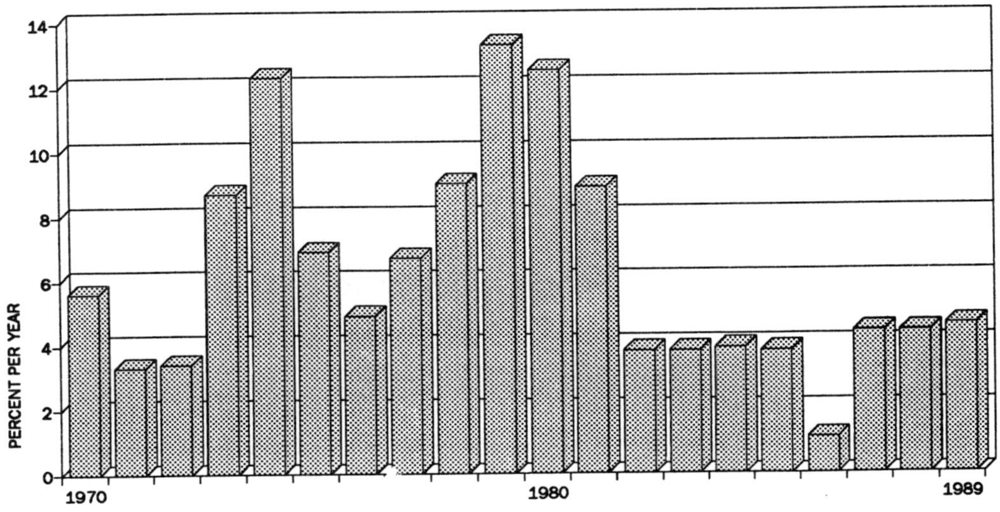

Source: U.S. Department of Commerce

It's evident that inflation will be a factor in your financial life. Check the following figures and fill in the blanks in the last column.

	1969 Cost	1979 Cost	Today's Cost
Hospital room/day	$ 47.00	$ 137.00	________
Regular gas/gallon	.39	.97	________
New home/median price	24,600.00	64,000.00	________
First class postage	.06	.15	________
New car	3,400.00	6,910.00	________
White bread	.23	.43	________
Man's haircut	2.50	4.25	________
Cigarettes/pack	.37	.62	________
Eggs/dozen	.53	.81	________
Hamburger/lb.	.62	1.52	________
Doctor office fee	6.75	14.50	________
Weeks food/four persons	36.90	77.50	________

Source: U.S. News & World Report, *October 1, 1979.*

Today most of those items are much higher than in 1979 — a direct impact of inflation over time. I remember one occasion, while teaching a class, that a woman spoke up and stated inflation did not concern her. When I questioned her as to why that was, she replied, "I just don't buy the items that go up." I silently chuckled as I thought how her grocery list must be dwindling. No one can escape inflation's toll on spending power.

Again, the important issue in evaluating how inflation will impact your future is to incorporate it into your planning by:

- Recognizing that money in the future will buy less than money today.
- Build an inflationary factor into all long range planning.
- Try to establish more than one source of income which will be responsive to changes in inflation.

PROCRASTINATION

I've often said that procrastination is the enemy of success and the great friend of the IRS. Procrastination impacts every facet of our lives, including financial planning, and has caused more people to fail than any other obstacle. Here's my list of all the excuses I've heard from individuals who seek to justify delays in confronting their personal financial management needs face to face:

I'm not interested.

I have a friend in the business.

My widow can work it out — she can remarry.

I'm not ready yet; call me in a few months.

Times are too turbulent.

I don't need professional advice.

Financial planning? I can't even get out of debt.

I'll think about it.

I need more time to get organized.

I've got a broker/banker/accountant.

I don't think anything can help.

My husband takes care of everything.

I can retire off of my business.

I don't have any money.

I got this far, I guess I'll make it the rest of the way.

I'm worth more dead than alive.

The details are too personal.

I'm too busy.

Why is it so important? According to statistics published in the past by the U.S. Department of Health and Human Services, fifty-five percent of the population retire with a median income of only $16,000. Although these statistics are becoming dated, many people still reach retirement without the means to live comfortably.

As a financial planner, I usually see more people with average to above average incomes rather than those in the $16,000 range. But I also have seen pending retirees reconsider their target retirement date once they review the reality of dollars today versus dollars needed in the future. One of the primary reasons many individuals are not financially fit by their projected retirement date is that they have neglected to spend either time or money on their financial plans. They have procrastinated.

The reasons for this common malady are various, but the most common behaviors that cause procrastination are as follows:

1. <u>The quest for perfection</u>: Trying to make the best possible decision often leads to unnecessary delays and lost opportunities. A client considering a potential investment may insist on a specific return or even a guarantee from his/her financial advisor. While the client sits on the fence and the advisor continues the search for the Holy Grail, economic conditions may change and the financial oppor-tunity that was nearly perfect slips away.

2. Sequential thinking: This is one I've heard often. "I've got to get my taxes done, organize my papers, get married, get divorced, get a raise, wait until my wife/husband goes back to work." The list goes on and on. This type of client has an unending list of excuses. They will never finish their financial planning because there will always be something else to consider first.

3. Pain avoidance: No one likes thinking of painful subjects, such as death and disability. Consequently, protecting incomes with adequate insurance coverage and making plans for what happens after death (estate planning) is often neglected. Yet considering these risks is an essential part of financial planning, and money must be spent in these areas to bullet proof a plan.

Here's a common list of the excuses for procrastinating categorized by lifestage. Do you recognize any of these?

- Mid-20s: "We can't spend money on investments yet. Our life's just starting and we don't make much money. Besides, we deserve some fun before we get serious. What's the rush, anyway?"
- Mid-30s: "The children are growing, our debts are still too high. When the kids get past this phase, it will be less expensive. Then, we'll start to think of our future. We just can't do it yet."
- Mid-40s: "Our two children are in college and we're strapped. Books, tuition, phone calls for money — it seems we have less spending money now than when we were 25."
- Mid-50s: "We realize it's time to think of spending on investments for retirement, but the house needs remodeling. And it takes all we have just to live. Besides, it's time we had some fun again."
- Mid-60s: "Who us? Sure planning was a great idea, but we never sat down to figure out how much we needed. Now Social Security isn't enough. It seems to be too late for us now. We should have started spending wisely years ago."

THE ROAD TO FINANCIAL FAILURE

The road to financial failure is broad and easy to follow. It can be summarized as follows:

- Forget the experts — get your financial advice from friends, neighbors, and relatives.
- Put off planning until you think you have enough time to do it right.
- Put all your money on the sure thing.
- Forget about inflation; it doesn't matter.
- Ignore tax advantages; just pay your bills.
- Live for today; tomorrow will take care of itself.

There are many excuses for not organizing one's financial affairs. Though the road to financial success is more challenging than daily procrastination, there are two overwhelming reasons to take steps down that road: peace of mind and financial self-sufficiency at retirement.

If you take it one step at a time, the road is simple to follow. It's your choice.

CHAPTER 3

FINANCIAL HOUSEKEEPING

"He who would climb the ladder must begin at the bottom."
English Proverb

Though not an immediately rewarding task, organizing one's financial papers is the first step to take to start clarifying options and defining financial realities. A few good reasons to be organized financially are:

- To document your assets and debts as of a certain date so you can ascertain progress in the future;
- To have your insurance coverages readily evident in case you need to make a claim and to ensure adequacy from year to year;
- To know where your estate documents, such as the will, bequest list, etc., are located;
- To have a list of credit card numbers so you can take immediate action to cancel the cards in case of loss or theft.

ORGANIZATION FROM CHAOS

What's the worst thing you can envision happening that would cause you to want to be organized? A household fire? A burglary? Both of those events would be fairly traumatic for anyone. If either were to happen, could you reconstruct and replace the lost information easily?

What if you became incapacitated? Who would know where your important documents are kept or what your wishes in a particular situation might be?

In 1983, while teaching a class at a major corporation, I asked the group if anyone had ever experienced an event in which they wished their financial papers had been safeguarded. One hand shot up and a woman shared that just one month prior to this class her home had burned to the ground.

Though not impossible, it had been very inconvenient for her to trace the records through her various advisors. Recreating her financial documents involved numerous phone calls, time out from her busy schedule, and lengthy waits. It would still have been a difficult situation, but the process could have been expedited if she had followed these rules:

- Store copies or originals of important papers outside the home.
- Create a Money Book.

SAFE STORAGE

If you don't have a fireproof safe, you will want to rent a safe deposit box for storing your valuables and certain papers. The safe deposit box is the best outside storage choice for safeguarding duplicates or originals of your records. If you are worried about access to the safe deposit box in case of your death, injury or illness, arrange to rent it jointly with another person. Of course, you would want the joint tenant to be a trusted friend or relative.

In your safe deposit box, place the following:

- A listing of your household inventory, including pictures or a videotape of antiques, exotic pieces of furniture, collections, and other valuables to support their worth in case you ever have to file a casualty loss report.
- Your will or a copy of it. Though it is often suggested to leave the original will in the hands of the attorney who drafted it, it's better to keep your will in the safe deposit box. When you die, the bank officials will allow your "next of kin" to enter the box in order to retrieve the will. This may vary from state to state, so check with your bank.
- Personal documents, including your marriage certificate, birth certificates, military discharge papers, and other papers that you feel would be irreplaceable if destroyed. There is really no right or wrong here — just make it convenient for yourself. Keep the papers you don't need to refer to frequently in the bank, and the others at home.
- Properties and securities such as Great Aunt Emma's broach or that diamond ring you wear only during the holidays, your stock and bond certificates, bank deposit certificates, and so forth. Some people also place their insurance policies here for safekeeping.

The remainder of your documents can be kept at home in a metal strong box or safe. The important part of making the storage decision is to remember later where you put what.

THE MONEY BOOK

To remember where you put what, create an organized notebook with information on your financial position and directions on where to find all your documents.

How do you organize your papers now? Does one of the following sound familiar?

- The "Toss It" approach: To trash or not to trash, this is the question as you hold the paper in your hand, moving it slowly toward the waste can.
- The "Later" approach: Throw the paper in a drawer and organize it later, or as a variation of this sentiment, throw the paper in a drawer and hope you'll never have to find it again.

- The "Color Coordinated" approach: This is the infamous file folder with a tab. The dazzling array of colors available makes you want to forsake fame and fortune just to spend time with this system. But does it really work?

Creating a system to control the paper flow into your world is easy with nothing more than a three ring binder notebook. Hole punch your information or use a plastic sleeve to store material that can't be punched. This is the Money Book. Start by dividing it into five sections:

IS THIS IT?

1. Goals and action plans: If you've identified your goals, list them and the steps you are taking to achieve these goals. For example, if taking a major vacation in five years is the goal, list the actions you must take in order to achieve that trip.
2. Net worth and spending analysis: In this section place your updated list of assets/ debts, and current income/expected outgo.
3. Listing of retirement accounts: List your IRAs, how much they are earning when they mature, and the year each was purchased. Other retirement assets, such as employer provided accounts, should be listed here also.
4. Insurance coverage limits: The easiest way to handle this is to copy the front page of both your auto and property policies. This page details the limitations of the policies. Your life, disability, and medical policy information should also be included.
5. Asset location records: This is the physical location of important documents. Any other personal information, such as personal and family data, can go here too.

The role of the Money Book is to keep you organized, make it easy to evaluate your progress with goals, enhance your ability to stay on track with net worth growth and spending controls, and provide a document which brings all the important financial information together in one place.

Think about the consequences should you die before taking this important step. You will have put your heirs in the unenviable position of creating order from chaos while coping with one of the most traumatic experiences in their lives.

Not only will you benefit from this step, but your significant other or children will also. Be sure you inform those who have a need to know where to find your Money Book in case of an emergency.

You can create your own forms. They don't have to be elaborate. The important part is to put down all the facts on paper — all the things you need to look at to evaluate where you are each year. Once you've visited with a financial advisor, these documents will be valuable in helping you update your direction semi-annually. Some advisors may even give you the forms to get started.

This is work, but it will make the next steps easier. And, it is a legacy of love you can provide your family. They'll thank you later.

CHAPTER 4

THE ROAD TO WEALTH – ONE STEP AT A TIME

"Everything should be made as simple as possible, but not simpler."
Albert Einstein

Up to this point, you have explored the meaning and value of money, reviewed your money attitudes, and considered the effects of procrastination and inflation on your ability to prosper. You have learned what it is to be financially organized and an easy-to-implement method to achieve that state. Now you will briefly assess your financial health to identify specific elements which need improvement.

DO YOU HAVE A FINANCIAL FEVER?

The following three-minute quiz is designed to evaluate your "financial temperature."

FINANCIAL WELLNESS QUIZ

	Yes/No
Do you have a will and has it been revised since 1981?	_______
If you become disabled or die, do you know exactly how your family will replace your lost income?	_______
Have you estimated your income taxes for the current year and adjusted payroll withholding or quarterly payments to reflect the expected tax bill?	_______
Can you trace your expenditures for the past 12 months?	_______
Does your investment portfolio reflect the results of a deliberate mix with regard to risk and asset diversification?	_______
Within the past year, have you added up what you own and compared it to what you owe?	_______
If you have a company-matching profit-sharing or 401(k) retirement program, have you spent enough here to qualify for their matching percentage?	_______
Do you understand the pros and cons of basic estate documents such as the will, durable power of attorney, community property agreement (where applicable), living trust and living will?	_______
Are you absolutely sure you will have enough money at retirement to have the lifestyle of your dreams?	_______
Have the after-tax returns on your investments over the last ten years exceeded inflation by at least two to three percent per year?	_______

If you marked every question affirmatively, you can put this book down and hang up your shingle as a financial planner. If not, what is your financial temperature?

1-3 NOs:	Starting to have a fever. Get out the aspirin.
4-6 NOs:	Several degrees above normal. Sick enough to ache all over.
7-9 NOs:	Fully infected. Treatment will be extensive.
All NOs:	Could be financially terminal!

If you marked eight or more questions Yes, you scored better than most persons. Attribute it to wise choices. If you marked more than four questions No, you may be inclined to blame it on poor economic conditions, fraud, your spouse, your neighbor, your boss or the moon cycle, but you're going to have to attend to it before it gets worse.

Why look at financial wellness as if it were medical? Because taking care of your finances is like taking care of your health. You start by consulting a professional. The professional examines the situation, makes a diagnosis, and offers a prescription.

It is at this point that you have two choices. The first choice is to hold your breath, wait for a turn of events, and see what direction the winds of fate take you — perhaps drifting into financial desperation. A second choice is to take charge and plan your financial life. It is up to you to take the actions that get you back on the road to financial health.

PLANNING YOUR WEALTH STRATEGIES

Now you're ready for the planning process. The steps to attaining wealth are often thought to be dry, detail-oriented, analytical, and even negative processes. Many people believe planning deals with dying, disability, and financial insecurity. In actuality, these steps should be viewed as a way to open opportunity's door just a little wider — to be ahead of the situation and in control instead of behind the eightball.

It is the process of examining your spending, insuring, investing, tax planning, and estate protection needs. The purpose is to make you wealthier year-by-year as you move toward your future goals. If you are financially astute, you can attempt to do your own planning. But most individuals find it to be an enormous task to coordinate all the elements, uncovering every available option and taking complete advantage of all appropriate opportunities. One key to understanding the process is to look at it in steps.

- Step one — Goal Formation: If you aren't excited about where you want to be financially, you probably won't get beyond procrastination. Most of us do have a mental list of goals and objectives. But putting these thoughts on paper forces us to think through the reality of our priorities. Goals can then be broken down into easy-to-swallow components of spending. This process will bring to light the importance of coordinating goals with significant others. Goals then have to be reviewed each year. What is different? Are your financial aspirations still the same? Is your ultimate destination still at the end of the road you're traveling on?

- Step Two — Data Gathering: This is where all the number crunching material must be compiled to prepare the financial statements, cash flow analysis, and other pertinent information. Sometimes this step is a hurdle that stops all but the most diligent. Persevere and you will be rewarded.
- Step Three — Identification of Obstacles: Explore the obstacles which have kept you from getting what you want. Some common obstacles are unplanned spending, poor investment choices, disorganization, procrastination, lack of knowledge, and low resolve.
- Step Four — Recommendations for Change: Once you've identified your financial problems, the solutions may become obvious. Strategies can be devised to eliminate problems or detour around them.
- Step Five — Implementation: It is up to you to activate your plan of action once you've decided on the important issues. This is where determination must take over. Good plans can be destroyed by lack of action.
- Step Six — Periodic Review and Revision: Financial planning is not an event but a process. Your action plans must be periodically reviewed in light of personal, political, and economic changes. Personal finances and goals are subject to rapid change; it is important to keep your plans tuned up by at least an annual review, although quarterly reviews are better.

Should you consult with a professional? Information on how to choose a planner is covered in Chapter 21. But how do you decide how much or how little help you need? Understanding how financial planning is delivered is paramount to choosing what kind of help you need.

Financial planning advice is readily available in a variety of ways: from informal verbal counseling to highly structured and documented reports. It can encompass a comprehensive financial physical exam with exhaustive data gathering and analyses or an isolated financial strategy addressing an immediate issue.

There is no right or wrong here. It depends on whether or not you have a pressing concern, such as buying versus renting, how to invest an unexpected sum of money, or whether you are ready for retirement. For these and similar situations, immediate answers are desired. But for a thorough, long term plan, a comprehensive financial physical is necessary. A complete review brings to light your financial strengths and weaknesses and, depending on the circumstances and complexity of your situation, outlines simple or sophisticated actions to follow. Anything else is a band-aid approach.

A comprehensive analysis is, however, difficult to absorb all at once. It's like trying to cram a seven-course meal into a 30-minute lunch break: you can digest only a small amount of each course — the rest is left untouched. As a result, many planners have developed systems in which staged financial analysis takes place. Regardless of how it gets done there are some basic elements which are always covered. Following are the areas addressed in a comprehensive financial analysis:

- Goal Setting: The development of financial destinations that are achievable within your lifetime. These goals help establish the motivation to make financial changes.
- Cash Flow Management (otherwise known as budgeting): The process which allows you to understand personal and family spending habits. The objective is to reduce non-essential spending and increase spending for net worth growth.
- Financial Statement or Net Worth Analysis: The accurate determination of your assets and liabilities at a particular time. This analysis helps form the basis for analyzing future potential and current concerns.
- Risk Management: Life, health, disability, and casualty insurance coverages. All of these have their costs, however, the cost of unpreparedness is even greater. Don't gamble in this area; play it safe. Spend your money carefully here.
- Investment Management: A pre-determined mix of growth and income assets. After determining how much risk you wish to take with your investments, you can decide how much income, growth, tax advantages or guarantees are necessary to help you achieve your desired returns.
- Tax Planning: Ensuring you defer, deduct and avoid taxes. Without denying Uncle Sam's due, there are some things that even Uncle Sam agrees we should consider. Tactics such as shifting the tax burden to others when possible, postponing taxation, or converting taxable income to tax-free income.
- Retirement Planning: Determining how much money you will need to fund the last third of your life and what to do about it. Getting started early is the secret. Spending dollars now for investments which will be spent again in retirement. You can take your chances and let the chips fall where they may, or you can plan for when you want to be financially independent.
- Estate Planning: Ensuring that your estate documents are adequate and liquidity is sufficient to cover the immediate needs of your survivors. Survivor income and security must also be addressed.

In order to complete the above analysis, planners not only must be technically competent but must know everything about you. It's time for you to get financially naked. Your advisor needs to know your age, assets, debts, goals, income, outflow, retirement program availability, insurance coverages, levels of taxation, methods you have or haven't used to reduce taxes, and which estate documents are in place. Once that information is revealed, the planner must be able to communicate solutions in understandable terminology. Much of his/her time will be spent educating you on the finer points of money management appropriate to your case.

PLANNING FLOWCHART

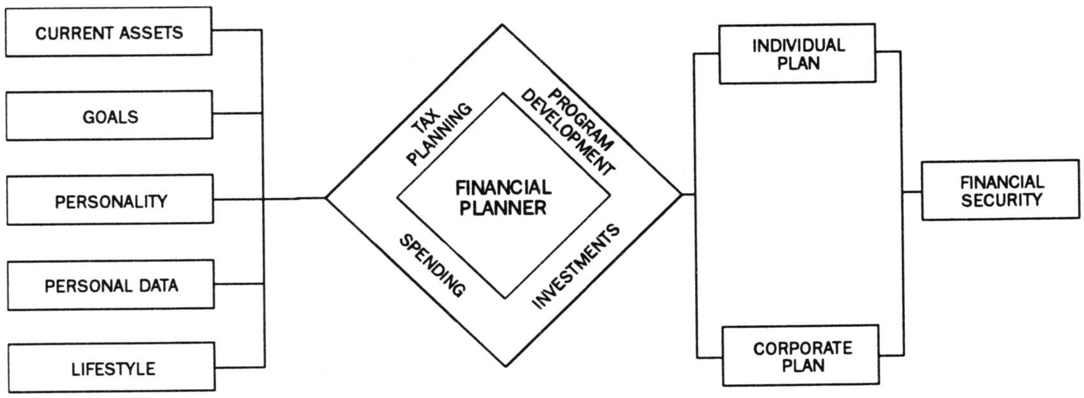

THE FUNDAMENTALS OF FINANCIAL PLANNING

Understanding the fundamentals of financial planning will not necessarily send you skipping happily down the road to financial independence. The majority of people will not take action until some life circumstance forces them to seek help. Death, disability, divorce, investment losses, overwhelming debt, negative cash flow, excessive taxes, college expenses, and pending retirement are all situations that disturb us enough to seek professional assistance.

However, understanding the fundamentals of financial planning, called here "Wealth-Building Secrets," will help you get on that road sooner. It's the same basic information advisors have been preaching for years.

Seven Easy Wealth-Building Secrets

1. Pay yourself first: This does not mean spending more on material items. It's been said that Americans are consumer spenders first and investment spenders second. Ideally, place at least 10% of your net income in an investment account before you lay your earnings at the feet of the god of consumer gadgets.
2. Maintain liquidity: In strict accounting terms, you usually want enough cash available to cover your short term debts (those that must be paid within the next year). But life doesn't always go as planned, so a prudent person keeps enough immediate cash available to satisfy his or her expenses for three to six months. This money should be set aside before any non-liquid investment is considered. Cash is king and liquidity can be the key to taking advantage of solid investment opportunities in the future.
3. Pay Uncle Sam only what he demands, nothing more: Everyone pays taxes — even the most practiced and educated financial planner. Wise planners, though, delay paying their taxes as long as possible.

If you owed $1,000 in taxes, would you rather pay that $1,000 with today's money or the money of 50 years ago when a dollar could buy several times as many groceries as today?

This is not to suggest that you defer your payment for 50 years (the IRS won't wait forever), but inflation makes it advantageous to defer tax payments until the dollar decreases in value. Incidentally, keeping that $1,000 from the IRS also frees it up for more interesting work, such as making your net worth grow.

Tax avoidance is totally dependent on what Congress has left of our tax system. It amounts to this: write off investment losses when practical, defer investment gains, seek tax-sheltered income, make maximum contributions to tax-advantaged retirement programs, and keep good records. Capitalize on all the legal tax-avoidance methods you can before Congress changes the rules once more.

4. Use time advantageously: Spenders have the same amount of time available as "spendsible" spenders. From conception to the grave, we all have a life span of approximately 70-90 years in which to achieve our financial goals. We have different ways of going about it — the spenders will get around to building net worth tomorrow if he/she has any money left at the end of the month; "spendsible" spenders understand the equation "Time + Money = Financial Success," and start buying investments immediately. The more you spend here, the better. This doesn't mean if you got started late, you don't have opportunities. It is just more difficult. As Vince Lombardi stated, "I never lost a game, I just ran out of time."

It's easier to understand the power of time on money by seeing examples. For instance, John and Mary have a goal of accumulating $500,000 by age 60. They both assume they can earn a 10% average return on their investments. At age 35, Mary has to spend $373 per month on investments to reach the goal. On the other hand, John who is 10 years older, is penalized by his lost time. His monthly investment spending quota must be $1,196. Ouch!

5. Use the power of compounding: Smart spenders understand the Rule of 72 when trying to determine how hard their money should work. The number 72 is the magic doubling number into which you can divide an expected interest rate and find how long it takes for your money to double:

72	÷	8%	=	9.0 years
72	÷	10%	=	7.2 years
72	÷	12%	=	6.0 years

Visualize how powerful it would be to have your money doubling every 6-9 years. The real power of compounding becomes clearer when following the growth of actual dollars over a period of 20 years.

Beginning Deposit	**Interest Rate**	**20 Years Later**
$10,000	6%	$32,071
	8%	$46,609
	10%	$67,274
	12%	$96,462

Simply seeking to increase the investment returns from 6% to 10% has more than doubled the potential. Remember that at 10%, money doubles every 7.2 years. Look at the difference between the 6% result and the 12% result: 12% returns three times more than 6%. While money at 6% only doubles every 12 years, money at 12% doubles every six years. What a difference a rate makes.

Money at 12% Compounded	
Year 1	$10,000
Year 6	$20,000
Year 12	$40,000
Year 18	$80,000
Year 20	$96,462

6. Know the rules to win: Understanding your financial options can go a long way toward keeping you on the winning team. If you know the rules from basic financial processes to tax laws and investment trends, you won't strike out. Being informed will help you make educated, practical, and positive choices of financial strategies and investment selections. Even if you don't wish to be your own advisor, you must know enough to distinguish between good advice and faulty advice. Knowledge is power.

7. Hedge your bets: Always protect what you have by wearing a parachute. It's not likely the plane will crash, but if it does and you have nothing to soften the landing, the impact may destroy you.

   Protecting family security means spending money wisely on disability, life, property and medical insurances, while diversifying your financial assets. In other words, don't bet the farm on a gamble; diversify your financial assets. Also, don't neglect your estate planning. Maybe you won't lose any money if you overlook this aspect, but your heirs might.

There is one final element in the magic formula for financial success which we haven't mentioned yet motivation. You can't legislate it, buy it, learn it in school, or read it in the newspaper. The motivation to improve your finances can only come from within.

CHAPTER 5

FROM DREAMS TO REALITY

"If you don't know where you're going, you'll probably end up somewhere else."

The Peter Principle

When Alice in Wonderland asked the Cheshire Cat which path she needed to take, he answered, "That depends a good deal on where you want to go."

"I don't know," said Alice.

"Then, it doesn't matter which road you take, any road will do," replied the cat.

Floating through life without clear goals leaves your financial destination to the whims of fate or chance. Failure to set meaningful, quantifiable goals will lead you, in a financial sense, to forks in the road where, as the Cheshire Cat said, it doesn't matter which road you take since you don't know where you want to go.

CHOOSING THE HIGH ROAD

Dreams will not become a reality until you act upon them. You must be excited about estimating the cost of a future lifestyle, future acquisition, or specific financial destination before you will be motivated enough to take steps toward its achievement. As a start, write a mission statement which describes your financial objective in general terms. For example, here's a mission statement appropriate for just about everybody:

"Financial success is ensuring that my present lifestyle is protected and the necessary steps are being taken to create a financially secure retirement."

The mission statement is a method to articulate your long-term strategic planning views. Tactical goals and actions are the next step in planning. A good analogy would be to consider how you plan a driving trip. You start by stating where you want to go (e.g. Seattle to Denver). The next step is to look at a map and determine which routes to take, what stops to make, what time to leave, and how long to drive each day. Those tactical decisions will control the outcome, including satisfaction with and length of the effort.

Financial Destination Map

#1 Mission Statement
#2 Goals
#3 Actions/Implementation Steps

How about you? What is your financial mission statement? To start the discovery process, complete the following statement:

"Financial success is ____

____

____

____

This financial mission statement is the beginning. From it, you develop an action plan, step-by-step. The first step is to develop definitive goals. Write down those goals, free your imagination. Visualize the material items you've always wanted, the lifestyle you wish you were born into, the security you want for your family, your early retirement, and so forth. But make your goals attainable within your lifetime.

Next quantify only the achievable goals. Ask yourself such questions as: How much capital must I accumulate to accomplish my goals? When do I want my goals to be achieved? How important is this financial destination?

When teaching a financial class for GTE in the mid-80s, I asked the group to write down their most important goals. I then requested they voluntarily share these with the group. On one particular evening, a gentleman in the back of the room shot up his hand and stated, "I want to retire in five years and sail around the Caribbean." What motivation — for me! I don't know about the rest of that class, but he struck a nerve in me because I love to travel. The purpose of the exercise was to create an atmosphere of positive expectation — and it did.

Here are the goals of Larry and Susan Young, a couple introduced in Chapter 2:

Reduce debts and taxes
Protect current lifestyle
Educate the children
Plan a major vacation
Start long term investing
Retire at age 55

The Youngs are in their mid-30s, have three young children and a considerable financial challenge ahead of them.

John and Clara Elden, also introduced in Chapter 2, have these immediate goals:

Retirement
Protection of net worth
Increase of investment income
Estate Planning

Now, it is your turn to articulate your major goals. Worksheet 5A found at the end of the chapter can be used. Either check off those filled-in goals that appeal to you or write in your own version. Spend some time with this — it is important. Remember the comment of the Cheshire Cat, if you don't know where you are going, "any road will do."

If you have a significant other, your major goals should reflect a dual vision. To paraphrase a quote from another financial author, Venita Van Caspel, "When it comes to achieving financial goals, love is not looking in each other's eyes, but looking in the same financial direction." Mutual goal setting will avoid misunderstandings and help achieve a commitment from both parties. It is also permissible for each of you to have your own goals — it depends on how many surplus dollars you have.

You can have short-, intermediate-, and long-term goals on your list. Short-term goals can be achieved in 1-5 years; intermediate-term goals, 6-15 years; and long-term goals, 16-30 years. Not all the goals on your wish list will be achievable or carry the same degree of importance. The next step is to prioritize your goals. If you do not have enough surplus income to invest to meet all of your goals, ask yourself "What is really important to me? When do I want this goal to materialize?"

Dig deep into your value system as you go through this process. You may need to switch a goal from the long-term section to the short-term section or expand on some of the categories. High accuracy when you assess your true needs and wishes will help you complete a financial plan. Take a close look at the list and strike off any goals that are attainable only with the assistance of a winning million-dollar lottery ticket. A miracle may occur, but setting goals based on divine intervention usually leads only to frustration.

If I were able to survey your answers, I would wager that 90% of you named financial independence — the freedom to work or not work — as your first priority.

Now sort your essential goals chronologically. Here's an example of Larry and Susan's prioritized essential goals:

Goals	Funds Needed	Target
Trip to Europe	$ 4,000	5 years
College for 3 children	$ 60,000	10 years
Retirement at age 55 with $2,500/month in today's dollar.	$ 400,000	20 years

The college funding is a healthy chunk of change and must be started now. The dilemma they face is how to provide for the education, take a trip or two, and still allow retirement investing to continue. How much should they put where? How hard must their money work? Should any of the goals be modified?

These are the types of questions you must ask yourself if you have multiple goals. For answers, you'll have to determine the impact of the goals on your monthly spending plans. Each future dollar amount needed can be broken down into annual savings increments if you know two things: 1) when you want the goal, and 2) what investment growth to expect.

For example, Larry and Susan's vacation illustrates how to use Worksheet 5B at the end of this chapter. It is helpful to have a financial calculator to solve these problems. If you don't have one, pick up your pencil.

DETERMINING ANNUAL SAVINGS TO ACHIEVE GOALS

A.	Goal:	European vacation
B.	Number of years until needed:	5
C.	Amount of money needed in a present dollar figure:	$4,000
D.	Inflation factor from Appendix Table I (6% = 1.3) x line C:	$5,200
E.	Investment return assumed:	10%
F.	Dollars already dedicated to the goal, $1,000 x Table I factor (10% = 1.6):	$1,600
G.	Total remaining dollars required to accumulate (line D - line F):	$3,600
H.	Annual investment amount necessary to accumulate remaining dollars assuming a 10% growth rate for 5 years. Divide line G by the factor found in Table II under the assumed growth rate (10% = 6.1):	$ 591

In the Appendix, there are present and future value tables with percent rates across the top and years down the left side. At the intersections of the percent rates and years are the factors used in the above example. Table I factors are used for inflation and growth of dollars already accumulated. Table II factors are used to determine the annual effort necessary in order to accumulate the remaining dollars needed.

Take a few of your goals and use Worksheet 5B to determine the savings needed for each. Don't worry about your retirement goals until later. Those will be addressed in Chapter 17.

FOUR ELEMENTS TO SUCCESSFUL GOALS

Your goals will be easier to achieve if you recognize and act upon these four important elements:

1. <u>Money to put aside for future spending</u>: This obvious step becomes easier after you have delved into this chapter. Freeing money from the consumption machine for more interesting work is crucial.

2. <u>Time for compound interest to work</u>: Money, even in lazy investments, can multiply rapidly when investment returns are reinvested and time is on your side. This doesn't mean you can't succeed if time is getting short, but you or your money will have to work harder

DISCIPLINE, DISCIPLINE, DISCIPLINE

3. <u>Discipline</u>: A penny a day is the idea, although you'll actually need to invest quite a bit more than that on a monthly basis. To make this point, consider that $100 per month, earning 6, 8 or 10% over a 35-year span, can win the race against a $10,000 lump sum deposit with the same interest and same time span:

RETIREMENT WITHIN 35 YEARS

Interest Rate	$100 Per Month	$10,000 Lump Sum
6%	$142,471	$ 82,125
8%	$229,388	$162,925
10%	$379,663	$326,386

(Rates compounded monthly)

4. <u>Desire (in the form of quantified goals!)</u>: It's been said that "Whatever you vividly imagine, ardently desire, sincerely believe, and enthusiastically act upon must inevitably come to pass." Wisdom passed on, no doubt, by someone who achieved success.

Ideally, you will work with a trained professional who can help you deal with ever-changing tax laws, a fluctuating economy, and a myriad of new investment choices each year. But, these four elements — investing, compounding interest, discipline and desire — are critical to that financial success. And they each depend on you.

WORKSHEET 5A

GOAL PLANNING

IMMEDIATE GOALS

Estimated Funds Needed	Approximate Date Needed	Goal	Essential	Very Important	Important
______	______	Investing for long term	______	______	______
______	______	Paying off credit debt	______	______	______
______	______	Reducing taxes	______	______	______
______	______	Vacation	______	______	______
______	______	Home furnishings	______	______	______
______	______	Sports equipment	______	______	______
______	______	Hobbies/collections	______	______	______
______	______	Insurance	______	______	______
______	______	Emergency fund	______	______	______
______	______	______________	______	______	______
______	______	______________	______	______	______

MAJOR OR LONG-TERM GOALS

______	______	Financial independence or retirement	______	______	______
______	______	New car	______	______	______
______	______	Down payment for home	______	______	______
______	______	Down payment for vacation home	______	______	______
______	______	Boat/recreational vehicle	______	______	______
______	______	Major home improvements	______	______	______
______	______	Extended vacation	______	______	______
______	______	Return to school	______	______	______
______	______	Child's education	______	______	______
______	______	Child's wedding	______	______	______
______	______	______________	______	______	______
______	______	______________	______	______	______
______	______	______________	______	______	______

WORKSHEET 5B

DETERMINING ANNUAL SAVINGS TO ACHIEVE GOALS

A. Goal: ____

B. Number of years until needed: ________________

C. Amount of money needed in a present dollar figure: ________________

D. Inflation factor from Appendix Table I x line C: ________________

E. Investment return assumed: ________________

F. Dollars already dedicated to the goal, $__________ x Table I factor listed under investment return desired: ________________

G. Total remaining dollars required to accumulate (line D - line F): ________________

H. Annual investment amount necessary to accumulate remaining dollars assuming a ______ growth rate for ______ years. Divide line G by the factor found in Table II under the assumed growth rate: ________________

CHAPTER 6

WHAT YOU OWN VS. WHAT YOU OWE

"Capital is past savings accumulated for future production."
Jackson Martindell

Where are you financially? Have you accumulated assets? Does the sum total of those assets outweigh your liabilities? If so, you're now the proud owner of a net worth. Your net worth, however large or small, reveals pertinent information about you: your financial actions to date and potential for the future. It illustrates your spending trend in personal and investment areas, and is a snapshot of how far you have progressed in the accumulation of assets compared to liabilities.

NET WORTH STATEMENT

The term net worth can be an obstacle to getting started on this exercise. In simpler language, it is a what you own versus what you owe comparison. Other terms you may hear for the same thing are: balance sheet and financial statement. The headings on a net worth statement can be organized in different ways. For example, you might see assets categorized as 1) loaned versus owned, 2) liquid or illiquid, or 3) variable and fixed. The net worth statement which follows in this book will use the following terms.

Cash Reserves

Money positioned for ready use in case of an emergency is called cash reserves. These funds can be held in savings, money market accounts, Series EE bonds, life insurance cash values, or short term certificate of deposits for opportunity investing.

Invested Assets

All those assets you have accumulated for future goals are your invested assets. Your list could include money set aside for your children's college, a new home or remodel job, monthly savings into a mutual fund for a major vacation, or your long-term retirement funding. Assets on this part of the net worth statement are those that do nothing more than earn money. Under the Investment Asset area, certain assets are identified as loaned and others as owned.

1. <u>Loaned Investments</u>: Money loaned to a third party in exchange for a return of principal and interest. These assets are also described as fixed assets due to the predictability of getting back in the future the amount you invested plus interest.

A good example is a Certificate of Deposit held at a bank. You gave the bank your money, and they gave you a piece of paper with a promise to pay a guaranteed interest rate for a predetermined period of time. At the end of that time, they'll give back the money along with the earnings.

2. Owned Investments: Ownership of an asset and participation in profits or loss. These assets are also known as variable assets due to their changing market values. The perfect example is common stock. When you purchase 100 shares of IBM, you're a partial owner of the company and have voting rights at share-holder meetings. You can't run the company, but you can participate in its growth or lack of growth.

Assets held in retirement plans can be either loaned or owned. Make a pencil note identifying those assets which are held in your retirement plans (403(b), 401(k), IRA, or pension/profit sharing programs).

Personal Use Assets

All assets meant to be used for personal enjoyment (boats, campers, collectibles), shelter (home, furniture, household goods), transportation (automobiles), adornment (jewelry, furs), etc. are listed as Personal Use Assets. Whatever you own that isn't intended to help you meet your financial goals belongs on this list. To help you determine which assets fit here, follow this golden rule: If you plan to use it, live in it, or never sell it, it belongs in the personal use section.

Liabilities

Get ready for the bad news. How much do you owe? Do you have real estate mortgages, consumer credit, automobile loans, loans from relatives, etc.? These are your liabilities. When you list these, don't spend a lot of time worrying about where to place the loans. Just be sure to account for every dime you owe.

BOTTOM LINE REVIEW

What part of your asset base is devoted to your future financial security? It is important to evaluate the amount of liquidity you have. Investment opportunities often arise unexpectedly and a cache of dollars immediately available to take advantage of these opportunities can provide efficient fuel for net worth

WHAT IS YOUR NET WORTH ?

growth. To find your net worth, subtract the sum total of all your liabilities from your assets. It is this figure that must grow to meet your goals.

Every person's net worth is distinctly different. The positioning of assets between loaned and owned can reflect different life stages or risk comfort levels. The following summarization of both the Young's and the Elden's net worths illustrates this point:

SUSAN AND LARRY YOUNG
NET WORTH STATEMENT

ASSETS		**TOTALS**
CASH RESERVES (less than 12 months maturity)		
Checking Accounts	$ 2,000	
Money Market Funds	1,600	
Life Insurance Cash	1,467	
Other: Series EE Bonds	3,000	$ 8,067
INVESTED ASSETS (loaned and owned)		
Tax Deferred Annuities	$ 10,750	
Individual Stocks	500	
Stock Mutual Funds	36,360	$ 47,550
PERSONAL USE ASSETS		
Home @ Market Value	$ 180,000	
Household Furnishings	5,000	
Automobiles	6,500	$ 191,500
TOTAL ASSETS		$ 247,177
LIABILITIES (Debts)		
Charge/Credit Balances	$ 1,500	
Automobile Loans	3,500	
Mortgage on Residence	100,000	
TOTAL LIABILITIES		$ 105,000
NET WORTH		
Total Assets less Total Liabilities		$ 142,177

JOHN AND CLARA ELDEN
NET WORTH STATEMENT

ASSETS		**TOTALS**
CASH RESERVES (less than 12 months maturity)		
Checking Accounts	$ 10,000	
Money Market Funds	20,450	
Life Insurance Cash	15,000	
Other: Series EE Bonds	7,000	$ 56,450
INVESTED ASSETS (loaned & owned)		
Tax Deferred Annuities	$ 90,000	
Municipal Bonds	86,000	
Individual Stocks	22,500	
Stock Mutual Funds	150,000	
Investment Real Estate	100,000	$ 448,500
PERSONAL USE ASSETS		
Home @ Market Value	$ 200,000	
Household Furnishings	25,000	
Automobiles	15,500	$ 240,000
TOTAL ASSETS		$ 744,450
LIABILITIES (Debts)		
Mortgage on Residence	$ 12,500	
Mortgage on Rental	60,009	
TOTAL LIABILITIES		$ 72,500
NET WORTH		
Total Assets less Total Liabilities		$ 671,950

There's quite a difference in these two net worth statements, most of which can be attributed to age disparity. The mid-30s Young family still have a long trek ahead of them to achieve all their financial destinations. The 55-year old Eldens are on the way to an early retirement by at least age 60.

Now that they have tallied their scores, how do you think they feel? Better or worse than when they started? Since both their bottom lines came up looking pretty good, perhaps they'll save the memory and let it motivate them to do more. Here are three steps to make net worth grow:

1. Save more: This step requires adjusting current expenditures in order to achieve future desires. In other words, cut back on pleasure spending and increase investment spending.

2. Decrease debts: Paying off indebtedness doesn't come easy. It is only accomplished by changing spending habits to free more funds for debt reduction.
3. Seek higher investment returns: This is the riskiest action to take because increased returns usually go along with increased risk. Sometimes, though, minor adjustments can increase the returns on your investments within your comfort zone (more about this later).

The net worth statement is a revealing picture. To an astute advisor, it exposes life-styles and financial philosophies. Here are a couple of my more memorable clients whose net worth statements spoke loud and clear.

Joe and Susie Gettenspend were an up-and-coming young couple with a lot of figures to add up in the personal assets section. They owned a boat, a new sports car, a 23-foot camping trailer, and an ever-increasing assortment of appliances, electronic gadgets, and furnishings. Their discretionary dollars, which could have been directed toward growth in net worth were instead dedicated to consumption. Other characteristics of this couple were their lack of long-term goals and an ever-present wail about high taxes.

Joe and Susie didn't need to tell me what their personal financial philosophy was. I could see immediately that they weren't motivated for the long-term. In fact, they were not even contributing to a retirement savings program at work, where they would have received three percent of their salaries free as a retirement contribution from their employers. It was obvious that Joe and Susie preferred instant gratification.

Mildred and Orville Safensound were just the opposite. They had a little to include in their net worth statement, but they could have had much more. They were living mentally in a depression, whether or not they lived through that historical period. Accordingly, they concentrated all their assets in areas with two characteristics in common — a guarantee and low returns. I'm surprised they didn't have their assets buried in their backyard.

For the Safensounds, frugality and a doomsday attitude resulted in a net worth of loaned assets they were afraid to touch, even though they were retired. They had a very modest life-style in relation to their net worth size, and their investments were generating inordinate amounts of taxable income. Still saving for that rainy day, this couple may die with all their assets intact.

Of course, these two couples are extreme examples. Perhaps you, like the Youngs and the Eldens, will find yourself somewhere in between the Gettenspends and the Safensounds. When I evaluate a net worth statement, I usually look for a balanced mix of loaned and owned assets. It's not good to have everything invested in either toys for today's joys or the equivalent of the backyard. Neither allows money to grow and multiply.

KEY ANALYSIS FACTORS

Reviewing key factors from your net worth statement will give you a clue or two about your own financial fitness.

1. Cash reserves: You need enough cash in your ready reserves to pay 3-6 months living expenses in case of unemployment, illness, accidents, or other catastrophes (flood, famine, or your extended vacation if boomerang children return).

   Add up your available cash and divide that number by your fixed monthly expenses as follows:

Monthly Expenses	$2,500
Cash Reserve $$$	$6,000

   $6,000 ÷ $2,500 = 2.4 months

   In this example, the cash reserve isn't quite enough, using the 3-6 month guideline. The final decision here is heavily dependent on personal circumstances. Is your job stable? Are you a one-income or two-income family? Are both jobs stable? Do you live up to your income? Are you covered by long-term disability insurance? Have you insured your income? Do you have a large mortgage or other debts? Do you have dependents? How much risk do you want in your life? An adequate cash reserve equals lower risk to your life-style.

2. Debt to equity ratio: To determine the relationship of debt to equity, or liabilities to assets, simply divide your total debts by your total assets. The answer will be expressed in a percentage. For example, $80,000 of debt and $150,000 in assets equals a 53% debt to equity ratio.

   $80,000 ÷ $150,000 = 53%

   The debt to equity ratio will vary according to one's lifestage. A younger person may have a much higher percentage due to a recent acquisition of a residence. An older couple will have a lower percentage if their goal has been to pay off debts prior to retirement.

   This ratio is commonly used to evaluate your risk exposure. The higher the percentage, the higher the risk.

3. Market values: It's easy to fudge here. What is your house really worth? Don't just guess, do a little research. It may be more or less than your tax assessment, so don't rely on it for a realistic valuation. There are other assets which are equally hard to value: Grandpa's coin collection, Grandma's jewelry, the fur you've had 15 years, and so forth. It's not quite as important if you never plan to spend the asset, but if you do , evaluate carefully. Business values are also frequently overstated and,

for many business owners, that asset — their business — may be a major part of their net worth. Particular attention must be paid to the method of business valuation. Is it realistic?

Start now to prepare a net worth statement using Worksheet 6A. It is tangible evidence of spending, wisely or unwisely. Quite a few people never bother with this exercise until they apply for a loan from a financial institution. Do it now; you may be surprised at the result. While your personal attributes may make you monetarily worth more than most individuals in your community, unless those attributes are backed up by a growing net worth, you may not be taken seriously in the banking boardroom.

WORKSHEET 6A

NET WORTH STATEMENT — "What You Own Minus What You Owe"
As of ________________, 19____

			TOTALS
	ASSETS		
L	CASH RESERVES (less than 12 months maturity)		
O	Checking Accounts	________	
A	Savings Accounts	________	
N	Money Market Funds	________	
E	Treasury Bills	________	
D	Life Insurance Cash	________	
	Other ________________	________	________
L	INVESTED ASSETS (loaned/fixed or owned/variable)		
O	Certificates of Deposit	________	
A	Notes Receivable	________	
N	Tax Deferred Annuities	________	
E	Bonds	________	
D	Bond Unit Trusts	________	
	Bond Mutual Funds	________	________
O	Individual Stocks	________	
W	Stock Mutual Funds	________	
N	Investment Real Estate	________	
E	Limited Partnerships	________	
D	Collectibles	________	
	Business Value	________	________
	PERSONAL USE ASSETS		
	Home @ Market Value	________	
	Second Residence	________	
	Household Furnishings	________	
	Automobiles	________	
	Campers/Boats/RVs	________	
	Time Share Assets	________	
	Jewelry/Furs	________	
	Other ________________	________	________
	TOTAL ASSETS		________
	LIABILITIES (Debts)		
	Charge/Credit Balances	________	
	Automobile Loan	________	
	Other Installment Credit	________	
	Mortgage on Residence	________	
	Other Real Estate Loans	________	
	Brokerage Margin Loans	________	
	Retirement Plan Loans	________	
	Other Debts	________	
	TOTAL LIABILITIES		________

NET WORTH: Total Assets less Total Liabilities ________

CHAPTER 7

SPENDING SOLUTIONS

"What each of us calls our necessary expenses will always grow to equal our incomes unless we protest the contrary."

The Richest Man in Babylon

Do you need to gain more control over your money? Do holidays torpedo your spending direction? Do you panic when the economy changes for the worse? Is money like a guest in your house — here today and gone tomorrow? Do you spend impulsively?

If you answered any of these questions with a yes, then it may be comforting to know that you are not alone. It's been estimated that as many as two thirds of the public live paycheck to paycheck. This creates a slight problem, such as never being able to satisfy your future goals through net worth growth. To put it succinctly, if your outgo exceeds your income, soon your upkeep will be your downfall. Planned spending is the most powerful weapon the wealthy have used to get rich.

MONEY MATTERS

Picture your life without financial worries. Acquiring positive spending habits will change your financial outlook by relieving guilt, creating financial options, and helping you reach your financial destinations. Here is what it takes to plan a successful cash flow:

- Your plan should develop as a result of your own experiences.
- Your plan must fit within your income resources and spending needs.
- Your plan should be structured so that you can begin to meet your individual goals.

Money matters, such as spending or charging for life-style needs versus spending for investments, must be faced frankly. A "spendsible" plan is the first essential part in that process.

Why does it seem that certain individuals have a knack for making ends meet and building assets, while others, in the same circumstances, are pinched for money? The answer is that the first group of people know how to manage money and have learned to plan spending. Even if you don't feel you overspend on a current basis, unless you are spending for the future, you are unlikely to see much financial progress. Just about everybody could do a better job in this area.

Before going into the mechanics of cash flow management, complete the following exercise. Rank the statements according to the degree of urgency you feel. If you're part of a couple, your partner should also do this exercise separately. Then compare notes to see where your attitudes differ.

DO YOU CONTROL YOUR MONEY OR DOES IT CONTROL YOU?

Circle the number under the column which reflects your attitude.

KEY:
A = Not at all like me
B = Marginally like me
C = Neutral
D = Very much like me
E = Describes me perfectly

	A	B	C	D	E
I like to know where every penny goes.	1	2	3	4	5
I think it is important to keep good records.	1	2	3	4	5
My charge balances don't concern me.	5	4	3	2	1
I have guidelines for spending in certain areas.	1	2	3	4	5
I enjoy material items and price is not an issue.	5	4	3	2	1
When it comes to gift giving, I work from a plan.	1	2	3	4	5
I think it is okay to use charge cards but I pay them off every month.	1	2	3	4	5
It is very important for me to keep up socially with my friends no matter what it costs.	5	4	3	2	1
I am concerned about my ability to save and invest.	1	2	3	4	5
I am an impulsive spender.	5	4	3	2	1
I often am late with my debt payments.	5	4	3	2	1
I watch the papers weekly for shopping bargains.	1	2	3	4	5
I don't know where my pocket cash disappears.	5	4	3	2	1
When I call long distance, I don't think about the charges.	5	4	3	2	1
When I get a pay raise, I still never seem to have extra dollars.	5	4	3	2	1

Add up your score, then look at the following descriptions and match your score to the appropriate paragraph.

Score

15-35 — You have difficulty dealing with money issues and have not fully, if at all, defined your spending priorities. Money has never been your favorite subject and, in fact, you don't think much about it unless circumstances — such as money-end before month-end, spousal arguments over money, or debtor notices — demand your attention. You could use a spending overhaul, starting with defining spending behaviors.

36-55 — You seem to get by OK. True, you have moments when you evaluate your income level and wonder why it's not being accumulated, but generally speaking, you're not overspending your income. If asked, you could estimate your expenses fairly accurately. You probably have taken stabs at accumulating money, but have never put enough systems in place so that it was accomplished. You can do better, if properly guided.

56-75 — You either are in control of your income and outgo, or you're very close to it. Your nature is such that you demand accuracy and accountability with your personal record keeping. Your potential to accumulate money is great and you may have already taken advantage of your abilities by "spendsible" investing. Your biggest challenge may be determining where to place the dollars that you have available for investment spending.

NEEDS VS. GREEDS ANALYSIS

It would be nice if we could skip this part of the job and get on with the growth in net worth. But we can't do that because this is the key to building net worth.

Many people confuse wants and needs, especially when rationalizing an expenditure. It's easy to tell the difference. We all need certain things in order to sustain our life-styles — food, clothing, shelter, utilities, transportation, medical/dental/auto/ property/life insurance coverages, and household and personal supplies. Other things we simply want — more steak dinners and pizzas (especially when we don't have to cook them), vacations to Hawaii and Europe, new living room furniture, sailboats, campers, a new VCR or camcorder, and so forth. These are the discretionary and irresistible greeds in life.

Understanding how and where you spend money is critical to success in this area. The ten steps which follow will help you "spendsibly" build a more productive future.

10 EASY STEPS TO CASH MANAGEMENT

1. The first step is to take a stab at estimating your mandatory expenses each month. List your debts, estimate your utilities, food and so forth. The intent is to see how familiar you are with the realities of your monthly cash flow. This area may hold surprises for those that have never analyzed their cash flow. Do you think you have dollars left? Are these discretionary dollars or necessary variable expenses which fluctuate from month to month?

2. Use Worksheet 7A to record the actual monthly amount of your fixed, necessary variable and purely discretionary expenditures. What is your monthly income? Was there anything left? If it looks as though there was an excess on paper, did you shift that excess to your net worth? If not, keep reading. You may wish to perform this step by using computer software such as Quicken, or other similar programs for tracking cash flow.

3. Visualize where you want to be in five years. Will you still be struggling to make ends meet, or will you be on the way to building wealth? What are your goals? If you are to put more money aside for the future...retire debt early...and make goals a reality, putting the brakes on certain spending is mandatory.

4. Make two copies of Worksheet 7B. On the first one (the second copy is referenced under item 7), try to document your spending pattern for 12 months. Audit last year's spending results by reviewing and categorizing checkbook entries, receipts, charge card statements, cash machine receipts, and other reminders of where your money has gone. Don't forget to include quarterly, semi-annual, or annual expenses you incur, such as auto licenses, insurance premiums, property taxes, gifts, the IRS, etc. This month-by-month estimate will serve as a guide to future spending. You can also use software, such as discussed in Step 2, for this exercise.

5. Establish immediately three cash management accounts:

   A. A cash control account — ideally a tax-free or taxable money market with checking privileges.

   B. A checking account for monthly fixed and mandatory variable expenses.

   C. A second money market or savings account for sporadic expenses. This is your come and go account.

6. Divide each paycheck amount between the three accounts. This is the critical component in your spending success and must be done in this order.

   A. Deposit your paycheck into the cash control account (this is the first account listed above).

   B. Now write two checks:

      1) The first should equal the total of your mandatory fixed and variable, but necessary expenses. Deposit it in your checking account, but only deposit the bare minimum you absolutely need to make it to the month's end.

      2) The second check must equal 1/12th of your annual sporadic expenses (car insurance, license tabs, property taxes, gifts). Put this check in the come and go account.

   C. Divide the remaining discretionary dollars in half. Allocate the first half to investment spending and the remainder to the pursuit of pleasure or non-essential purchases. This is a very easy way to divide your discretionary dollars between current wants and future needs, but it may not be a large enough investment expenditure to catapult you into financial independence. To see if your investments are large enough, read Chapter 17. If you don't have a cash reserve equal to 3-6 months of your expenses, make that the first goal for this money. Dollars available above this amount are candidates for serious investments.

7. If you haven't been successful in staying within your self-imposed limits, plan to monitor your discretionary and variable spending for at least 12 months.

Worksheet 7C is a form that is useful in keeping track of the detailed spending that takes place in your variable but necessary or discretionary categories. Use the second copy of Worksheet 7B to record actual results each month. Every three months evaluate the results. Where did you overspend and why? Make appropriate changes in variable expenses to customize your spending plan to your needs. But do not change your three-account system.

8. Faithfully monitor any depletion of your cash stash or investment accounts. Note what you did with that money — paid for unexpected medical bills, extra food, auto maintenance, home repair, vacation, and so forth. After a few months, you may see a trend which indicates you have underestimated required needs in one or more areas. If so, adjust your spending targets and shift dollars from overfunded to underfunded categories.
9. Some people do better at managing their monthly cash flow when they assign certain fixed expenses to specific weekly, biweekly, or semi-monthly pay periods. If it helps you to visually strategize your spending, use this technique to connect income to specific outgo.
10. Reward yourself with a tangible treat (but don't charge it) when you have accomplished 12 months of deficit-free spending.

As you strive to complete Worksheet 7A, realize that each of your expense items will fall in one of three areas: fixed and mandatory, variable but necessary, and discretionary expenses. The discretionary areas could be eliminated and the variable but necessary expenses trimmed. At the end of each expense line, circle the appropriate description of the expense: Fixed (F); Variable (V); or Discretionary (D). Don't forget that consumer debt payments must be broken down by category. For example, if you are paying $150/ month on furniture, place that amount in the Major Purchase category and note the credit company. Your VISA/MasterCard expenses also must be itemized by category.

The purpose of this exercise is to find and identify lost dollars that can be redirected into net worth growth — future spending — and used to satisfy your financial objectives. These objectives might include retiring at age 55, sending your children to a four-year state college, ferreting out a few extra dollars to blow each week, or all three.

Take a few minutes and review the worksheets at the end of the chapter. It will take time, but this discovery mission will be worth the effort if you can improve spending results. If you find your cash flow to be negative, it may be a result of investing too heavily in plastic.

CONTROLLING THE OPEN-ENDED CATEGORIES

You may want to monitor your variable and discretionary expense areas, such as entertainment, food, clothing, personal care, allowances, etc. The easiest way to accomplish this is to take Worksheet 7C, copy it and establish a looseleaf notebook for tracking purposes. The form is self-explanatory and will help you limit spending in one area so that you can devote extra dollars to another priority, such as future spending — retirement, education funding, travel, asset purchases. As an example, this control device can be used to monitor a clothing account with a $200/month allotment. Throughout the month, whenever a clothing item is purchased, it is recorded with the new balance carried forward. If the account is dry by mid-month, the clothing purchases simply cease until the cycle starts again.

That's it in a nutshell. But how do you deal with the realities of everyday life? You don't necessarily need to be a penny pincher, rather you need to enjoy money today and money tomorrow. Debt reduction and growing cash and investment reserves are the objectives.

Here are ten specific ideas to help you pull in the spending reins.

Spending Tips

1. Write checks for every item above $3.00. Account for allowances by keeping receipts. Categorize your credit card expenses, cash, and checking activity, and record these monthly.
2. Eliminate some or all discretionary items if you are in a crisis situation.
3. Spend less for certain expenses, such as gift giving, purchasing convenience foods, attending first-run movies, etc.
4. If you can, make use of your skills instead of paying for services, such as washing your car, chopping your wood, and doing your own home repairs. Brainstorm the possibilities.
5. Bring your lunch from home rather than eat out.
6. Take advantage of free community services for education and recreation, such as concerts, parks, lectures, libraries, recreational centers, and art exhibits.
7. Plan the year's purchases — even next year's holiday gifts — so you can look for values throughout the year.
8. Cut down or eliminate the so-called sin habits such as cigarettes, alcohol, and gambling (the lottery).
9. Don't get suckered by promotions that give you gifts with a purchase. For example, if you want a clock radio, buy it rather than subscribe to a magazine you're not particularly interested in that offers it with a subscription.
10. Try to appeal your property tax assessment if it appears unfair.

CURING CREDIT CARD BLUES

A credit card is a means for buying something unneeded at a price you can't afford with funds you don't have. If that sums it up for you, it's time to clean up the results of investing too heavily in plastic. Consumer interest is no longer tax deductible and is certainly not economical. If you want to make 15-18% on your money, it's easy — simply pay off consumer debt. Wouldn't it be nice to loan out your money and receive 18% interest on it? This is another secret of the wealthy!

Credit cards are a convenient but dangerous way to spend. I've counseled too many people who have obligated themselves with overwhelming levels of fixed credit payments. I remember one couple particularly well.

John and Georgia were card addicts who came to see me several years ago. They suffered the plight of many upper-income wage earners — "incomitis." They not only lived up to their income, they used 32% of it to fund consumer debts. This wasn't a deprivation to them necessarily, as their income levels allowed for luxuries, but it was what I called underwater debt. It kept them from doing other more important things with their money, such as adequately protecting their family from the risks of life and saving for their impending retirement. This family eventually paid off their debts and, as a result, created much more flexibility with spending choices.

If you want to find out whether you are over your head in debt, calculate your Consumer Debt Ratio. This ratio should be no more than 15% of your net income. The lower the better. Start by listing the mandatory minimum debt payments required on all loans, with the exception of your home mortgage or other investment oriented loans. Add these to get a total and divide that number by your monthly income after taxes. If you are carrying $300 of debt payments per month and your after-tax income is $2,000, the equation is as follows:

$$\$300 \div \$2{,}000 = 15\%$$

Many people, though, who are not over their heads according to this rule of thumb, nevertheless suffer from a monthly crunch on cash flow. Consider that 15% of a net income of $5,000 per month may leave more than enough money to live comfortably, but 15% of $1,500 per month may cut the margin too close to necessities.

Charging Tips

1. Visualize three other things that you can do with your money before you charge an item.
2. Reduce the number of credit cards you carry — keep just one major credit card and a couple of minor cards, such as a gas card and department store card. Use these only for essential purchases.

3. Pay off your credit card balances and keep them paid off monthly.
4. Write all charges in your checkbook and subtract the amount of each and every charge from the balance. This is a very visual way to see how easy it is to spend with plastic. If you follow this advice, at the end of the month, you should have adequate dollars left over in your checkbook to pay off the credit charges. Don't forget to add the charges back to the running total if you balance your checkbook before you actually write a check to pay off the credit accounts.

DEBT REDUCTION

Reducing consumer debt increases net worth, but which debt should be reduced first? Logic will lead you to the conclusion that the highest interest loans should go first — VISA, MasterCard, Sears, Penneys, etc. There is another way to attack the problem, one that works better psychologically. Pay off the smallest balance first. Otherwise, you may have to drastically cutback on other items in order to reduce your debt burden, and you may become discouraged; so don't pick the largest balance.

It is hard work. Every time you pay off a balance completely, reward yourself — but not by using a credit card.

If the idea of reducing your debt burden by systematic pay-offs is overwhelming, you may need to consider paying off the high interest loans with less expensive money.

Cost Effective Borrowing

1. Borrow against securities in a brokerage account. You can deduct the interest as long as it doesn't exceed your net investment income.
2. If you have cash value life insurance, check the cash balance. This may be a source of low-interest loans which you never have to pay back. Loans are simply deducted from the cash benefit at your death.
3. Refinance your primary home mortgage or add a home equity loan to turn non-deductible debts in fully tax deductible. Mortgage loans are fully deductible within certain limitations. Criteria for a deductible mortgage is discussed in Chapter 9.
4. Borrow against your bank certificate of deposit. A collateralized passbook loan may be only one or two percent more than your bank deposit may be earning. A line of credit tied to the prime rate is another option.
5. Borrow against your retirement accounts; but be careful, this is sacred money. You may be able to access money in certain pension plans, such as a 401K or employee thrift plan. These loans are also not deductible but can be one of your lower interest options.

DO YOU NEED HELP?

There are a multitude of ways to improve your cash flow. The first step is to evaluate your situation realistically.

There are two kinds of people who need help with their money:

1. Those who are in a crisis: They are over their head in debt and unable to purchase even essential items due to poor money management or other circumstances out of their control. These individuals should contact the Consumer Credit Counseling Service in their area. This non-profit service specializes in crisis management.

2. Those who know they could do a better job of managing their money: These people's primary objective usually is to pay off consumer debt and spend wisely in the future.

I'M SORRY, IT SAYS HERE YOU FILED FOR CHAPTER 11

In evaluating whether or not you need help, think about your strengths and weaknesses. Do you have the ability and want to manage your cash flow? Then what you've read may help you with that task. Or do you have the ability but don't wish to deal with the problem? You may want to have a professional assist you. Or perhaps you do not have the necessary discipline to get the job done. Then you definitely are a candidate for professional guidance.

According to the National Center for Financial Education, "When it comes to saving money, some people will stop at nothing (zero)." Don't let this be you!

WORKSHEET 7A

AVERAGE MONTHLY INCOME VS. EXPENDITURES

KEY: F = Fixed Expense; V = Variable; D = Discretionary

Monthly Average Income

Salaries	
Husband	________
Wife	________
Self-employment income	________
Dividends & interest	________
Capital gains & losses	________
Rents, annuities, or pensions	________
Alimony, child support	________
Tax refunds	________
Bonuses, gifts, misc. income	________
Total Income	________

Monthly Average Outgo			**Notes**
Federal income tax	________	F, V, D	________
FICA tax	________	F, V, D	________
State/local income tax	________	F, V, D	________
Housing			
Mortgage payments	________	F, V, D	________
Monthly rent	________	F, V, D	________
Utilities			
Electricity	________	F, V, D	________
Oil or gas	________	F, V, D	________
Water	________	F, V, D	________
Telephone	________	F, V, D	________
Maintenance/repairs	________	F, V, D	________
Insurance			
Homeowners	________	F, V, D	________
Renters	________	F, V, D	________
Property tax	________	F, V, D	________
Groceries	________	F, V, D	________
Restaurant meals	________	F, V, D	________
Clothing			
Purchases			
Husband	________	F, V, D	________
Wife	________	F, V, D	________
Children	________	F, V, D	________
Laundry	________	F, V, D	________
Dry cleaning	________	F, V, D	________
Repairs	________	F, V, D	________
Transportation			
Auto payments	________	F, V, D	________
Auto insurance	________	F, V, D	________
Gasoline	________	F, V, D	________
Repairs/maintenance	________	F, V, D	________
Auto licenses	________	F, V, D	________

Medical		
Health insurance	________F, V, D	________
Uncovered medical	________F, V, D	________
Prescriptions	________F, V, D	________
Child care expenses	________F, V, D	________
Education		
College	________F, V, D	________
Other tuition	________F, V, D	________
Life insurance prems.	________F, V, D	________
Disability ins. prems.	________F, V, D	________
Major purchases		
Appliances	________F, V, D	________
Furniture	________F, V, D	________
Other	________F, V, D	________
Support maintenance	________F, V, D	________
Child support	________F, V, D	________
Vacations	________F, V, D	________
Entertainment	________F, V, D	________
Gifts		
Holidays	________F, V, D	________
Birthdays	________F, V, D	________
Other	________F, V, D	________
Charitable contributions	________F, V, D	________
Miscellaneous		
Newspapers	________F, V, D	________
Magazine subscriptions	________F, V, D	________
Toiletries, cosmetics	________F, V, D	________
Personal care	________F, V, D	________
Allowances	________F, V, D	________
Other	________F, V, D	________
Other	________F, V, D	________
Other	________F, V, D	________
Other	________F, V, D	________
	Total Expenses	________
	Total Income Less Total Expenses (+ or (-) Result)	________

WORKSHEET 7B
TWELVE MONTH CASH FLOW CALENDAR

INCOME	JANUARY	FEBRUARY	MARCH	APRIL	MAY	JUNE	JULY	AUGUST	SEPTEMBER	OCTOBER	NOVEMBER	DECEMBER
SALARY NO. 1												
SALARY NO. 2												
SELF-EMPLOYMENT INCOME												
DIVIDENDS & INTEREST												
CAPITAL GAINS/LOSSES												
RENTS OR ANNUITIES												
PENSIONS												
SOCIAL SECURITY BENEFITS												
ALIMONY, CHILD SUPPORT												
TAX REFUNDS												
BONUSES, GIFTS, MISC.												
OTHER												
OTHER												
OTHER												
TOTAL												

WORKSHEET 7B
TWELVE MONTH CASH FLOW CALENDAR

EXPENSES	JANUARY	FEBRUARY	MARCH	APRIL	MAY	JUNE	JULY	AUGUST	SEPTEMBER	OCTOBER	NOVEMBER	DECEMBER
FEDERAL INCOME TAX												
FICA (SOCIAL SECURITY) TAX												
STATE/LOCAL INCOME TAX												
MORTGAGE PAYMENTS												
MONTHLY RENT												
ELECTRICITY												
OIL/GAS												
WATER												
TELEPHONE												
MAINTENANCE/REPAIRS												
HOMEOWNERS INS.												
RENTERS INS.												
PROPERTY TAX												
FOOD AT HOME												
RESTAURANT MEALS												
CLOTHING/HUSBAND												
CLOTHING/WIFE												
CLOTHING/CHILDREN												
LAUNDRY												
DRYCLEANING												
REPAIRS												
AUTO PAYMENTS												
AUTO INSURANCE												
GAS/OIL												
REPAIRS/MAINTENANCE												
AUTO LICENSES												
HEALTH INSURANCE												
UNCOVERED MEDICAL												
PRESCRIPTIONS												
CHILDCARE												
COLLEGE TUITION												

WORKSHEET 7B
TWELVE MONTH CASH FLOW CALENDAR

EXPENSES	JANUARY	FEBRUARY	MARCH	APRIL	MAY	JUNE	JULY	AUGUST	SEPTEMBER	OCTOBER	NOVEMBER	DECEMBER
OTHER TUITION												
LIFE INSURANCE												
DISABILITY INSURANCE												
APPLIANCES PURCHASES												
FURNITURE PURCHASES												
OTHER PURCHASES												
SPOUSAL SUPPORT												
CHILD SUPPORT												
VACATIONS												
ENTERTAINMENT												
GIFTS/BIRTHDAY												
GIFTS/CHRISTMAS												
GIFTS/OTHER												
CHARITY												
NEWSPAPERS												
MAGAZINES												
TOILETRIES												
COSMETICS												
HAIRCUTS												
OTHER PERSONAL												
ALLOWANCES												
OTHER												
OTHER												
OTHER												
OTHER												
TOTAL												
TOTAL INC												
TOTAL EXP												
(+) OR (-) R												

WORKSHEET 7C

VARIABLE/DISCRETIONARY EXPENSE CONTROL SHEET

______________________ (Expense Category)

______________________ (Budgeted $$$ Amount)

Date	Transaction	Monthly Expenditure	Running Balance

INSTRUCTIONS: For every spending category you need to track, set up one of these pages. Use of this spending control tool can be a great aid in helping you accurately track your spending patterns.

CHAPTER 8
SAFEGUARDING YOUR WEALTH

"Insure for surgery, pay for the runny nose."
Unknown

Insurance is the great protector of wealth. Yes, it does cushion some unpleasant facts of life — death, catastrophic losses, disability, and poor health — the circumstances you think will never happen to you. But these situations do occur, and the cost can be devastating.

Why is it then that people will risk their future wealth instead of protecting it with insurance that may cost only pennies day? Perhaps it is because the issues of one's own death, disability or major illness are hard to face. Insurance is always behind the scenes and does not provide flashy cocktail party conversation. When the rich share how they became wealthy, they only discuss their renown as wheelers and dealers or their nonchalant acceptance of large inheritances. Rarely do they brag about their insurance strategies. But the wealthy do understand the art of preserving their wealth through adversity. You can also. The example which follows provides immediate clarity and, it is hoped, motivation.

An infantry battalion was due to ship overseas. The captain was given responsibility for seeing that everyone in the battalion signed up for their $10,000 of insurance. He stood in front of the group and said, "Men, you're due to go overseas. You need this insurance. It will cost you $6.50 per month, and you can sign up at the end of the field."

No one signed up. The captain said the same thing every day for a month and still no one signed up. At the end of the month, a sergeant was transferred in and the captain delegated this miserable assignment to him. His instructions were "Sergeant, your job is to see to it that each of these men signs up for $10,000 worth of insurance." The sergeant proceeded to talk to the men for just one minute and everybody in the battalion signed up.

The captain, understandably, was mystified and said: "I have tried this for a month, and nobody signed up at all. You talked for one minute and everybody signed up. What did you say?"

The sergeant replied, "I just told the facts. I said, 'Men, you're in the infantry now, due to go overseas, and you don't have any insurance. If you get over there and get killed without any insurance, the government isn't going to lose a penny. But, if you take out your insurance and you're killed, the government will be out $10,000. Now who do you think they're going to place on the front lines? The men they're not going to lose a penny on, or the men they're going to have to pay $10,000 on?'"

This story is frequently circulated in financial seminars to illustrate the power of fear. We are most motivated to act when we are empowered by the fear of dying, becoming disabled or seriously ill, losing property, or being sued. Consider Murphy's Law — just when you think you have your life in order, a monkey wrench surfaces. Murphy's Law, "Anything that can go wrong, will go wrong," rules. It is never timely.

You have several options with which to manage risks. For instance, you can ignore the risk, mitigate it by some action you take to lower the risk, share the risk, or assume the risk. When you weigh the potential cost of ignoring or assuming the risk entirely, insurance is really a bargain. It's an inexpensive way of placing a safety net around you and your family until you have acquired sufficient wealth to diffuse the effects of unexpected disasters.

I learned this firsthand when I was just a novice in financial advising. Back in 1982, I delivered a life insurance check to a client who had just lost her husband. I had never met the woman before, but her distress was so intense it could not be hidden, even from a stranger. I can still remember how her eyes misted over as she sat at her kitchen table. She shared with me that the $5,000 check I had given her and her Social Security were all she had in the world. Her husband hadn't believed in insurance, and they had never managed to accumulate assets for retirement.

It was grim, but there are other choices. Widows or widowers don't have to be left destitute. They can and should be left with enough insurance so they can be self-sufficient and free to make reasonable choices as to life-style. Those that are disabled can and should have had the courage to protect their life-style. Sickness can but should not devastate life savings. A fire can but should not leave you homeless. Insurance can protect your wealth/ savings and help manage your risks.

LIFE OR DEATH INSURANCE

I always wondered why life insurance was so named, when it is only activated upon death. Death is the most certain of all realities and every day we live, we are one day closer to dying. Some of us are lucky and die a peaceful death at an advanced age, while others die accidently or from poor health at too young an age. As Venita Van Caspel wrote in her book, ***Money Dynamics for the 80's***, "The great mystery of life is the length of it! You need a plan if you live a normal lifetime and you need a plan if you die prematurely." Since we all know we'll die eventually, the mystery is how to plan for something when we don't know when it will happen.

Who Needs It?

To start thinking about your needs, review these common questions asked by concerned individuals:

"I'm single, do I need life insurance?"

"Do you recommend that I buy a policy for my baby?"

"We're both working and living up to our incomes. What do you think?"

"Should we convert our company group insurance when we retire?"

The purchase of life insurance is often a subjective decision made as much with emotion as with logic. Consider my long-standing position that children do not need life insurance protection because they don't have an earnings value yet. When I shared this conviction firmly in a seminar several years ago, a young mother told me that her son had been killed the year before and she was unable to work for some time due to her extreme grief. The $50,000 policy on his life allowed her time to grieve and helped put her life back in order. After that night, I started rethinking my position. If it is important to your emotional peace of mind to carry insurance where it doesn't appear to be economically mandated, do it.

Here are five rules of thumb to help you determine if you need life insurance:

1. If you have an income flow that beneficiaries require to maintain their life-style and future goals.
2. If excessive debts would be a burden to your heirs.
3. If you're contemplating retirement and want the flexibility of self-insuring the survivor pension rather than paying your employer to provide the survivor pension.
4. If you're so wealthy that Federal estate tax will be assessed.
5. If you want to be sure to leave an inheritance for your beneficiaries.

You may have a valid reason to think about covering those needs with life insurance.

Providing Family Security

The objective of performing a family security needs analysis is to guarantee that your family can maintain the same standard of living after your death. How much coverage you need is determined by calculating the after-tax income for the rest of your working years. This is what will vanish and will need replacement with a lump sum of income producing cash.

There are so many variables involved in determining your insurance needs that it's impossible to give a quick answer to the question, "How much insurance should I buy?" Worksheet 8A (end of chapter) attempts to develop the concept for you, but there is more. The answer should be formulated after having calculated the income needs of your survivors. These questions can get you started: How heavily dependent is your life-style on your income? Will your survivors be able to produce enough income to support themselves? If they don't work, can they? How many years do you believe your family will need extra income? Are you concerned about providing your family with a standard of living after your death similar to that enjoyed now? Financial counseling may be required to help you sort through these issues.

The last assumption needed to determine the face amount of the life insurance is your expectation on how well your beneficiary can manage the money. The higher the return you believe he or she can achieve, the lower the death benefit necessary. I usually recommend an interest rate which does not exceed 3% over long-term inflation. For example, if the long term average inflation rate has been 5%, don't expect earnings above 8%.

Calculating the insurance for Larry and Susan Young will serve as an example. Larry is the primary wage earner with a net income of $3,600 per month. Susan is presently a homemaker caring for their three minor children.

Without insurance on both lives, things would be bleak. Susan would probably have to sell the home to rid herself of the $1,029 per month mortgage payment, and the family would have to downscale their housing expenses. The required addition of a nanny for the children if Susan predeceases Larry would stretch his income to the breaking point.

How can Larry and Susan avoid such a dark future? The first step is to determine what their required income needs are for life-style in addition to their long term goals. They start out by determining they need to have at least $30,000 available upon the death of either parent for each child's college education.

The next item they want to protect is their ability to keep the children in familiar surroundings. This means the surviving spouse would need adequate money to either make the mortgage payments or pay it off. Rather than purchasing mortgage insurance as a separate policy, their advisor suggests that life insurance policies on each be structured to produce enough income to cover all mortgage expenses.

The last item to discuss is how much other income would be needed to maintain the family's standard of living. With three children under age 16, the surviving spouse would receive Social Security benefits as a widow/er as long as her/his earnings don't exceed the maximum allowed. Neither Larry nor Susan would probably draw this benefit. Larry earns too much and Susan would be forced to join the working ranks also. In any case, once the children reach age 16, spousal Social Security income ceases until age 60 when each would have the choice of drawing against the deceased spousal benefit. If they draw as early as age 60, the benefit would equal 71.5% of the spouse's age 65 benefit. The children also would receive a benefit up to their age 18.

This information forms the basis for the following example illustrating Susan's income needs. This calculation was performed using Worksheet 8A. You may be surprised at the amount of insurance needed.

LIFE INSURANCE NEEDS ANALYSIS

THE INCOME NEED		
Immediate Expenses		
Federal estate taxes	$ -0-	
State inheritance taxes	-0-	
Probate costs	1,000	
Burial fees	10,000	
Uninsured medical costs	-0-	
Repayment of selected debts	3,500	
Total Final Expenses		$ 14,500
Future Expenses		
Family income needs[1]		
$24,000 divided by .08 (8%)	$ 300,000	
Emergency fund	10,000	
Child care expense	-0-	
Education funding	60,000	
Total Future Expenses		$ 370,000
Total Immediate & Future Needs		$ 384,500
CURRENT ASSETS		
Cash & savings	$ 7,500	
Equity in real estate excluding home	20,000	
Securities (stocks/bonds)	2,500	
IRA/Keogh plans	12,000	
Employer savings plans	35,000	
Lump sum pensions	-0-	
Current life insurance	100,000	
Other assets	-0-	
Total Current Assets		$ 177,000
INSURANCE NEEDED		
Total needs minus total assets		
Total Immediate & Future Needs		$384,500
Total Current Assets		- 177,000
Additional life insurance needed		$207,500

1. To estimate the lump sum of capital needed to produce the income shortfall, divide the annual income need by a reasonable interest rate such as 7-8%. In this example, the children were assumed to collect Social Security benefits of $1,000 per month. This example provides for enough capital to supply income needs from the interest earned. Expenses will be forced up by inflation and the principal will be invaded eventually to sustain the standard of living.

Now that the Young family has determined additional insurance is necessary, where should they look first? The obvious source would be to check out Larry's employment benefits. Or any group or association they belong to could be another source of group term insurance. If Larry can purchase additional insurance, these sources could be the least expensive place to buy it. The big drawback is that Larry can't take it with him if he quits, is terminated, or drops out of the association, unless it is converted to permanent insurance.

Some permanent insurance, an amount to carry around through life like a warm, fuzzy security blanket, may also be a desirable option. It can help protect us from our own human frailties, such as poor investment decisions or a lack of discipline in saving money. It can also protect us from medical catastrophes that strike, consume money, and result in death.

Life Insurance Choices

There are many creative labels placed on life insurance, but under all the razzle dazzle, only three basic types emerge:

1. <u>Whole life — protection plus savings</u>
   Characteristics: Low interest, fixed premium, and frequently, dividend options.

   Whole Life insurance is still alive and well. It may seem archaic in composition, but it does carry the lowest risk of all cash value insurances. The interest rate is guaranteed and if dividends are part of the plan, they can be used to partially pay premiums or be returned to the policy holder. Don't confuse a life insurance dividend with a taxable investment return. They're not the same thing. A life insurance dividend is only a return of part of the premium paid; the portion the company does not need for current operations. Dividends are not guaranteed but a trend can probably be established.

   The only appropriate use of a dividend is to reduce premiums or make a deposit in your checkbook. Purchasing paid up additions, PUAs in insurance lingo, is probably one of the most expensive ways to accumulate additional insurance. It can be useful, though, if you become uninsurable and you wish to buy teeny pieces of additional insurance without proof of insurability. Dividends held on deposit are another mistake. You are taxed on the interest from the dividend pool and only earn interest equivalent to money market rates — if that. Unless you are uninsurable, avoid succumbing to the temptation to let the insurance company use your dividends.

2. <u>Term — annual renewable or 5/10/15 year level term</u>
   Characteristics: Pure insurance just like your health, auto, or homeowner policies. There is no return of cash after the term of insurance has ended, which is the sole reason the cost is so reasonable.

Term aptly describes the use of this type of insurance because the insurance will terminate after a predetermined period. It can be used quite wisely, though, to insure for periods of up to 20-40 years, depending on how old you are when you start. One of the most popular configurations of term is level premium term from 5 to 20 years. The cost should be guaranteed so you can avoid ugly surprises when premium notices arrive.

Mortgage insurance is another type of term insurance which eventually disappears just like your mortgage. The kicker is that you pay a level premium for decreasing insurance. It is one of the most expensive types of term insurance, and more of a convenience than a wise buy. Don't insure your mortgage, insure your life. Provide enough insurance so that your survivor can maintain his/her standard of living, make the mortgage payment, send the kids to college, and not have to get remarried for financial reasons. For those that insist on having mortgage protection as a separate policy, I recommend the purchase of level term insurance with guaranteed premiums for 15-20 years.

Term insurance is always a good choice when funds are tight. For those who may have a permanent insurance need, a guaranteed convertible and renewable policy can be purchased and converted later to permanent insurance regardless of health history. It is the item of choice when insurance is needed only for a short period of time rather than permanently. Term insurance has always been recommended for those that have the financial discipline to save the difference between the higher whole life premium and the term premiums. Unfortunately, most people don't follow through with the necessary discipline.

3. Interest Sensitive — Term plus Cash Value Accounts
Characteristics: Flexible premiums, current mortality table rates, adjustable death benefit and premium payment periods, guaranteed cash accounts or variable investment choices (i.e., safety vs. growth).

While it may sound like the whole life insurance described under No. 1 above, interest sensitive life insurance is a different configuration founded on the same principles — term insurance married to a tax deferred cash value account.

The most common type of interest sensitive life is Universal Life. It is also one of the most flexible policy structures you can buy. Premium payments and death benefits can be increased or decreased plus you can borrow from your cash values.

Fixed versions of Universal Life can be purchased from most life insurance companies. Premiums will vary dramatically from company to company depending on the mortality assumptions used, interest rate credited to the cash earnings of the policy, and internal company expenses. Be careful when relying on policy sales illustrations — there is ample room with this type of policy to be overly confident with policy performance projections. If you are going to purchase an interest sensitive product, ask your agent to run the illustration at an interest rate two percent below that which is currently credited. If the policy you are considering runs out of money in the cash account prior to your age 85, the premiums aren't sufficient to fund the insurance. At some future point, you would have to increase your premium to keep your current level of death benefits. It is a delusion to expect present interest rates will continue for the next 40 years yet that is what is purported on these sales illustrations. Be careful!

Another choice for your universal life policy is the variable version. Within variable life policies are multiple pools of managed stocks and bonds. The primary advantage of a variable policy is that the income and capital gains produced by holding stocks and bonds can be tax deferred. Tax deferred compounding combined with a tax free death benefit could be profitable.

There is another type of interest sensitive insurance — Current Interest Life. This product credits competitive interest rates to a fixed cash account like the universal life product above. Premiums are fixed and guaranteed, and death benefits are not adjustable. One model has a disappearing premium which vanishes after six years if the policy continues to earn at the stated rate. If not, premiums would be paid for a longer period, but they would vanish eventually.

You can shop and compare policies, but you will have to be an astute shopper. Of the total premium, find out how much is attributed to the mortality and expense costs and how much of the premium is transferred to the cash account. Ask for a internal adjusted rate of return on the cash account. This will disclose the rate of growth on the savings component after expenses and mortality costs. It will never be the same as the interest rate declared by the company. If you have chosen a variable product, the confusion can be even greater. In addition to the mortality and insurance expense costs, there are money management fees.

Here are some thoughts to help you make a good buying decision. If you want to be sure that your insurance will still be in effect when you die, you need to buy either whole life or interest sensitive life. If you just want to protect certain events from risk that have an easily defined time frame, purchase term.

The above information is meant to be a broad summary of what is available so you'll be able to make the right decision when it comes to protecting your family. Life insurance coverages can be confusing. Exhibit 8A (end of chapter), a life insurance product analyzer chart reprinted with permission of Ben G. Baldwin, CLU, clarifies types of coverages available and options which belong to each type.

The key to choosing life insurance is to find the model that fits your needs. It's not always the least expensive or the priciest, but rather a good policy at a reasonable cost from a quality company. For information on financial ratings, see Exhibit 8B. Additionally, try and work with an experienced broker (three plus years in the industry) who can shop among multiple companies for the product which fits your needs rather than an agent tied to one company.

BELLS & WHISTLES

Most policies come with bells and whistles sold as options: accidental death rider, term riders for other family members, waiver of premium, and guaranteed purchase options.

Some of these extra options can be attractive, but keep in mind, the more options you purchase, the higher your premium will be. Consider the purpose of the options and whether they are appropriate for your needs. Many people buy for emotional reasons rather than the value of each option as applied to their lives.

Here are some options worth considering:

- Waiver of Premium. For a very small monthly charge per $1,000 of death benefit, this option can guarantee payments of your premiums in case of disability. After you have been disabled for 90 days, your premium will be paid by the waiver of premium insurance option you purchased.
- Guaranteed Purchase Options. If you feel that your health might deteriorate in the future and there is a remote chance you will want to increase your insurance coverage, buy this option. It guarantees the insurance company will provide additional insurance for you in the amount of the option you purchased, even if you no longer qualify for new coverage.

Here is an option that is less worthy:

- Accidental Death. This option is always vetoed unless the insured is employed in a highly dangerous line of work or is accident prone. Do you know why this coverage is dirt cheap? It is because insurance companies rarely have to pay off. Statistically speaking, a very small percentage of the population dies accidentally each year. Before you sign on the dotted line, ask yourself, "Will my survivors need more money if I die accidentally rather than of natural causes?"

Let's Make a Deal

Many companies and insurance agents encourage clients to replace their old policies with new products. Should you trade in those old-fashioned policies for the latest design? It could be to your advantage, but don't make this choice without a thorough numerical analysis of the economics of trading your old insurance coverages for one of the latest models. Most insurance agents will assist you in calculating the real costs of maintaining your old policies versus acquiring a new policy. In most states, insurance agents and brokers are required to have you sign a disclosure statement which compares the economics of the suggested policy against your existing policy.

WILL DISABILITY STRIKE?

Many working adults make a common mistake when it comes to insurance: they buy life insurance but ignore their need for disability insurance.

Disability can strike just as quickly as death. Paul learned this the hard way. He was dumping the garbage one morning when he slipped and landed on a pane of window glass. The impact sliced his arm lengthwise and crosswise. Many stitches and eight to nine weeks of healing later, he began six hours of therapy a day. This kept him from working for 18 months more. Who would have thought a trip to the garbage container could prove so financially devastating?

Today, Paul is a walking advertisement for the benefits of carrying a disability policy. Yes, he's back at work, but the road back was extra long due to the frugalities imposed by living on a greatly reduced income. If he had been covered by disability insurance, the outcome of the story could have been much more pleasant.

Your ability to earn income is a very important asset and deserves protection. A disruption of income could be disastrous (unless you're already independently wealthy). All your plans for the immediate future would screech to a halt.

Statistically speaking, you are more likely to be disabled than die, but only about one-quarter of the population is insured against this risk. The odds are about six to one in favor of disability over premature death. If this area is of concern to you, the logical place to investigate purchasing coverage is with your employer. Many large corporations offer long-term disability to their employees at costs greatly subsidized by their largess. Typically, a corporation may provide a plan that starts paying 55-60% of your wages three months after you are disabled. These policies are based on a definition which states if you can't perform the duties of your own occupation for a stated period of time, usually 18-24 months, they'll pay you. After that period, you must be unable to perform the duties of any job or any job for which you are suited by education and experience.

There's some risk involved in these programs. For instance, if you can't work at your own occupation after the initial period expires but can perform the duties of a janitor, you may find that a janitor is exactly what you've become.

Read your company plan carefully. If you're not comfortable with the extent of the coverage, purchase a wrap-around policy. These policies provide expanded coverage which dovetails with the underlying policy. Again, weigh the risks against your other financial goals to see how far your investment and insurance spending can be stretched. Features that affect your coverage include:

- Definition of Disability: The policy must explain the definition of disability. You'll see the terms own occupation (OWN OCC) or any occupation (ANY OCC) used to describe conditions which must be present to activate the policy. The OWN OCC language is the strongest. If you can't work at your own job or a job for which your training and experience qualifies you, they'll pay. The ANY OCC is the weakest. If you can work in any capacity, you must.

- Elimination Period: The elimination period extends from the first day of disability to the beginning of benefits. It can be 30, 60, 90, or more days. The longer the elimination period, the lower the premiums.
- Length of Benefits: The benefit period defines the term of coverage: one year, five years, or up to age 65. The longer the coverage period, the higher the premiums.
- Amount of Benefits: Generally, coverage is desired for 60% of one's gross income. Premiums can be greatly reduced if an integrated policy is selected. This allows the insurer to reduce the disability payment if the insured starts to collect Social Security disability income.
- Partial Disability Benefits: Be sure the policy you consider allows for partial payments in case you return to work at less than full capacity.
- Cost-of-Living Rider or Future Purchase Options: If you want to keep your benefits in step with inflation, one of these options is necessary. Either feature can assure you that if you do become disabled in the future, the income you draw will buy the same amount of groceries as when you purchased the policy.
- Other Areas of Concern: The policy must be non-cancellable and guaranteed renewable.

Remember, Social Security doesn't pay benefits unless your disability is expected to last at least one year or result in death. Even then you must wait five months for payments to start, and these cease as soon as you are able to perform <u>any</u> kind of work. The key word is "any."

An incidental consideration is the tax treatment of the disability income. If your employer pays the premiums, the proceeds are fully taxable to you when received. If you pay the premium with after-tax dollars, the benefits are received tax-free.

Estimate your disability needs by filling out Worksheet 9B. Be realistic. Disability means you can't go out and earn a living. It doesn't necessarily mean the disabled will be a vegetable. Contemplate the effects on your family of six months or more of lost income. The result from the worksheet will reflect your deficit income during disability. This is the extra amount you need to provide through a disability policy. Remember, it can't be more than 60% of your gross income.

Here is what Susan and Larry discovered about their disability needs. If you have a concern in this area, Worksheet 8B can be used to review your disability income exposure.

DISABILITY INCOME NEEDS

LIVING EXPENSES		
Housing (utilities, insurance, taxes, maintenance, rent/ mortgage payment)	$ 18,000	
Food	4,200	
Clothing	2,400	
Transportation	3,600	
Entertainment/recreation	1,200	
Uninsured medical expenses	500	
Insurance premiums	600	
Debt payments	1,200	
Miscellaneous	3,000	
Annual Living Expenses		$ 34,700
INCOME DURING DISABILITY		
Spousal after-tax income	$ 13,000	
Dividends and interest	1,500	
Rents, annuities, pensions	-0-	
Annual Income		$ 14,500
NET ANNUAL DISABILITY INCOME NEEDS		$ 20,200

Fortunately, Larry has 60% of his earnings protected with a disability policy through his employer. It would provide $30,000 a year to them and perhaps negate Susan's need to work full-time. But like most employer provided policies, it will only insure Larry for his OWN OCC for the first 18 months and then the definition of disability reverts to ANY OCC. If Larry and Susan want stronger coverage, they could purchase an additional policy with OWN OCC coverage which has an 18 month waiting period. This would give them a solid disability insurance package.

MEDICAL

High deductibles along with high co-insurance limits will keep your costs down. Protecting your family against catastrophic medical expenses is a must. Remember to insure for surgery but pay for the runny noses. Read your policy carefully to see what is covered and what is not — you don't want any surprises to greet you on your hospital bed. You need a policy with at least a million dollars in benefits. With today's skyrocketing costs of hospitalization, physicians' treatments and medicine, this risk is not to be left uncovered.

LONG-TERM CARE

Will you spend your final years being cared for by professional caregivers? According to statistics, about 40% of all persons over age 65 will require some form of long-term care. Of persons over age 85, roughly 25% are in nursing homes. This could be a problem as more and more people will reach these ages and beyond.

You may think you'll never end up in a home because you're healthy. That's what 50% of the nursing home population also once said — the 50% who have some form of dementia. Senility, Alzheimer's, or whatever you wish to call it, is one of the leading causes of incapacity as the population ages.

Will Medicare take care of your long-term care needs? No. In fact, Medicare will pay for very little and then it is just for skilled care. The first 20 days are paid up to an approved amount, and the next eighty days are fully paid except for a $74 daily deduction. Beyond 100 days, there is a zero payment. Worse yet, most admissions to nursing home facilities are at the custodial level for which Medicare pays nothing.

What makes long-term health care such a risk? Money, money, money. The average cost is $40,000. Knowing this, you might wonder why 80% of the people over age 65 have one or more Medicare supplement plans, but only 3% carry long-term health care. Again, refer to the axiom: pay for the small items and insure the large risks. It makes good sense.

Most long-term care policies cover both a specified stay in a long-term care facility and certain home health services. These policies are generally sold individually, though some large employers have discovered that offering them as an employee benefit encourages workers to sign up. Insurance carriers divide long-term care into four main categories:

1. <u>Skilled care</u>: The highest level of medically necessary care provided by a licensed, skilled medical professional working under the supervision of a doctor.
2. <u>Intermediate care</u>: A level requiring medical supervision and skilled nursing on an intermittent basis.
3. <u>Custodial care</u>: The level of care given primarily to meet personal needs. It can be provided by persons without professional skills or training and includes help walking, getting out of bed, eating, and taking medicine. Even if this care is provided by a professional in a skilled nursing facility, it is still considered custodial care.
4. <u>Home health care</u>: Home care covers everything from homemaking and chore services up to professional services of medical personnel. This is one area where there is great disparity between policies. Be sure and review services, frequency, and expense limitations carefully.

Buyer's Guide

Here are a number of considerations which will affect the cost:

Number of years benefits will be paid.
Per day benefit ceiling
Length of elimination period
Cost-of-living benefits
Age of applicant and, in some cases, marital status.

Other important questions for you to ask:

Is there a waiver of premium?
What are the restrictions for Alzheimer's or other forms of dementia?
Are pre-existing conditions excluded? If so, for how long?
Does the policy cover all levels of care?
Is the policy guaranteed renewable for life?

Look for a policy with as few gatekeepers as possible. Gatekeepers are those hoops you must jump through prior to qualifying for coverage. Two examples are: 1) The insuring company's definition of the Six Activities of Daily Living, and 2) hospitalization for at least three days prior to admission to a nursing home. There are more. Once you have narrowed the field, start comparing the money. You will be surprised at the great variance in policy costs.

Should you spend a few dollars now to avoid major expenditures later? Yes, with the following two exceptions: 1) you are already mega-rich and can pay for care for years without any noticeable depletion of your estate, or 2) you have little investment assets which would be consumed. In the latter case, Medicaid, under present laws, would soon come to the rescue.

PROPERTY INSURANCE

Homeowners policies cover two areas of loss: 1) to the dwelling, related properties, and household furnishings, and 2) losses where you were at fault. You want an all-risk policy that insures your home's contents and property for replacement cost. This is the amount of money you would have to pay to rebuild your home, excluding the value of the land and foundation if the home were to be destroyed. The cost to replace just your home furnishings and personal belongings could be considerable.

Keep your deductible small. It is difficult under current tax laws to qualify for any loss deduction on uninsured casualty losses.

If you own expensive jewelry, silver, furs, computer equipment, etc., you must add a floater to cover these items. Wise homeowners take photos of their possessions and store these photos or videos in a safe place outside of the home.

What about liability? If a visitor slips on the proverbial banana peel in your home and sues for damages, how much will your policy pay? You should probably take the upper limit your insurance company has to offer.

AUTO INSURANCE

Automobile insurance must cover some big losses: loss of the auto itself, medical bills, and exposure to suit. Don't try to trim the costs by cutting liability coverages. We live in a litigious society.

Here's a summary of the common coverages:

- Bodily injury liability: This coverage pays claims and legal defense costs if the policy holder's car injures or kills another person. Maximum coverage is recommended to cover what could be a devastating expense.
- Property damage coverage: Claims and defense costs are paid if the policy holder's car damages the property of others. Same recommendation as above.
- Uninsured and underinsured motorists: Uninsured motorist insurance pays for injuries which are caused by uninsured motorists or hit-and-run drivers to policy holders and their families. Underinsured is similar, but is activated only after the other driver's coverage is exceeded. Many people do not know the difference between these areas so, consequently, they have inadequate coverage. It is advisable to match the uninsured and underinsured coverage to the coverage carried for bodily injury protection (at least $100,000 each person or $300,000 each occurrence).
- Collision: This is the area people worry most about, and for good reason. For example, last year, I had the unfortunate experience of totalling my late model sports car. And it hurt, not just me, but also my insurance company which had a sizeable claim to pay.

  This coverage comes with a deductible, and you should take as large a deductible as you can comfortably self-fund from your current cash flow. Weigh the risks. Here as well, try to insure big losses and carry the little risks in life. A $500 collision deductible isn't a big risk, but it can carry a disproportionate cost in increased insurance premiums. It makes sense to price policies with different levels of collision deductibles to see how much gain there is when a larger deductible is chosen.

  For cars older than 6-7 years, it may be better to drop collision and save the difference. Insurance companies won't pay a claim greater than the car's market value. For instance, if your son's 1981 Ford Fairlane is covered for collision, you are wasting your money. One fender-bender and the car is totalled. What is it worth? Does it make sense to insure it for collision?

- Comprehensive: This area covers a variety of losses, including vandalism, theft, fire, and damage from the elements. Again do not cover 100% of this risk. Take as high a deductible as it makes sense to self-fund.

If you configure your automobile policies as suggested above, you will potentially reduce your overall costs. If you go for years without an accident, you'll have saved a nice amount. On the other hand, if you have an accident immediately after making such changes to your policies, you'll be kicking yourself. Risk is what it is all about. How much do you want to assume and how much do you want to give away to your insurer?

Don't blindly act on these suggestions without reviewing cost comparisons from several companies.

UMBRELLA LIABILITY COVERAGE

This is the last wealth protector. Dollars spent in this area are wisely invested to shelter your growing or established wealth from adversity. Liability coverage protects you against a litigious society over and above the maximum limits in your home, auto, boat, or motorcycle policies. Depending on your net worth, an excess liability policy of a million or more may be recommended. Umbrella liability policies are offered through property and casualty insurance agencies and they are very inexpensive. Don't neglect this one.

WEALTH BUSTERS

By stocking up on the most expensive models in each insurance category, you can easily become insurance-poor. On the other hand, purchasing insurance from a weak company can be a waste of money in addition to a financial gamble. Be sure the insurance you consider is offered by a company rated A or A+ by A.M. Best. Insist on at least one other rating by an agency issuing claims paying ratings (Moody's, Standard and Poor's, Duff and Phelps, Weiss). Exhibit 8B will help you define categories of ratings from rating agencies.

It is important to evaluate the trade-offs in every type of coverage available. Your ultimate goal is to cover all the big risks and still have money left to spend for other needs. Consider carefully the magnitude of a potential loss in each area discussed in this chapter. Ask yourself if you could recover financially if you gamble and lose. If you can't, paying insurance premiums can be a very small price for shielding you from wealth damaging financial losses

MISUSED PROTECTION CAN SOMETIMES BE INCONVENIENT

EXHIBIT 8A

THE "MENU" OF LIFE INSURANCE PRODUCTS

Term Only = Mortality & Expenses ONLY

	GENERAL DESCRIPTION	INVESTMENT VEHICLE	INVESTMENT FLEXIBILITY	PREMIUM FLEXIBILITY	FACE AMOUNT FLEXIBILITY	APPROPRIATE FOR
NON-GUARANTEED TERM	Lowest Cost *No Control*	NONE	N/A	NONE *Increases*	NONE	*Very Limited Situations*
YEARLY RENEWABLE & CONVERTIBLE TERM	Policy Owner *Control*	NONE	N/A	NONE *Increases*	NONE	*Limited Cash Flow Temporary Needs Protection NOW*

Term PLUS = Mortality, Expenses AND Investment

WHOLE LIFE	FIXED LIFE *Basic Coverage* *Dividends Provide Investment Return*	*Primarily Insurance Co. selected Long term bonds and mortgages*	**NONE** *To Change investment, borrowing and reinvesting is required.*	**NONE** *Dividends can reduce or eliminate fixed, billed premium.*	**NONE** *Want More?... Buy new, IF you can pass a physical.*	*The Conservative Older Insureds* *Substandard Insureds*
VARIABLE LIFE	*You Direct the Investment*	*Common Stock Bond Funds Guaranteed Interest Rates Zero Coupons Money Markets etc., etc. ...*	**MAXIMUM** *Your Decision, Split It, Move It, Etc.*	**NONE** *Fixed premium remains level. Loans Available*	**NONE** *Want More?... Buy new, IF you can pass a physical.*	*The Investor. An alternative to ... Buy Term, Invest Difference.*
UNIVERSAL LIFE	*Current interest rate Flexibility Transparency*	*Short Term interest investments*	**NONE** *Borrow or Withdraw*	**MAXIMUM** *Enough for mortality and expenses, or AS MUCH AS LAW ALLOWS.*	**MAXIMUM** *Increase or decrease ... Stay Healthy for major increases.*	*Younger Insureds Variable Needs Like Short Term interest rate investments.*
UNIVERSAL VARIABLE LIFE	*Disclosure Flexibility Control*	*Common Stock Bond Funds Guaranteed interest rates Zero Coupons Money Markets etc., etc. ...*	**MAXIMUM** *You Name It. You Split It. You Move It. You Withdraw It.*	**MAXIMUM** *Enough for Mortality and expenses, or AS MUCH AS LAW ALLOWS.*	**MAXIMUM** *Increase or decrease ... Stay Healthy for major increases.*	*The Investor. An alternative to ... Buy Term, Invest Difference. I want it MY WAY!*

EXHIBIT 8B

LIFE INSURANCE RATING AGENCIES

Rating Category	A.M. Best	Standard & Poors	Duff & Phelps	Moody's	Weiss
Superior	A++	AAA	AA	Aaa	A+
Excellent	A+	AA+	AA+	Aa1	A
	A	AA	AA	Aa2	A-
	A-	AA-	AA-	Aa3	B+
Good	B++	A+	A+	A1	B
	B-	A	A	A2	B-
	—	A-	A-	A3	C+
Adequate	B	BBB+	BBB+	Baa1	C
	B-	BBB	BBB	Baa2	C-
	—	BBB-	BBB-	Baa3	D+
Below Average	C++	BB+	BB+	Ba1	D
	C+	BB	BB	Ba2	D-
	—	BB-	BB-	Ba3	E+
Weak	C	B+	B+	B1	E
	C-	B	B	B2	E-
	—	B-	B-	B3	—
Nonviable*	D	CCC	CCC	Caa	—
	E	CC	CC	C	F
	F	C	—	—	—

* Below minimum standards or under state supervision

WORKSHEET 8A

LIFE INSURANCE NEEDS ANALYSIS

INCOME NEED

Immediate Expenses

Federal estate taxes	$ ________	
State inheritance taxes	________	
Probate costs	________	
Burial fees	________	
Uninsured medical costs	________	
Repayment of selected debts	________	
Total Immediate Expenses		$ ________

Future Expenses

Family income needs[1] ________ divided by ______%	$ ________	
Emergency fund	________	
Child care expense	________	
Education funding	________	
Total Future Expenses		$ ________
Total Immediate & Future Needs		$ ________

CURRENT ASSETS

Cash & savings	$ ________	
Equity in real estate excluding home	________	
Securities (stocks/bonds)	________	
IRA/Keogh plans	________	
Employer savings plans	________	
Lump sum pensions	________	
Current life insurance	________	
Other assets	________	
Total Assets		$ ________

INSURANCE NEEDED

Total needs minus total assets	
Total Immediate Needs	$ ________
Current Assets	- ________
Additional life insurance needed	$ ________

1. To estimate the lump sum of capital needed to produce the income shortfall, divide the annual income need by a reasonable interest rate such as 7-8%. This capitalizes the income.

WORKSHEET 8B

ESTIMATING DISABILITY INCOME NEEDS

LIVING EXPENSES		
Housing (utilities, insurance, taxes, maintenance, rent/mortgage payment)	$ ________	
Food	________	
Clothing	________	
Transportation	________	
Entertainment/recreation	________	
Uninsured medical expenses	________	
Insurance premiums	________	
Debt payments	________	
Miscellaneous	________	
Annual Living Expenses		$ ________
INCOME DURING DISABILITY		
Spousal after-tax income	$ ________	
Dividends and interest	________	
Rents, annuities, pensions	________	
Social Security disability pay	________	
Annual Income		$ ________
NET ANNUAL DISABILITY INCOME NEEDS (Excess expenses over income)		$ ________

CHAPTER 9

REAL ESTATE DOLLARS AND SENSE

"The best investment on earth is earth."
Louis Glickman

Your home may be your castle, but will it make you king or queen? The answer to that question depends on whether the country was in a recessionary or inflationary period when you bought or sold. Most experts agree the purchase of a residence should be the mainstay of any financial program.

BUY RIGHT

The number of people purchasing real estate to make a quick kill in the market usually increases after their area has experienced a hot market. The unfortunate part of this scenario is that short-term profits are hard to make in real estate because of the high cost of buying and selling. For those that want to buy and hold, however, real estate is a very attractive investment option which can keep pace with or exceed the inflation rate.

If you purchase a home in a deflationary cycle and hold it for three years or less, you probably would have been better off renting. If the home does not appreciate over a period as great as 10 years, you still would be better off renting. This is because the increase in equity as a result of principal payments on the mortgage is very small in the first 15 years or so of a 30-year mortgage. Before you commit to purchasing your dream house, be sure you're going to be anchored to it for a long enough period to reap the benefits of home ownership.

In my practice, I have met very few people who complained about the returns they had achieved in real estate. Usually, they will say something like this, "Our home has been a great investment. We paid $80,000, and now it's worth $200,000." When I ask for the date of the purchase and analyze their annual compound return, these terrific returns often have just slightly outpaced the long-term average inflation rate.

Even though it has not always been the greatest investment since the Texas gushers — most of us want to own the great American dream — a home of our own. What other asset can we live in, love, work on, change according to our own designs, age with, and still have it be worth more than when we purchased it?

A GREAT TAX SHELTER

Despite the trap doors and dimly-lit staircases, your home is one of the best tax shelters around. Consider these eight compelling reasons for home ownership:

1. Current taxation on the growth in value of the property is deferred until you sell it.
2. The interest is tax deductible. You may carry up to one million dollars in acquisition debt on a primary residence and up to $100,000 on a second home equity loan.
3. If you buy an equal or higher priced home than the adjusted sales price of the one you sold and do so within 24 months, you can continue to defer unrecognized gain on the previous residence.
4. You can exclude $125,000 in gain if you sell a primary residence after your age 55 (more about this in a moment).
5. Mortgage payments build equity. Each month, you are placing a portion of your mortgage payment into a large piggy bank, your home.
6. The home is exempted in many states, when you qualify for Medicaid benefits. This is especially important to older individuals who might be faced with unfunded long-term care needs.
7. Depending on the state, the home will provide varying degrees of protection from creditors.
8. In case of your death, all unpaid tax on the appreciation of your home is forgiven. This feature is further explained in Chapter 15.

The over-55 benefit mentioned above deserves expansion. Every person is entitled to exempt $125,000 of profits from taxation when they liquidate a home after age 55 unless they've been tainted by the strange quirks in this IRS code. For example, if you're married and one of you is over 55, you can use the exemption. However, although both you and your spouse are over 55, together you are entitled to one exemption, not two. In this area, the government discriminates against married couples. Even after a divorce and remarriage, new partners are painted with the same brush used earlier. Though they may have never used their exemptions, they won't be allowed to as long as they're married to someone who has.

This could make for an interesting discussion among the over 55 who are contemplating marriage. Picture the first date between two aspiring romantics, "By the way, have you used your over-55 capital gains exclusion?" If the answer is yes, the gentleman or lady in question must decide between lasting romance or tax-free profits if they own a home and have not yet used the exclusion. When both own a home and neither have used their own exclusion, they should each consider selling, taking advantage of the tax laws while single, and then purchasing a joint residence.

Keep in mind that to qualify, homeowners must have owned the home for the last five years and occupied it three out of those five years. Tax advisors can provide more details on the exception or two that apply to the above rule.

A HOME OF YOUR OWN

There are many issues to consider when you buy real estate, but one important consideration is determining how large a monthly payment you can afford. There are two rules of thumb commonly used by realtors and prospective buyers: 1) your mortgage payment (principal, interest, taxes, and insurance or PITI) shouldn't exceed 28% of your gross monthly income, and 2) all of your monthly credit obligations, including your new mortgage payment, should not exceed 36% of your gross income. This is the criteria most lenders will use to judge your ability to meet the payments on their proposed loan. You are also limited by IRS rules which state the maximum loan which qualifies for interest deductions is $1 million

Susan and Larry Young used Worksheet 9A to estimate their ability to carry the loan on their present house. They pay $1,029 a month on the home and qualified for the loan by earning $50,000 a year as shown on the following worksheet.

ESTIMATING QUALIFYING LIMITS ON MORTGAGE PAYMENTS

Gross Monthly Income (before taxes)	$4,166
	x .36
Subtotal	$1,500
Subtract monthly debt payments on all loans except proposed mortgage payment	-375
Maximum Mortgage Payment (PITI)	$1,125

OR

28% of gross monthly income, whichever is less.

How much can a mortgage cost up front? There are two major cash outlays to completing a real estate transaction: the down payment and the closing costs. The total of these two figures can be 10% plus of the loan value, depending on the lender and the type of financing utilized.

How to Calculate Payments

Spreading the cost of loan principal and interest payments over a period of years is called amortizing your loan. Exhibit 9A can be used to estimate monthly payments required to amortize a loan over a 15- or 30-year period at various interest rates.

First determine the amortization factor, using the first three columns. Find the interest rate under Column I, then locate the appropriate factor in Column II or III. Now divide the loan amount by 1000 and multiply that number by the appropriate factor. The result is the monthly payment to amortize that size of loan over a 15- or 30-year period.

The most baffling decision for many prospective buyers seems to be whether to take a loan for 15 or 30 years. I generally recommend the 30-year variety because it can always be shortened to 15. There is no way to stretch a 15-year to a 30-year loan once you sign on the dotted line.

Now let's use Exhibit 9A to find the monthly payment on a new mortgage of $125,000 for both 15- and 30-year terms at 9% interest.

9% factor @ 15 years = 10.14
9% factor @ 30 years = 8.05

$125,000 ÷ 1,000 = 125.0

Monthly payment for 15 years 10.14 x 125 = $1,267.50
Monthly payment for 30 years 8.05 x 125 = $1,006.25

You can easily see the difference between a 15-year and a 30-year fixed rate. Would you save the $261.25 per month difference? If so, and you could average 9% or better on your investment returns, you should take the 30-year term. In 15 years, you could have adequate liquid assets to pay off the loan if desired. In reality, most people just aren't disciplined enough to get the job done. Does that ring a bell for you? If so, you had better opt for the mandatory payment method if a 15 year mortgage term is desired.

Another flexible way to reduce the term of your mortgage is to split your monthly payment by half and pay biweekly. The biweekly payment strategy will reduce your loan term about one-third. Without costing you any more, you can drop a 30-year mortgage to a 20-year by paying one-half of the mortgage every other week. Check with your mortgage holder to see if they will accept biweekly payments. If not, you will have to implement this strategy through a service firm established for this purpose.

THE TRUE COST OF BORROWING

How much does a home loan really cost? Here's a rule of thumb computation to determine the typical after-tax cost of a loan:

Interest Rate (A) x Tax Rate (B) = Tax Reduction (C)

(A) - (C) = After-Tax Cost

A 12% loan only costs 8.64% with tax adjustments. But the cost is truly only 8.64% if the entire amount of the interest on the loan is tax deductible. This may not be the case. Taxpayers who itemize on Schedule A of their personal tax return know that each taxpayer receives a free Standard Deduction from the government in amounts which vary according to filing status. But the sum total of all items listed as allowable expense deductions on Schedule A must exceed the free amount prior to being deductible. The standard deduction is also indexed to inflation and, in the future, the standard deduction could exceed most taxpayers' itemized deductions.

This is one reason it is difficult to generalize about the after-tax cost of a mortgage. The entire sum of interest paid probably is not deductible.

If Susan and Larry's loan were 12%, would they come out ahead by refinancing? Should they release some of their equity dollars to do bigger and better things? If they could refinance at 9%, money borrowed in excess of their present mortgage loan balance would have to earn at a rate of 9% or more before taxes. In order to achieve that return, the Youngs would undoubtedly have to assume some volatility risk with investments. As aggressive investors, refinancing might provide them with an opportunity to propel their net worth to new heights.

Refinancing Break-Even Analysis

When it comes to refinancing, the after-tax value isn't the end of the story. If your mortgage debt was acquired before October 14, 1987, you can only refinance the amount of the mortgage at time of refinancing. If your mortgage debt was acquired after that date, you can refinance the original amount of the debt. Additionally, you are restricted to a maximum of $100,000 for post October 13, 1987 home equity debt.

How does one determine the real cost of refinancing to decide if it is a wise alternative? One rule of thumb states that if interest rates are more than 2% lower than the interest rate on your current mortgage, you are better off with a new loan.

The KISS (keep it simple...) method takes your total closing costs and divides this sum by the monthly savings in your mortgage payments. This method, however, ignores two important factors: 1) the tax ramifications, and 2) opportunities for investing the money you would have spent on closing costs. The decision to refinance depends on how long it will take the homeowner to recoup the closing costs, plus interest forfeited on that sum, in lower monthly payments.

If you could invest the money you spent on closing rather than refinancing, the real break-even point comes when the cumulative monthly savings exceeds the after-tax cost of refinancing plus the lost opportunity cost. Completing Worksheet 9B will clarify this point. The following example helps the Youngs compare the after tax cost of their current mortgage to a new mortgage.

ESTIMATING REFINANCING BREAK-EVEN POINTS

Assumptions: Larry and Susan Young are trading in their $100,000 12% mortgage for a new $100,000 9.13% mortgage. Closing costs are 4%. For this illustration, forget the fact that part of their monthly payment is principal.

1.	Current monthly mortgage payment	$1,029	
	Less tax savings (.28[1] x $1,029)	-288	
	Current monthly after-tax cost	$ 740	(a)
	New monthly mortgage payment	$ 814	
	Less tax savings (.28 x $814)	-227	
	New monthly after-tax cost	$ 587	(b)
	After-tax savings from refinancing (a - b)	$ 153	(c)
2.	Calculate the after-tax closing costs		
	Total closing costs	$4,000	
	Deductible points[2]	2,000	
	Less tax savings (.28 x $2,000)	-560	
	After-tax closing costs	$3,440	(d)
3.	Provisional break-even point		
	Divide after-tax closing costs (d) by monthly after-tax savings (c) ($3,440 ÷ $153)	22.5 mos.	(e)
4.	Adjust for the opportunity cost of refinancing.		
	The after-tax closing costs can be invested over the break-even period. Calculate the annual return on after-tax closing costs (d) at an appropriate after-tax opportunity cost such as 7%. ($3,440 x .07)	$ 241	(f)
	Divide the after-tax opportunity cost (f) by 12 = $20.07/month and multiply by the provisional break-even months 22.5 (e)	$ 452	(g)
	$452 (g) divided by the monthly after-tax savings of $153 (c)	2.95 mos.	(h)
	Add 22.5 (e) and 2.95 (h) for the estimated break-even point	25.45 mos.	

1. .28 equals 28% tax bracket. 15% bracket would be .15.
2. May be disallowed by the IRS.

Worksheet reprinted with permission of Steven Enright, CFP, Enright Financial Advisors, River Vale, New Jersey.

Deducting points for refinancing would be an aggressive tax maneuver. The IRS has issued Revenue Procedure 92-12 effective for loans closed after December 31, 1990, to clarify the five key criteria which make points deductible in the year they are incurred: 1) points designated as loan origination on the settlement sheet, 2) calculated as a percentage of the loan amount, 3) within the normal charges for your area, 4) paid for the acquisition of the residence and secured by it, and 5) were paid by your check or cash rather than deducted from the loan proceeds.

You can not deduct but rather must capitalize (deduct prorata over the term of the loan) points paid for 1) refinancing, 2) home equity loans, 3) home improvements, 4) second home, vacation, business or investment property loans, 5) or points attributable to the excess over $1 million mortgage loan.

What can be learned from such financial aerobics? In a nutshell, the Youngs will not break even on their mortgage refinancing unless they keep their home for 25 months or longer.

If they thought their investment results would exceed 7%, the opportunity cost would be driven up and the break-even point stretched even further. An exercise like this is proof that rules of thumb are not accurate enough when making big decisions like refinancing. The variables — cost difference between mortgage payments, opportunity costs, and amount of closing fees — all affect how long a house must be kept to recoup the refinancing costs.

DOES IT PAY TO BE A LANDLORD?

Susan and Larry have decided to take out a home equity loan of $30,000 and put on their landlord hats. They locate a home in a slightly rundown condition for $80,000 that can, with minor renovation, be ready to rent shortly. The home has 3 bedrooms, 1-1/2 baths, a single car garage and is located in a metropolitan area. The following information represents their costs to close the deal.

Sales price	$80,000
Down payment	$20,000
Mortgage amount	$60,000
Monthly payment at 10% for 15 years	$645.00[1]

1. From Exhibit 9A, Amortization Factor Chart (10.75 x 60)

The closing costs of 4% of the mortgage amount would force Susan and Larry to ante up another $2,400. They now have $7,600 cash left. They are going to use $5,000 to spruce and polish the rental so it will command a monthly rent of $750. The remaining $2,600 will be placed in a cash account as a cushion against unexpected vacancies and repairs.

Yield on Rental Activity

Using an estimate of rental income and expenses, Larry and Susan determine the net result of this investment decision.

Annual income from rents	$9,000
Annual expenses	
Interest payment	$7,363
Fire/liability insurance	300
Property taxes	1,000
Repairs/cleaning	250
Total cash expenses	$8,913
Cash flow before taxes	$ 87

With hard cash in the pocket, the before-tax return would equate just 0.32% on their total investment in the property of $27,400. This is not enough. The property must appreciate, as it will in time.

The next step is to calculate the tax benefits available as a result of the straight line depreciation expense. Part of the yield on Susan and Larry's real estate rental will come to them in the form of reduced taxes today. Of course, they will have the pleasure of paying those taxes eventually, but not until they sell the property.

The property is valued at $80,000. The allocation of cost to the land is 20% ($16,000) with 80% to the structure ($64,000). To calculate their yearly depreciation loss, they divide 27.5 years into $64,000. The answer, $2,327, is the annual depreciation expense deduction for tax purposes.

Here's how these two investors finish their analysis of the potential return on their $27,400 investment.

Income from rents	$9,000
Hard (cash) expenses	-8,913
	$ 87
Soft (depreciation) expense	-2,327
	<$2,240>

Susan and Larry can now report a loss of $2,240 on their income tax return. In fact, they could deduct losses of up to $25,000 as long as their adjusted gross income remains under $100,000. To qualify for this exception in the tax law, they must actively participate in the management of the rental. Since they are in the 28% tax bracket, their federal income tax is reduced by $627 (.28 x $2,240). Added to their previously pocketed $87, the total yield on their invested dollars is 2.61%.

So far, they are in the hole. Remember they borrowed $30,000 at a 10% interest rate. Their adjusted after-tax cost of the second equity loan on their mortgage is 7.2% (10% x .28).

But what if the rental property appreciates by 5% annually? This makes a very dramatic difference. Their total first year return would be 17.21%, which is the result of 5% appreciation on $80,000 plus the $87 cash flow and $627 of reduced taxes. That sum, $4,714, divided by their investment of $27,400 equals 17.21%. Take away their cost of borrowing the original capital (7.2%) and they actually gain 10.01% on the rental investment.

Susan and Larry may be scratching their heads trying to decide whether the lack of liquidity, the time and attention required to be landlords, the risk of destructive tenants and the unknown future value of real estate make this investment a wise choice. Their investment returns may be impacted yearly by income realized, inflation's effect on their expenses, and surprise repair bills. The element of risk is ever present. It is probable, however, that with annual rent increasing to stay abreast of inflation, equity building through principal payments and the market value appreciating, this investment will be a wise choice.

TOO MUCH REAL ESTATE CAN BE INCONVENIENT

EIGHT PITFALLS FOR REAL ESTATE INVESTORS

Investors frequently make mistakes and learn from them. But this type of lesson can be an expensive tutorial. To help you avoid some of the more common mistakes, review the following points:

1. Calculating yields on the yearly cash results rather than evaluating the impact of appreciation on the entire value of the property.
2. Leaving too big a cash stash in a home bank.
3. Not knowing the optimum time to sell.
4. Selling rather than trading under Section 1031 and possibly deferring taxes on investment real estate.
5. Keeping poor records which can result in the loss of tax deductible items and/or depreciation on the property.
6. Renting real estate for below market rates.
7. Believing that a monthly negative cash flow equals a good tax shelter.
8. Expecting real estate values to repeat history.

EXHIBIT 9A

AMORTIZATION FACTOR CHART

Column I Percent Interest Rate	Column II 15-Year Term Amortization	Column III 30-Year Term Amortization
7.0	$ 8.99	$ 6.65
8.0	9.56	7.34
8.25	9.70	7.51
8.50	9.84	7.69
8.75	9.99	7.86
9.0	10.14	8.05
9.125	10.22	8.14
9.375	10.37	8.32
9.5	10.44	8.41
9.625	10.52	8.5
9.75	10.59	8.59
9.875	10.67	8.68
10.0	10.75	8.77
10.125	10.82	8.87
10.25	10.90	8.96
10.375	10.98	9.05
10.5	11.05	9.15
10.625	11.13	9.24
10.75	11.21	9.33
10.875	11.29	9.43
10.9	11.30	9.45
11.0	11.37	9.52
11.25	11.52	9.71
11.5	11.68	9.90
11.75	11.84	10.09
12.0	12.00	10.29
12.25	12.16	10.48
12.5	12.33	10.67
12.75	12.49	10.87
13.0	12.65	11.06
13.5	12.98	11.45
14.0	13.32	11.85
15.0	14.00	12.65

$$\text{Factor} \times \frac{\text{Loan Amount}}{1000} = \text{Monthly payment}$$

WORKSHEET 9A

ESTIMATING QUALIFYING LIMITS ON MORTGAGE PAYMENTS

Gross Monthly Income (before taxes)	$________________
	x .36
Subtotal	$________________
Subtract monthly debt payments on all loans except proposed mortgage payment	-________________
Maximum Mortgage Payment (PITI)	$________________

OR

28% of your gross monthly income, whichever is less.

WORKSHEET 9B

ESTIMATING REFINANCING BREAK-EVEN POINTS

This worksheet is a tool to determine how low interest rates must drop to make refinancing a viable economic move.

1. Current monthly mortgage payment ____________
   - Less tax savings (tax bracket x current payment) - ____________
   - Current monthly after-tax cost ____________(a)

   - New monthly mortgage payment ____________
   - Less tax savings (tax bracket x new payment) - ____________
   - New monthly after-tax cost ____________(b)
   - After-tax savings from refinancing (a - b) ____________(c)

2. Calculate the after-tax closing costs
   - Total closing costs ____________
   - Deductible closing costs ____________
   - Less tax savings (tax bracket x deductible closing costs) - ____________
   - After-tax closing costs ____________(d)

3. Provisional break-even point
   - Divide after-tax closing costs (d) by monthly after-tax savings (c) ____________(e)

4. Adjust for the opportunity cost of refinancing
   - After-tax closing costs can be invested over the break-even period
   - Calculate the annual return on after-tax closing costs (d) at an appropriate after-tax opportunity cost such as 7% ____________(f)

   - Divide the after-tax cost (f) by 12 and then multiply by the provisional break-even point (e) ____________(g)

   - Divide (g) by (c) ____________(h)

   - Add (e) and (h) for the estimated break-even point ____________

Worksheet reprinted with permission of Steven Enright, CFP, River Vale, New Jersey.

CHAPTER 10

DESIGNING A PLAN FOR WEALTH

"Poverty and riches often change places. When riches take the place of poverty, the change is usually brought about through well conceived and carefully executed plans."

Napoleon Hill
Think and Grow Rich

Building a strategic mix of investments is not like completing a paint-by-number picture. There's no clear set of directions that anyone can apply to produce a predictable financial result. Although investments experts have developed tests to help people make the hard choices that color their financial picture, in reality, investment selection is a grey area that everyone deals with differently. Many of the choices made are governed by emotion rather than logic.

Tina, a widow, was bored a few years ago with the mundane and safe performance of her bank investments. She told me she was worried about inflation and looking for some different ways of investing for conservative growth. After collecting considerable information about Tina's cash flow, net worth, and personal objectives, I designed an investment portfolio for her that contained some utility and blue chip stock mutual funds. The potential for growth was good for the equity part of Tina's portfolio based on historical evidence of these particular mutual funds' skill in navigating through bull and bear markets.

Tina took the information home to discuss with her daughter and son-in-law. A couple of days later, I received a call. Tina was having trouble dealing with the potential variance in value that could occur as a result of being invested in the stock market. She was feeling anxious and wasn't sleeping. It was clear that the investments I recommended were not what Tina wanted. Intellectually, she understood the benefits of growth investing. Emotionally, she could not handle the transition from safe and secure stable investments to fluctuating growth investments.

Why didn't she say so in the first place? I suspect it was because I did not spend enough time educating her about stock and bond market volatility risks as opposed to purchasing power risks in a fixed-income portfolio. Also, Tina was oblivious to her extreme need for totally safe investments until we discussed the uncertainty of future returns when investing in growth areas. As Tina's case illustrates, even in the financial world, the old adage "Know thyself" applies.

I've had a few clients who, after purchasing growth investments in a volatile year have, wrung their hands and said, "I could have made more money in the bank." That is a possibility if you pick the wrong time to invest. Will it be next year, or the year after, when the market disappoints you? There will always be one or more years when you won't make money. In fact, you could lose some of the gains made in previous years. Growth investing can be a volatile experience but historically, 70% of the time, it has offered rewards outdistancing inflation for the patient and long term investor.

The intent of this chapter is to share risk reduction strategies through techniques known as asset allocation and diversification. Keep in mind, however, that developing a portfolio that fits you is more of an art than a science.

EVALUATING THE TRADE-OFFS

"What's the best way to invest my money these days?" This is the big question, but it has no single answer. Like life, investing is a series of trade-offs. One of those trade-offs is understanding that higher returns go hand in hand with increased portfolio volatility.

Another trade-off is allocating a portfolio so sudden changes in the economy do not destroy investment strategies. Where is the current economy? Where will it be next month or next year? Will interest rates drop? Is the stock market undervalued and poised to move forward? What steps should be taken now? These are all difficult questions to answer. Recessions can creep up on you. The stock market can drop 500 points in a day or gain 700 points in a month and, generally, make a fool out of anyone who tries to outguess it. In addition, the Federal Reserve Board can lower or raise the discount rate without warning.

The only way to deal with these concerns is to develop a realistic long-term perspective and a portfolio of investments which provides some protection against all of the elements.

Here is an analogy to make my point. Leon was about to jump out of an airplane for the first time and was evaluating his risks: "Umm, if my parachute doesn't open, I'll get killed. But the probability of that occurring is very low because I'm wearing two chutes. But then again, neither may open." One choice he has is to add more chutes, if possible. The more chutes he has, the better his chances are one will open to carry him safely to the ground.

Financial choices usually aren't so dramatic, but the process investors use to make their choices are the same ones used by Leon crouched at the open hatch looking down at 2,000 feet of sky. In financial jargon, the questions are: What is the probability of loss of capital? What impact will it have on my overall financial plans should it happen? How can I decrease the probability of loss?

The final trade-off is to accept less income from your portfolio today so that a portion of the capital can be devoted to investments which outperform inflation.

INVESTMENT OBJECTIVES

Investment objectives can be the starting point in determining what types of investments make sense for you. Start by marking the following list from 1-5 in order of importance.

1 = Most Important 5 = Least Important

	Investor #1	Investor #2
Safety of principal	________	________
Guaranteed returns	________	________
Tax free or deferred income	________	________
High income	________	________
Growth of capital	________	________
Liquidity	________	________
Stable principal value	________	________

Once you know your investment objectives, you can apply them to the more sophisticated concepts of diversification and asset allocation. A prudent advisor will recommend a mix of the two basic types of investments to develop an asset allocation strategy which stays ahead of inflation and taxes.

BACK TO BASICS

An easy way to start categorizing your investments is to arrange them by type — loanership or ownership.

Loanership or Debt Assets (fixed assets)

This category represents the loaning of funds by one party to another. Generally, these assets come with a guarantee of principal or an expectation that principal will be returned in the future. Included in this category are:

Savings Accounts
Certificates of Deposit
Corporate and Municipal Bonds
Treasury Bills, Notes and Bonds
Mortgage Backed Securities
Tax-Deferred Annuities
Real Estate Contracts

These are dollar denominated assets, each a different form of an IOU which pays income you can spend or reinvest.

Ownership (variable assets)

These represent an ownership interest in an asset; a correct expectation for this category is that total return will vary. How much variance occurs depends on many factors, most of which are out of your direct control. Representative of ownership assets are:

Stocks (equities)
Real Estate
Natural Resources
Precious Metals
Collectibles

Each of these positions convey a partial or total interest in a tangible asset, such as land, what is on the land (buildings and businesses), or what is in the land. While income may be produced, the primary purpose of the investment is to provide growth in excess of inflation.

ASSET ALLOCATION

Asset allocation strategies provide diversification among different asset classes. If you have one or more investments in each category, you have asset allocation — planned or unplanned. Later in this chapter there will be some ideas on how to plan an asset allocation appropriate for your situation. You will need to decide what percent of assets you should place in the loanership, or debt, category and what percent in the ownership, or equity, category. Many factors play a part in the formula for asset allocation: your age, goals, amount of investment capital, time frame and desired return and amount of risk you are willing to take to achieve returns.

INVESTMENT TRIANGLE

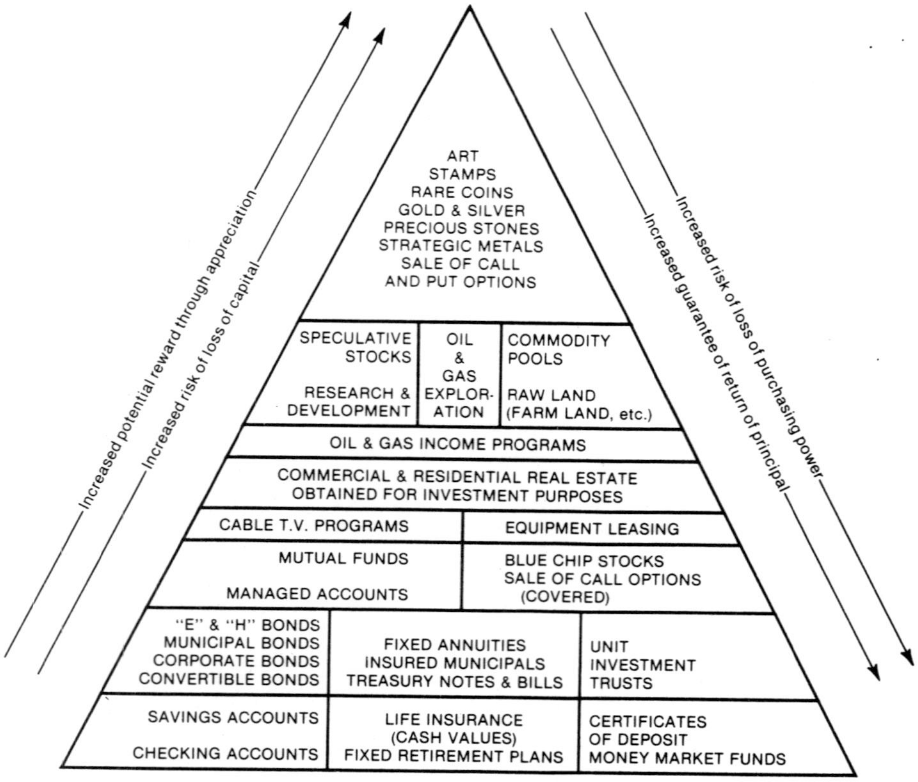

What the Egyptians Didn't Know About Pyramids

Structuring investments is sometimes done with high tech software and high tech minds. However, here is a visual method which provides a structural means of organizing investments effectively. This is an aid in allocating assets by risk levels.

Lower levels of the pyramid are reserved for defensive assets. These are assets which may be relied upon to meet liquidity needs and which are predictable in both the value of the principal and the income generated. Upper levels of the pyramid accommodate more aggressive investment objectives, the growth investments.

Two things occur as you move up the pyramid. First, invested assets become less stable with less safety of principal. Second, opportunity for capital appreciation increase, as do more options for inflation protection.

Here are three different ways to categorize your asset allocation choices. The first two relate more to comfort level than any measure of expected return versus volatility risk.

1. <u>KISS asset allocation</u>: Balance your investments the easy way. The formula is as follows:

   Age = Percent of investments to be held in loanership assets.

   For example, Susan and Larry, who are both 35 years old, will place 35% of their investment capital in loanership and 65% in growth areas. As they age, they will shift more assets to the loanership category, just as John and Clara, who are 62, have. John and Clara have 62% of their investments in the loanership area (guaranteed and fixed income investments) while 38% is in growth (stocks and real estate). If there are age differences between partners, add up both ages and find the average. For instance, Roger is 48 and Beth is 40. Their average age is 44, so they would have 44% in the loanership area.

   This is just a rule of thumb and may be more passive or aggressive than you wish to be, but it will get you started analyzing your investment mix.

2. <u>Basic Attitude Toward Life asset allocation</u>: This philosophical approach on four model portfolios is not statistically founded either. Rather, these conceptual models are based on risk aversion perceptions. The varying percentages help you understand the difference between a defensive versus aggressive allocation approach.

   A. Defensive orientation. This investor wants the majority of his/her portfolio invested in current income assets although some growth will be tolerated. There is a short time horizon (3 to 5 years) and a desire to minimize risk. Dividend and interest income are used to meet daily living expenses, usually in conjunction with other income sources. An ultra-conservative retired person, or someone with enough assets that they don't need to accept higher levels of risks, would be typical examples of investors in this group.

Cash Assets	10%
Fixed Income Assets	70%
Growth Assets	20%

B. Conservative orientation. This investor seeks a combination of income (interest and dividends) and capital growth. There is a moderate time horizon (5-10 years), but a reluctance to accept moderate to aggressive risk levels typical of the growth investor. Those individuals who are building retirement assets or who are retired and seek to outpace inflation with their investments might wish this type of portfolio allocation.

Cash Assets	10%
Fixed Income Assets	50%
Growth Assets	40%

C. Moderate orientation. This investor is interested in a balanced approach to investing with a weighting toward capital growth and is able to wait at least 10-15 years to achieve it. There is a willingness to accept considerable fluctuation in portfolio values. Mid-career professionals, dual income families with high discretionary income, and some pension plans might fit in this category.

Cash Assets	10%
Fixed Income Assets	30%
Growth Assets	60%

D. Aggressive orientation. This investor is not dependent on income from his/her portfolio but is primarily seeking growth and, thus, is unconcerned about price risk (volatility). There is a willingness to place approximately 50% of the growth position in small or international stock positions with minimal dividends. High income ($100,000+) young professionals or dual income families with no immediate need for capital usage may wish to consider this category. Time horizons should be 15-20 years.

Cash Assets	5%
Fixed Income Assets	15%
Growth Assets	80%

Although this is interesting information, it doesn't tell you what level of return to expect from the portfolio. Nor, does it give you a clue as to the differing degrees of portfolio volatility (value fluctuations). It also does not clarify whether, as you beef up the growth in your portfolio, the extra return achieved was worth the risks you bore (risk adjusted return performance). The following third approach does.

3. Modern Portfolio Theory approach: This is the high tech world of technobabble and numerical analysis where you learn about Alpha, Beta, R-Squared, Sharpe, and other statistical characters (explained in more detail in Chapter 12). This theory is not the one-dimensional process of selecting the right stock or bond, rather it is the combining of assets which are statistically efficient.

   The concept of efficient portfolio risk adjusted performance was originated in the mid-1950s with work done by Professor Harry M. Markowitz and the University of Chicago and enhanced by William Sharpe's Capital Assets Pricing Method — the beginning of Modern Portfolio Theory (MPT). In 1990, modern portfolio originators Harry Markowitz and Merten Miller, University of Chicago, and William Sharpe, Stanford University, were awarded the Nobel Prize in Economics for their achievements in this area. The premise for this theory is that portfolios will incur less volatility if assets are selected that correlate negatively with each other, i.e., one goes up and as another goes down. Modern Portfolio Theory lays the groundwork for statistically evaluating the effects of differing asset allocations. The objective is to find a portfolio which is statistically efficient — one where the highest return is milked from a portfolio with the lowest possible fluctuation of value.

   The first step in that process is to understand why asset allocation is so important. Studies completed in 1986 by SEI and First Chicago Investment Advisors revealed the value of Strategic Asset Allocation (SAA) to portfolio performance. This study analyzed the returns of 91 large U.S. pension plans from 1974 to 1983. The pension plans were measured against various active and passive investment strategies to determine which factors were primarily responsible for their investment performance. The study reached the following conclusions concerning the formation and adherence to an investment policy:

   - SAA is responsible for 93% of the variation of total returns.
   - SAA far outweighed the influence of any one individual investment or market timing.
   - It is the single most important element in the investment management process.

   Since 93% of a portfolio's returns are attributed to the asset allocation chosen rather than the specific investment selection, it is an important element in investment success. And, as such, is the part which deserves the most attention and planning.

   Tactical Asset Allocation is the next step and is a form of subtle market timing. While you can adopt a SAA which reflects your tolerance for risk by establishing limits in asset classes, you may wish to alter those limits from time to time within a predetermined range. For instance, when interest rates are dropping, allocating a greater percentage to bonds can be profitable. Or when the stock market takes a dive, increasing the weighting in equities can be profitable.

Institutional investors have utilized modern portfolio techniques for years to analyze different mixes of portfolios. Now, individual investors can also use MPT through database computer technology. Add this quantitative tool to common sense, research, realistic expectations, risk tolerance and review, and you are on the way to a sophisticated investment program.

THE POWER OF DIVERSIFICATION

Still part of the same tune, diversification is a different and powerful verse. A wide range of investments within one asset category equates diversification. This reduces the impact on a portfolio if the value of one or more investments remains static or declines. A mutual fund is a perfect example of good diversification. If you decide to purchase blue chip stocks, you could select one or two, such as General Electric, U.S. West or Boeing, or you could own a whole portfolio of similar stocks through a mutual fund. Prices on the portfolio would change daily. While some would drop, others would increase in value and cushion the fluctuation.

Consider the results of the following example comparing a mix of different growth investments with varying returns against a single guaranteed investment over a 25-year span.

YEAR 1		YEAR 25
Single Guaranteed Investment Choice		
$100,000 at 8% fixed return		$684,850
Diversified Growth Investment Choices		
$ 20,000 at a total loss	$ -0-	
$ 20,000 at 0% return	20,000	
$ 20,000 at 5% return	67,727	
$ 20,000 at 10% return	216,694	
$ 20,000 at 15% return	658,379	
Total Diversified Growth		$962,800

It's unlikely that you would want to use a diversified growth strategy without also placing part of your assets in guaranteed or fixed-income positions. Working together, a variety of investments will build a stronger financial program while cushioning risk and providing a greater opportunity for returns to outpace inflation.

BASIC INVESTMENT RISKS

Risk is a word of the future. It reflects the probability of future events based on historical evidence and belongs in the vocabularies of both the advisor and investor who want to establish realistic expectations. There are six real risks inherent with every investment opportunity:

1. Inflation risk: Since about 1940, the U.S. has experienced a steady inflationary trend. This makes a dollar in the future worth less than a dollar today. Fixed-income investments are impacted most by this risk and may not keep up with inflation. The longer the term of the fix, the greater the risk that money won't buy the same amount of goods and services when it returns to your pocket.

   A good example is to examine the future value of $1.00 if we experience 5% average inflation. In 10 years, a $1.00 will only purchase $.62 of goods and services. In 20 years, the dollar will only be worth $.38. This is a frightening and compelling reason to avoid placing 100% of your portfolio in long-term fixed-income assets.

2. Financial risk: This is the pure risk of losing all your investment. It does happen, even to Donald Trump, Eastern Airlines, and savings and loan companies. Several years ago, investors were burned by the demise of certain Washington Public Power System (WPPS) bonds thought to be safe. WPPS became commonly known as "Whoops." When you consider financial risk, you're looking at the stability and capability of the company behind the investment. You should ask if the business is viable and being managed competently.

3. Market risk: Stocks, or an entire area of the stock market, such as timber, technology, health care, energy, etc., can lose value due to fluctuating security prices. You may remember October of 1987 and fall of 1990. A major reason for this risk is making decisions at the wrong time, as did those who invested in gold in 1982 or bought stocks in early October 1987.

4. Interest rate risk: This very real risk impacts investments like bonds, preferred stocks, and interest sensitive stocks such as utilities. In 1990 interest rates began to drop. As a result, the above investments experienced increases in their market value (capital appreciation) and, for the year of 1990, outperformed the stock market. But the opposite can happen also. Rising rates cause a general decline in the price for existing fixed securities, first bonds and then stocks. When is the best time to invest in bonds? The next chapter will have an answer to that question.

5. Liquidity risk: This risk becomes real when you need your money immediately. Limited partnerships are illiquid unless sold to market makers at a discount. As Texans know well, real estate has its timing pitfalls too. Other investments, such as certificates of deposit and deferred annuities, also have penalties if tapped before their time.

6. Tax risk: Last, but not least, is tax risk. This risk became too familiar to those who owned real estate installment contracts in 1986. Congress changed the tax rules so that capital gains would be taxed as ordinary income. Of course, these investors could not know the rules would be changed mid-stream without warning. Various tax acts have turned the investment world topsy-turvy and severely limited

tax benefits of investing. It's definitely simpler now. Instead of focusing on tax benefits, investors focus on the total tax adjusted returns. Tax risk is always present. Congress works overtime to squelch tax benefits — don't expect the future to be the same as today.

To summarize, if you want a higher total return or the potential for a higher return, an increasing amount of volatility risk must be taken. Loanership assets usually have the lowest market and financial risks but because they have a fixed yield and term, they are more susceptible to inflation risk. In addition, bond values are subject to interest rate risks. Ownership assets have higher market and financial risk but, as indicated by examining past results, have less inflation risk.

Where's all the fun? It is fun to navigate through the risk if you invest knowledgeably.

Here's a quiz designed by money guru, William Donoghue, to help you determine your risk tolerance:

WHAT TYPE OF RISK TAKER ARE YOU?

Choose one answer for each question.

1. An investment loses 15% of its value in a market correction a month after you buy it. Assuming none of the fundamentals have changed, do you:
   (a) Sit tight and wait for it to journey back up?
   (b) Sell it and rid yourself of further sleepless nights if it continues to decline?
   (c) Buy more — if it looked good at the original price, it looks even better now?
2. A month after you purchase it, the value of your investment suddenly skyrockets by 40%. Assuming you can't find any further information, what do you do?
   (a) Sell it.
   (b) Hold it on the expectation of further gain.
   (c) Buy more — it will probably go higher.
3. Which would you have rather done:
   (a) Invested in an aggressive-growth fund that appreciated very little six months.
   (b) Invested in a money market fund only to see the aggressive you were thinking about double in value in six months.
4. Would you feel better if:
   (a) You doubled your money in an equity investment.
   (b) Your money market fund investment saved you from losing half your money in a market slide.
5. Which would make you happiest?
   (a) You win $100,000 in a publisher's contest.
   (b) You inherit $100,000 from a rich relative.
   (c) You learn $100,000 by risking $2,000 in the options market.
   (d) Any of the above — you're happy with the $100,000, no matter how it ended up in your wallet.
6. The apartment building where you live is being converted to condominiums. You can either buy your unit for $80,000 or sell the option for $20,000. The market value of the condo is $120,000. You know that if you buy the condo it might take six months to sell, the monthly carrying cost is $1,200, and you'd have to borrow the down payment for a mortgage. You don't want to live in the building. What do you do?

(a) Take the $20,000.
(b) Buy the unit and then sell it.

7. You inherit your uncle's $100,000 house, free of any mortgage. Although the house is in a fashionable neighborhood and can be expected to appreciate at a rate faster than inflation, it has deteriorated badly. It would net $1,000 monthly if rented as is, or $1,500 per month if renovated. The renovations could be financed by a mortgage on the property. You would:
(a) Sell the house.
(b) Rent it as is.
(c) Make the necessary renovations, and then rent it.

8. You work for a small but thriving privately held electronics company. The company is raising money by selling stock to its employees. Management plans to take the company public, but not for four or more years. If you buy stock, you will not be allowed to sell until shares are traded publicly. In the meantime, the stock will pay no dividends. But when the company goes public, the shares could trade for 10-20 times what you paid. How much of an investment would you make?
(a) None at all.
(b) One month's salary.
(c) Three months' salary.
(d) Six months' salary.

9. Your long-time neighbor, an experienced petroleum geologist, is assembling a group of investors (of which he is one) to fund an exploratory oil well, which could pay 50 to 100 times its investment. If the well is dry, the entire investment is worthless. Your friend estimates the chances of success at only 20%. What would you invest?
(a) Nothing at all.
(b) One month's salary.
(c) Three months' salary.
(d) Six months' salary.

10. You learn that several commercial building developers are seriously looking at undeveloped land in a certain location. You are offered an option to buy a choice parcel of that land. The cost is about two months' salary and you calculate the gain to be ten months' salary. Do you:
(a) Purchase the option.
(b) Let it slide — it's not for you.

11. You are on a TV game show and can choose one of the following. Which would you take?
(a) $1,000 in cash.
(b) A 50% chance at $4,000.
(c) A 20% chance at $10,000.
(d) A 5% chance at $100,000.

12. It's 1989, and inflation is returning. Hard assets such as precious metals, collectibles and real estate are expected to keep pace with inflation. Your assets are now all in long-term bonds. What would you do?
(a) Hold the bonds.
(b) Sell the bonds, put half the proceeds into money funds and the other half into hard assets.
(c) Sell the bonds and put the total proceeds into hard assets.
(d) Sell the bonds, put all the money into hard assets and borrow additional money to buy more.

13. You've lost $500 at the blackjack table in Atlantic City. How much more are you prepared to lose to win the $500 back?
(a) Nothing. You quit now.
(b) $100.
(c) $250.
(d) $500.
(e) More than $500.

Scoring

Total your score, using the point system listed below for each answer you gave.

1.	(a) 3	(b) 1	(c) 4		
2.	(a) 1	(b) 3	(c) 4		
3.	(a) 1	(b) 3			
4.	(a) 2	(b) 1			
5.	(a) 2	(b) 1	(c) 4	(d) 1	
6.	(a) 1	(b) 2			
7.	(a) 1	(b) 2	(c) 3		
8.	(a) 1	(b) 2	(c) 4	(d) 6	
9.	(a) 1	(b) 3	(c) 6	(d) 9	
10.	(a) 3	(b) 1			
11.	(a) 1	(b) 3	(c) 5	(d) 9	
12.	(a) 1	(b) 2	(c) 3	(d) 4	
13.	(a) 1	(b) 2	(c) 4	(d) 6	(e) 8

Below 21: You are a conservative investor who's allergic to risk. Stick with sober, conservative investments until you develop the confidence or desire to take on more risk.

21-35: You are an active investor who's willing to take calculated, prudent risks to achieve greater financial gain. Your investment universe is more diverse.

36 and over: You're a venturesome, assertive investor. The choices that are available to you promise dynamic opportunities. Remember, though, the search for more return carries an extra measure of risk.

Reprinted with permission from Donoghue'$ MONEYLETTER. *For a free sample copy, call toll free 1-800-445-5900.*

What did you find out? Do you feel that your score describes your attitude toward taking risk? A quiz like this can be a helpful tool to examine the degree of risk you are willing to take with your money. But, in actuality, many other factors will influence your risk profile such as degree of affluence, age, health and probably many other subtle but persuasive emotions.

HISTORICAL INVESTMENT RETURNS

After all the rhetoric about risk, you might wonder why invest at all. The same reasons that have always been important are still valid:

You want your money to grow.
You need income.
You want to defer or avoid taxes.
You want a hedge against inflation.

The goal of investing is to be rewarded sooner or later. Many would-be investors try to hit a home run with each investment and frequently strike out. Realistic expectations must be developed for those people who anticipate compounded rates of return of 20-30% a year. Those expectations are two to three times the actual rates of return that have been achieved over the long term. A realistic expectation for future returns would be to beat the rate of inflation by two to three percent.

The following table reveals the variances in returns between asset classes over the last seven decades:

	1920s	1930s	1940s	1950s	1960s	1970s	1980s
S&P 500 Index	19.2%	0.0%	9.2%	19.4%	7.8%	5.9%	17.5%
Small Company Stock	-4.5	1.5	20.7	16.9	15.5	11.5	15.8
Long-Term Government	5.0	4.9	3.2	-0.1	1.4	5.5	12.6
Long-Term Corporate Bonds	5.2	6.9	2.7	1.0	1.7	6.2	13.0
Treasury Bills	3.7	0.6	0.4	1.9	3.9	6.3	8.9
Inflation	-1.1	-2.0	5.4	2.2	2.5	7.4	5.1

Source: Ibbotson and Associates

Look at the difference from decade to decade in the returns between asset classes. A crystal ball would be necessary to know just where to be at any given time. Assets would have to be diversified among categories in order to reap the varying benefits from each. From the 1940s through the 1970s, bonds after inflation lost money, and in all decades except the 1930s and 1970s, stocks outpaced bonds by a margin of from 5-18%.

Perhaps an easier way to evaluate the merits of stocks, bonds, or cash is to determine how much reward is left from each of these investments after subtracting for inflation and taxes.

T-bills	6%	-	.28% tax	=	4.32%	-	5% inflation	=	-.68%
Government Bonds	8%	-	.28% tax	=	5.76%	-	5% inflation	=	.76%
Stocks	10%	-	.28% tax	=	7.20%	-	5% inflation	=	2.20%

Keeping abreast with and ahead of inflation is a challenge. In the above example, stocks performed 189% better than long term government bonds This will not always be true. Investments returns will vary and should be evaluated under current conditions.

The next chart is the average mean return of selected investment areas over the past 15 years. The standard deviation (STD) number, opposite each investment, reflects the potential variance from the mean (midpoint) return. If you add or subtract the STD to/from the mean return, you will be able to determine the range of returns that are probable 68% of the time. If you add or subtract the STD twice to/from the return, you can determine a range of returns statistically predictable 95% of the time. Notice how the standard deviation escalates at a faster rate than the returns increase. An unwritten rule of portfolio management is that the percent increase in volatility will always be greater than the percent increase in returns. This is another trade-off of investment realities.

AVERAGE MEAN RETURN

	1976-1991	STD
Small Stocks	14.40	23.14
Large Stocks	12.01	16.25
Long-Term Government Bonds	9.48	10.65
Long-Term Corporate Bonds	9.23	11.36
Treasury Bills	8.42	2.36

Source: **RAMCAP Asset Allocation System,** *Advanced Investment Software, Denver, Colorado*

This can be confusing, but a review of the following portfolio examples of hypothetical results based on 15 years of historical data may clarify things. You will see quite a difference among the defensive conservative, moderate, and aggressive models. Note the variance in return, standard deviation, and the Sharpe Ratio. The Sharpe Ratio is derived by taking the expected annual return less a risk free rate of, for example, 6% and dividing by the expected annual standard deviation. The higher the Sharpe Ratio, the more efficient the portfolio. Which portfolio would you prefer?

According to the Sharpe Ratio, the conservative portfolio is the most efficient from a risk versus return position. These results are skewed by the 12-13% bond returns achieved during the decade of the 1980s. If these allocations were calculated using 25-30 years of historical data, the Sharpe Ratios would probably get higher rather than lower as the growth assets were increased.

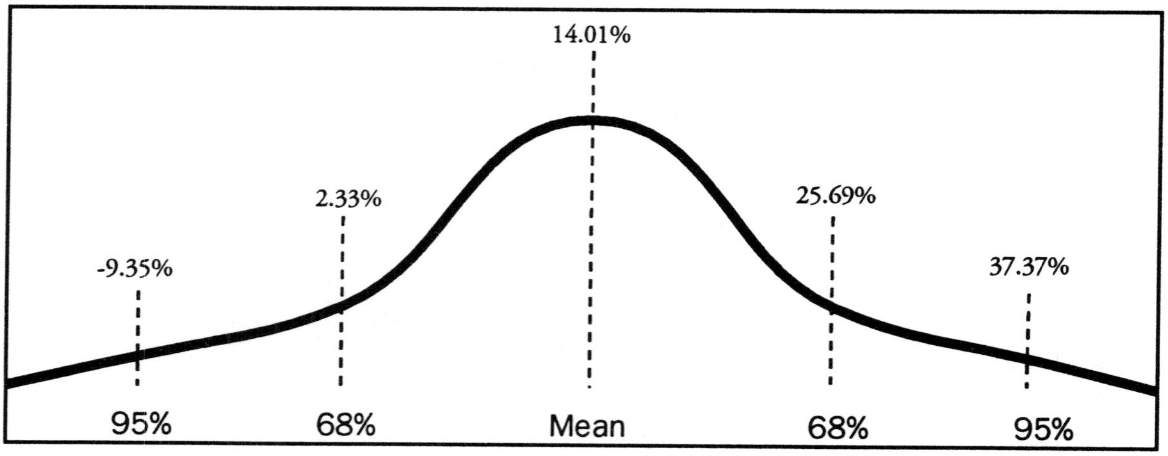

The standard deviation is a measurement of volatility as mentioned above. It is calculated by measuring the probability of the percent deviation from the mean average of the portfolio. Whew, that's a mouthful! Statisticians love this type of analysis and it is also a useful tool for investors. Examine the bell curve above which illustrates the standard deviation of the aggressive portfolio away from the mean average.

DEFENSIVE PLAN

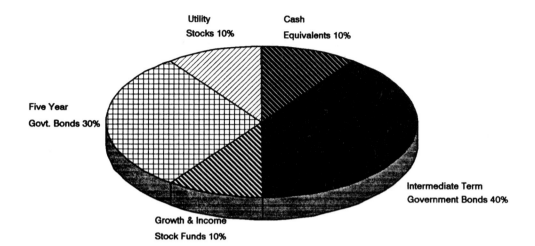

EXPECTED PORTFOLIO PERFORMANCE	
Mean Return	9.54%
Standard Deviation	4.65%
Sharpe Ratio	.76%

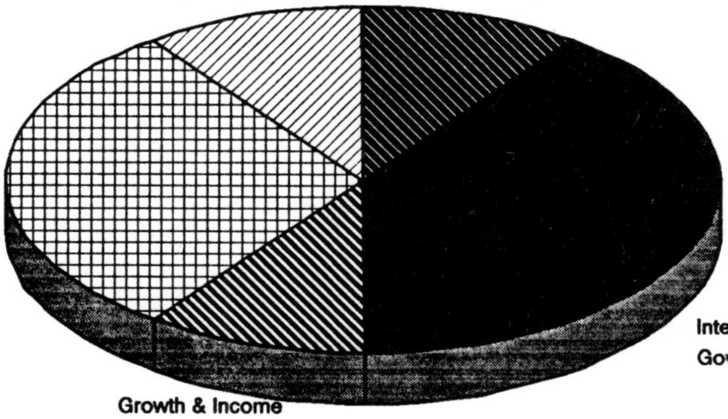

CONSERVATIVE PLAN

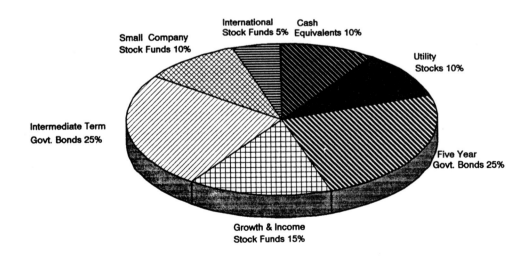

EXPECTED PORTFOLIO PERFORMANCE	
Mean Return	11.07%
Standard Deviation	6.28%
Sharpe Ratio	.81%

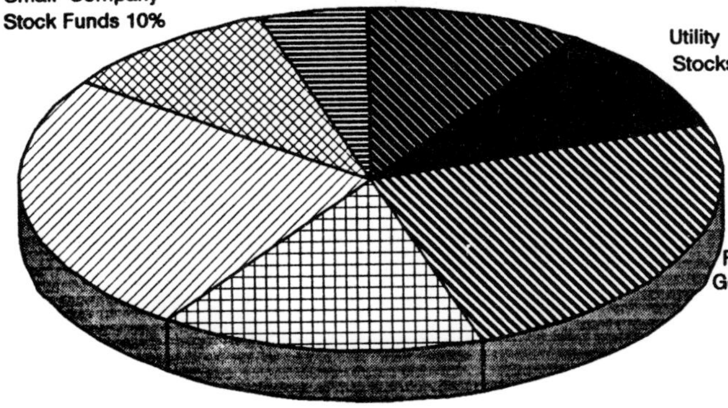

EXPECTED PORTFOLIO PERFORMANCE	
Mean Return	12.56%
Standard Deviation	8.78%
Sharpe Ratio	.75%

MODERATE PLAN

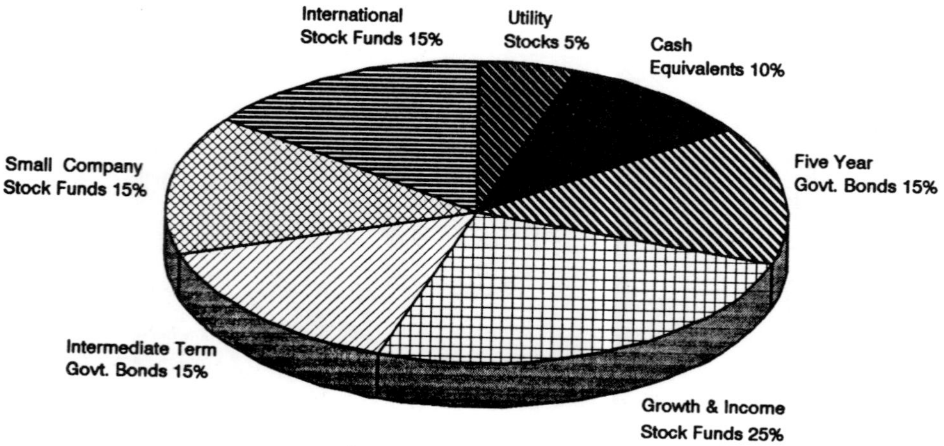

EXPECTED PORTFOLIO PERFORMANCE	
Mean Return	14.01%
Standard Deviation	11.68%
Sharpe Ratio	.69%

AGGRESSIVE PLAN

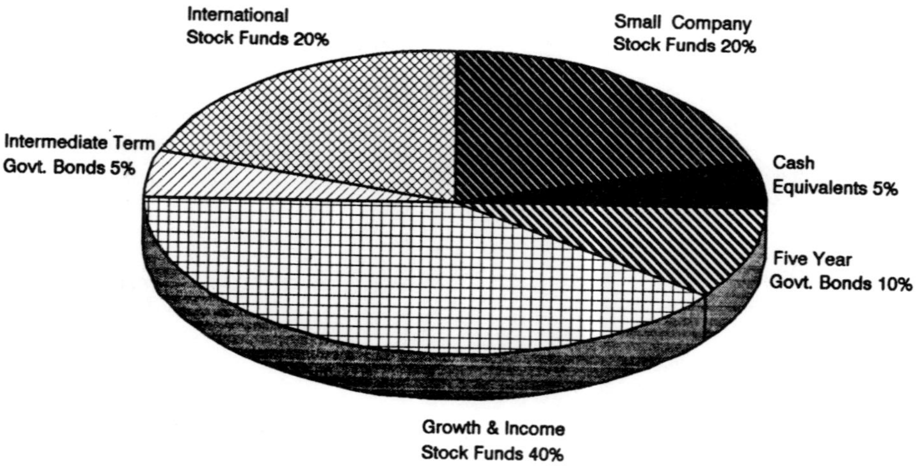

Source: RAMCAP Asset Allocation System,
Advanced Investment Software, Denver, Colorado.

As the standard deviation of the portfolio is 16.68%, the range of returns would be as follows:

68% probability = 2.33% to 25.69%
(mean average of 14.01% added to or subtracted from one standard deviation).

95% probability = -9.35% to 37.37%
(mean average of 14.01% added to or subtracted from two standard deviations).

I call this the swing factor because the portfolio results could swing between a wide range of returns. I prefer to use the 95% probability factor to determine if the potential volatility of a portfolio is suitable for a client. In other words, I do not want more than a 5% chance that the realized returns will fall outside the expected range of results.

These are the same examples which were listed under the Basic Attitude Toward Life asset allocations. All fixed income assets listed are guaranteed. All stock assets are intended to be further diversified through mutual funds. There are many other ways to diversify the same categories. Ideally, a customized portfolio would be developed to meet specific individual needs relating to a mix of income, growth, or tax-advantaged investments. Pre-mixed instant portfolios are good tools to help investors examine their comfort level with varying mixes of stocks, bonds, and cash. From these jump off points, tailored mixes can be developed.

PORTFOLIO ALLOCATION SCORING SYSTEM (PASS)

Allocating a portfolio is a highly complex, sophisticated exercise requiring both experience and knowledge of investment markets. You can start to determine the percentage in each category which might be appropriate for you by completing the following exercise. The PASS system is reprinted with permission of Dr. William G. Droms, CFA, Professor of Finance at Georgetown University. It was first published in his 1985 book, ***The Mutual Fund Handbook***. It has been refined and revised since and is widely used by CPAs and financial planners to educate clients.

This approach is not a foolproof method but offers a guideline for examining the placement of your existing investments versus the recommended placement resulting from your PASS score.

The PASS system captures the essence of Modern Portfolio Theory by recognizing that:

- There is a risk and return trade-off for all investments.
- Investors must diversify to reduce risks.

The score you achieve on the seven listed return and risk measurements determine your portfolio allocation picture. The higher your score, the more your portfolio will be skewed toward growth assets.

The first four objectives are measurements of the expected returns. A score of 5 in numbers one, two, and four would result if it were important to have high long-term total returns, deferred capital gains, tax advantages, and long term investment goals. If you rank number three as a 5, the result to your portfolio will be more growth than income investments.

When you score the last three objectives, you are quantifying your risk tolerance. A score of 1 on the last three objectives states that you are a low-risk taker. The result would be to slant your portfolio mix toward stable or guaranteed fixed-income investments.

To develop your PASS score, circle the number under the column which most closely reflects your expectations or comfort level. You may Strongly Agree, Strongly Disagree, or circle a number in between the two.

PORTFOLIO ALLOCATION SCORING SYSTEM (PASS)

	Investment Objective	Strongly Agree	Agree	Neutral	Disagree	Strongly Disagree
1.	Earning a high long term total return that will allow my capital to grow faster than the inflation rate is one of my most important objectives.	5	4	3	2	1
2.	I would like an investment that provides me with an opportunity to defer taxation of capital gains and/or interest to future years.	5	4	3	2	1
3.	I do not require a high level of current income from my investments.	5	4	3	2	1
4.	My major investment goals are relatively long term.	5	4	3	2	1
5.	I am willing to tolerate sharp up and down swings in the return on my investments in order to seek a higher return than would normally be expected from more stable investments.	5	4	3	2	1
6.	I am willing to risk a short-term loss in return for a potentially higher long-term rate of return.	5	4	3	2	1
7.	I am financially able to accept a low level of liquidity in my investment portfolio.	5	4	3	2	1

Add up your score to examine your hypothetical asset allocation. A PASS score of 35 indicates an investor who is seeking the highest possible returns with no regard for risk. The lowest possible score, 7, denotes an investor who is fearful of risk and desires income, minimal fluctuation in market values, and liquidity. His or her portfolio would be almost all insured and fixed-income assets.

Compare your total score to the score board below. Remember, score interpretation doesn't create a portfolio for you. Instead, it provides guidelines to consider when evaluating the trade-offs between risk and return. Return to page 93 for a basic description of each category.

Total Score		Cash and Equivalent Accounts	Fixed Income Accounts	Variable Growth Accounts
30-35	(Aggressive)	10%	10%	80%
22-29	(Moderate)	20%	20%	60%
14-21	(Conservative)	30%	30%	40%
7-13	(Defensive)	40%	40%	20%

Here is a list of the investments which I feel belong in those categories:

Cash and Equivalent Accounts	Fixed Income Accounts	Variable Growth Accounts
Savings Accounts	Corporate Bonds	Common Stocks
Money Markets	Municipal Bonds	Preferred Stocks
Certificates of Deposit	Bond Mutual Funds	Stock Mutual Funds
Deferred Annuities	Treasury Notes	Real Estate
Series EE Bonds	Treasury Bonds	Natural Resources
Treasury Bills	Ginnie Mae or other Government Agency Mortgages	Precious Metals
Annuities	Private Real Estate Contracts	

HOW TO BUILD AN INVESTMENT PORTFOLIO

Suppose, now, that you are ready to retire and find that you will have $200,000 distributed to you from your retirement plan. Your task is to place it for income and inflation protection. Use the following worksheet to allocate these dollars among investments in the three categories listed. **Before you start on this exercise, be sure and read the next three chapters on investments.** When you start, keep these rules in mind:

- The score you achieved on the PASS exercise should be used to help you decide how much to place in each of the three broad categories.
- Age is a factor to consider when determining placement of assets. A younger person can take more risks because he or she has adequate time to compensate for disappointing investment performance. As one ages, it is appropriate to be more defensive with investment placement.
- Do not put more than 10% in any one investment, such as a stock or a bond. Do not place more than 20% of your total portfolio in any one mutual fund. Because mutual funds are broadly diversified, the business risk of owning bonds or stocks is minimized.

- Do not place more than 10% of your entire portfolio in precious metals and natural resources.
- Limit your illiquid investments, such as partnerships or individually owned investment real estate, to not more than 50% of the whole.
- Diversify.

Cash or Cash Equivalents Accounts % Allocation	Fixed Income Investment Accounts % Allocation	Variable Growth Investment Accounts % Allocation
___ Savings	___ Corporate Bonds	___ Common Stocks
___ Money Markets	___ Municipal Bonds	___ Preferred Stocks
___ Certificates of Deposit	___ Bond Mutual Funds	___ Stock Mutual Funds
___ Annuities	___ Long-Term Government Bonds	___ Real Estate
___ Series EE Bonds	___ Ginnie Mae Bonds	___ Natural Resources
___ Treasury Bills	___ Real Estate Contracts	___ Precious Metals
___ TOTAL %	___ TOTAL %	___ TOTAL %

ECONOMIC HAZARDS

Once you have your investment portfolio together, you cannot just forget it. All investments behave better under certain differing economic conditions and require occasional changes. The best investments for deflation are long-term fixed income. Low inflation and decreasing interest rates provide fuel for stock and bond markets. High inflation rewards real estate the most, but excessive inflation (12%+) knocks out real estate because buyers can't afford the interest rates to finance purchases. Instead, excessive inflation rewards natural resources and precious metals. The following table illustrates how inflation affects asset categories:

ASSET REPOSITIONING

MULTI-ASSET ALLOCATION MODEL

	Inflation Scenario				
Asset Category	-5%-0%	0%-3%	3%-6%	6%-12%	12%-20%
Fixed Income:					
Bonds (Intermediate and Long-Term)	Excellent	Good	Good	Poor	Poor
Cash Equivalents	Fair	Fair	Fair	Fair	Fair
Equities	Excellent	Good	Good	Poor	Poor
Natural Resources	Poor	Fair	Fair	Good	Excellent
Real Estate	Poor	Fair	Good	Excellent	Poor[1]
Tangibles	Poor	Poor	Fair	Good	Excellent

Asset behavior definitions

Excellent:	Substantial real return
Good:	Reasonable real return
Fair:	Tend to track inflation
Poor:	Loss of purchasing power

1. Due to cost of financing. All cash deals would be profitable.

Source: J.L. Joslin, S.G. Lorant, and R.E.C. Wegner, "The Multi-Asset Allocation Model: A Financial Planning Framework for Long-Term Investment Management," **Tax Management Financial Planning Journal,** *October 21, 1986, p. 528. Reprinted with permission of Tax Management, Inc., a subsidiary of the Bureau of National Affairs, Inc. 1231 25th Street, N.W., Washington, D.C. 20037.*

Most people feel inadequate when it comes to interpreting economic signals. With just a little effort on your part, you can become more informed about financial and economic indicators. Start by:

- Reading the business section of your local paper daily.
- Reading the money section in the ***Wall Street Journal*** at least weekly.
- Reading at least one business magazine a month such as ***Money, Consumer Reports, Barrons, Forbes,*** or ***Business Week.***

...AND THEN YOU SWITCH INTO MONEY MARKETS, BUT IF THE GNP POINTS UPWARD, PLAY EQUITIES...

At the end of a month, see if you can answer the following questions:

- Which way are long-term interest rates headed?
- What is happening in the real estate market locally and nationally?
- What economic cycle are we in or shifting toward (growth, recession, inflation, depression)?
- Which investments make sense for the short term? The long term?

Interest rates are a primary force which impact investment results. If you keep tabs on rates you will start to see a pattern. Watch both 3-month Treasury bill rates and 30 year Treasury bond rates. The normal spread between the two is approximately 2.5%. When short rates start to rise, to match or to close in on long-term rates, it indicates that corporate borrowers think interest rates are on the rise and a credit crunch may be forthcoming.

Track the consumer price index (CPI) as an indicator of inflation. Watch it carefully. If it should rise above a 6% average for an extended period of time, stock market activity could be sluggish.

Stay on the trail of the Feds as they increase or decrease the money supply (M1). The Federal Reserve's monetary policies are among the stabilizing factors of our economy. Putting dollars into the economy lowers interest rates by making more money available and easing credit. Taking money out of the economy, or raising the financial institution's reserve requirements serves to tighten up credit.

Watch the Federal deficit. Think what would happen to it if interest rates zoomed up to 14% or beyond. The size of the deficit is one reason the Feds will work to keep interest rates low for the foreseeable future (or at least until something is done to control the deficit).

Other indicators — such as value of the dollar, crude oil price trends, outflows of foreign capital, federal policies, gross national product, and unemployment figures — also contribute to economists' analyses of economic trends. Even with all their knowledge and analytical tools, economists' opinions on the state of the economy vary dramatically from one to another. If they can't agree, how can lay people or even financial advisors cope with changing economic trends? It's difficult.

PRESCRIPTION FOR INVESTMENT SUCCESS

- Spend first for investments — spend last on life-style: Pay yourself first to make a dent in that burning passion you identified as a financial goal in Chapter 6. Commit at least one half of your discretionary cash or 10% of your net pay, whichever is greater, to the future.
- Develop achievable goals: Visualize where you want to be in 5 years, 10 years, or 20 years. Make your goal explainable. Be patient; a roaring fire starts first with twigs. Take responsibility for your future — no one else will.
- Diversify your assets among more than one asset category: If you are an expert in any one area such as real estate, value investing, growth stock selections, etc., your portfolio will probably be weighted heavier in your area of expertise. But, don't neglect the protection achieved through diversification — it can help protect you from relying on any one investment to make your fortune. You may miss the home run, but then you probably won't strike out either.

- Seek variety in your stock or equity mutual fund portfolio: Diversify within this category by establishing value, growth, blue chip, utility, small stock, or international stock positions.
- Ladder your fixed income investments: Rather than betting on interest rate trends, try to create a portfolio of fixed income investments which have staggered maturity dates. As bonds or certificates of deposit mature, you can reinvest the proceeds. Regardless of whether interest rates are in an incline or decline, this rolling maturity portfolio serves to hedge interest rates.
- Follow the economic cycles: Watch interest rates and inflationary trends. Keep your investment portfolio flexible enough to make gradual shifts toward investments you believe will respond well to changing economic conditions. Keep in mind that some conditions, such as sudden shifts in interest rates or drops in the stock market, will be beyond your control.
- Understand the risk to reward ratio: An investment with a small risk usually has a small reward. The reverse can also be true. Keep in mind the degree of volatility you are willing to endure. Vary your degrees of risk.
- Seek after-tax returns greater than inflation: Examine your investment returns after subtracting taxes. The average after-tax return should exceed the average inflation rate.

There is no such thing as a perfect investment. Each investment position you establish will have drawbacks under certain economic scenarios. Your job is to make sure your portfolio has adequate diversification to protect against illiquidity, extreme volatility, excessive taxation, or high purchasing power risks and still allow you to generate the necessary income or growth required to fulfill your financial goals. Use Worksheet 10A to review your present portfolio position and 10B to draft a model portfolio based on the foregoing information and your specific investment objectives.

WORKSHEET 10A

CURRENT INVESTMENT POSITIONS AS OF ____________________

Investment Category and Identification	Current Value	Total $ in Category	% of Category
Cash or Cash Equivalents Investment Assets			
________________	________		
________________	________		
________________	________		
________________	________		
________________	________		
________________	________		
________________	________		
________________	________	________	________
Fixed Income Investment Assets			
________________	________		
________________	________		
________________	________		
________________	________		
________________	________		
________________	________		
________________	________		
________________	________	________	________
Variable Growth Investment Assets Domestic Stocks			
________________	________		
________________	________		
________________	________		
________________	________	________	________
International Stocks			
________________	________		
________________	________		
________________	________		
________________	________	________	________
Real Estate, Natural Resources, Precious Metals, Other Inflation Hedges			
________________	________		
________________	________		
________________	________		
________________	________	________	________
Total Investment Values			________ 100%

WORKSHEET 10B

REVISED INVESTMENT POSITIONS DRAFT AS OF ______________________

Investment Category and Identification	Current Value	Total $ in Category	% of Category
Cash or Cash Equivalents Investment Assets			
____________________	__________		
____________________	__________		
____________________	__________		
____________________	__________		
____________________	__________		
____________________	__________		
____________________	__________		
____________________	__________	__________	__________
Fixed Income Investment Assets			
____________________	__________		
____________________	__________		
____________________	__________		
____________________	__________		
____________________	__________		
____________________	__________		
____________________	__________		
____________________	__________	__________	__________
Variable Growth Investment Assets Domestic Stocks			
____________________	__________		
____________________	__________		
____________________	__________		
____________________	__________	__________	__________
International Stocks			
____________________	__________		
____________________	__________		
____________________	__________		
____________________	__________	__________	__________
Real Estate, Natural Resources, Precious Metals, Other Inflation Hedges			
____________________	__________		
____________________	__________		
____________________	__________		
____________________	__________	__________	__________
Total Investment Values			__________ 100%

CHAPTER 11

WEALTH BUILDERS

"To be truly rich, you must inherit wealth, be successful in the investment world or be an exceptionally daring entrepreneur."
Unknown

The reader board of a Baptist church located in the South usually had a variety of uplifting messages, then one day this one appeared: "Getting rich is no longer a sin, it's a miracle." The author of that quote probably did not fully understand how to make wise investment decisions. Undoubtedly, there's a lot to know. And no one is ever so knowledgeable that he/she makes the right decision every time. Investments sometimes turn out differently than expected. Here's a story to illustrate this last point.

A ship, encountering thick pea soup fog, was blowing its foghorn. The captain on the ship suddenly saw a light approaching. Becoming concerned that a collision was probable, he radioed this message. "Ahoy there, correct your course 20 degrees to the north." A message came back immediately stating, "You correct yours 20 degrees to the south."

This exchange went on a couple more times during which time the light was coming perilously close. The captain, determined to make the other ship change course, tersely sent this last message, "Look, I am captain of this ship. Get your ship out of my way and right now!" The voice came back, loud and clear, "Look, captain, this is a lighthouse and you better move your ship 20 degrees to the south, and right now!"

Investments, like the lighthouse in the story, aren't always what they appear to be. For instance, government bonds are guaranteed against default, but did anyone mention their interest rate risk? Yes, stocks will probably provide an after-tax return well in excess of inflation, but did anyone mention their volatility? Gold is an inflation hedge, but did anyone mention that it has not kept pace with the long-term inflation rate since the early '60s?

As was discussed in the last chapter, to be a successful investor, a diversified blend of investments is necessary. Like building blocks, some will provide a firm foundation and safe haven for your money, others, the growth necessary to hedge your portfolio against inflation's erosion of spending power. A little of each is recommended even if you find certain investments to be about as exciting as television reruns. In fact, most people find investing rather ho-hum. They don't make money fast enough. They're looking for money excitement from winning the lotto, betting at the race track, or gambling in Las Vegas. Unfortunately, investments don't work the same way.

With most investments, you will not attain overnight wealth. It will take hard work, patience, persistence, and time to work — along with a good understanding of which investments will fulfill your needs.

It also takes a plan. Spending money on investments without a plan is like shopping without a list. You proceed down the aisle plucking items off the shelves as they strike your fancy. Soon you arrive at the checkstand with a cartful of groceries — none of which will work together to make a meal. It is the same with investments. If they do not meet your requirements for safety, growth, income, tax advantage, or ready cash, they will just gather dust and eventually be discarded.

MAKING MONEY MAKE MONEY

Above average returns are usually the primary goal when investing. Why then, from time-to-time, do individuals hold idle assets too long? Is it apathy or lack of time that causes this investment neglect? Leaving money invested in savings, or that stock which promptly lost money, may not feel like a huge mistake for the short term. Over an extended period of time, however, extensive investment idling will undermine your ability to prosper.

If you are determined to have $100,000 accumulated in 20 years and you are spending $100 a month to build up a 6% savings account, you're going to miss the boat. Look at the difference in $100 a month compounded at various investment returns:

Potential Return	Potential Reward
6.0%	$46,435
8.0%	$58,902
10.0%	$75,936
12.0%	$98,925
14.0%	$130,116

You must make a choice now — either to take more risk with your money or increase the amount of money you are spending in this area:

Potential Return	Savings Increment
At 6.0%, it takes	$215/month
8.0%	$170
10.0%	$132
12.0%	$101
14.0%	$ 77

You may not actually earn 14% or 12% on your investments, but an 8-10% return over 20 years may be achievable with a mix of investments.

INVESTMENT BASICS

If you want to start successfully navigating the investment maze, you could categorize your investments by expected returns under the two broad categories discussed in the last chapter — loaned and owned. The lowest returning investments usually will be those with less volatility risk and higher purchasing power risk. Investments which have a greater chance of outpacing inflation will be those with greater volatility. The following brief descriptions of investments does not represent the entire universe of candidates for a portfolio, rather those which are practical and easily attainable such as cash, certificates of deposit, bonds, and stocks.

LOANERSHIP ASSETS

The main risk of this group of investments is declining purchasing power. Their fixed interest rates, varying durations, and predictability can lull even the most sophisticated investor into ignoring the implications of inflation.

Money Markets

These savings instruments are available at some banks, brokerage houses, and most mutual fund companies. Taxable money markets are comprised of short-term debt investments, such as Treasury Bills, certificates of deposit, commercial paper, banker's acceptance notes, and repurchase agreements. Tax-free money markets are comprised of investments in short-term municipal notes issued by city, state and local governments.

The money market usually offers higher yields than savings accounts with minimal risk. Since money markets are available in taxable and tax-free varieties, it will pay you to spend your money on the right type. If you're taxed at the 28% or above tax bracket, you may find the tax-free money market to be more effective. In order to compare tax-free against taxable, you need to subtract taxes from the taxable fund. This will allow you to evaluate both on an equal basis. Multiply the taxable yield by the top tax rate you pay (i.e., 28% or 31%). If the taxable money market is paying 6% the formula is as follows:

$$6\% \times .28\% = 1.68\%;\ 6\% - 1.68\% = 4.32\%$$

Now you know the real return before inflation on the taxable money market — 4.32%. Put your money in the account with the highest tax adjusted rate. Money markets can be opened for as little as $25 up to minimums of $2,000 and many provide free checking privileges. There are no broker's fees and the accounts are 100% liquid. They are an excellent cash stash position for emergency money or opportunity funds.

Certificates of Deposit (CDs)

Fixed duration CDs are available through banks and brokerages in terms from three months up to five or more years. Banks have gotten quite clever in recent years in offering attractive terms and conditions on these investments. You might find CDs which guarantee renewal rates, accept further deposits, or allow interest to be withdrawn while the certificate is moving toward maturity.

Most people think of buying CDs at their local bank where it is convenient to do business, but there are other choices. Brokerages offer CDs from selected financial institutions throughout the country. These CDs have one primary advantage over bank CDs. They can be liquidated without penalty before their maturity date. How much money you receive when you liquidate early will depend on the time left of the term and prevailing interest rates.

The risk relates to increasing interest rates and inflation impacted purchasing power. If interest rates were guaranteed to be at the pinnacle of the interest rate cycle, investors would be glad to put their dollars on loan for as long as possible. I had one client who took that chance in the early 1980s and placed his Individual Retirement Account in a 10-year, 12% CD. He placed his bets on interest rates moving lower in the future and locked up his money. He smiled all the way to the bank for years.

Like bank savings accounts, CD accounts are insured up to $100,000 by the Federal Depository Insurance Corporation. As experienced in the late '80s and '90s, everything can go to %@•&!$# in a handbasket when a significant number of institutions fail. While investors panic at the thought of their savings institution failing, the federal government so far has kept investors' money intact in failed institutions when account balances were under the insurance maximum of $100,000. This experience is called the "bail-out." Avoid this risk by not keeping more than the insurable maximum in all accounts at one institution which are registered in your name.

Series EE Bonds

These bonds always have a face value of twice the purchase price and will eventually double if owned long enough. They are guaranteed a minimum return of six percent if held for five plus years or 85% of the average market yield on five-year Treasury Notes, whichever is greater. If cashed prior to five years, a lower interest rate is credited. Be aware also they cannot be redeemed prior to holding six months except for an emergency.

The main characteristics of this investment are the guaranteed minimum interest and tax deferral. The interest is reset each May 1 and November 1. Since they only credit the interest earned twice a year, be sure and cash these bonds after an interest crediting or you will lose several months of interest. Bonds purchased prior to December 1965 must be cashed in 40 years from their date of issuance or they stop earning interest. The same is true for bonds purchased after November 1965 except the interest payment period is limited to 30 years.

Series EE bonds are an easy investment choice for deferring taxes and building an emergency fund. You can buy the bonds through payroll savings, order them from your bank, or call 1-800-US-BONDS, for a minimum of $25 per bond and a maximum yearly purchase of $15,000. They also have some special tax advantages which will be discussed in Chapter 16, Managing College Costs.

Series HH Bonds

The sole function of this bond is to serve as an exchange for Series EE bonds. The years and years of deferred interest from EE bonds can continue to be deferred if exchanged for a set of HH bonds. Ten-year maturity HH bonds are purchased for full face value of $500 to $10,000. Unfortunately, they only pay a semi-annual rate of 6% which is NOT subject to market rate adjustments. Further, it is also taxable. The best place to get information on Series HH Bonds is at a Federal Reserve Bank.

Treasury Bills (T-bills)

The return from 90-day T-bills is commonly used as an index to replicate cash or cash equivalent returns. T-bills, purchased at a discount in three-, six- or twelve-month durations, grow to maturity. The minimum initial face amount is $10,000, but it doesn't take $10,000 to purchase a T-Bill. For example, when interest rates are 7%, you can buy a 12-month bill for $9,325. The 12-month holding period and the guaranteed interest rate will grow your $9,325 to $10,000. The main advantage is the ability to defer taxes on the maturing T-Bill until the tax year in which your T-bill matures.

Treasury Notes (T-notes)

The minimum purchase price is $5,000 for an investment with a term from two to three years. If a fixed return is desired longer than four years and up to ten years, the minimum investment is $1,000. The key characteristics are semi-annual, fully taxable interest payments and a rock solid guarantee. These can be purchased from a broker, banker, or the Federal Reserve Bank.

Zero Coupon Bonds

Guaranteed compounding is the main benefit with zeros. Purchased at a discount, they grow to maturity — compounding at a rate you can depend upon. Popular choices are treasury zeros for guaranteed fully taxable income and municipal zeros for tax free growth. The treasury zero is a great investment to place in an IRA account or other tax sheltered retirement program if you are not in need of income.

Bond Interest Rate Risk

Unlike the direct relationship between the value of savings accounts and interest rates, there is an inverse relationship between the value of bonds and changes in interest rates. Increasing rates will cause bond values to decrease. The reverse is also true. Whether or not this affects you will depend on your immediate need for liquidity. The price value fluctuation is illustrated below.

The bond in the illustration was issued with a 10% return. If new bonds are issued in the future either above or below that stated rate, the principal value of the existing bond will change as shown. This change in value is only for that moment in time. The bond,

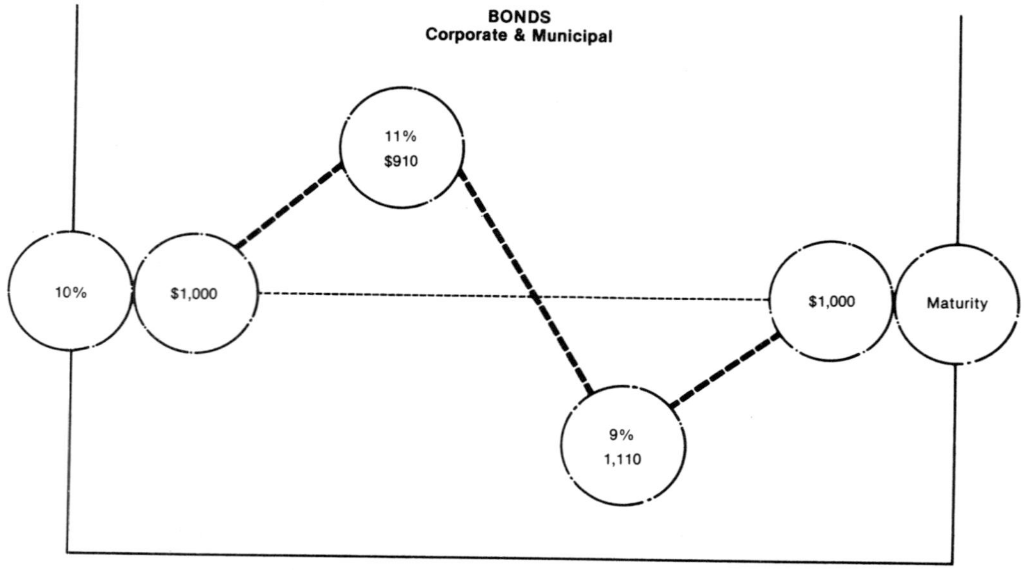

if held to maturity, will be redeemed at full face value. Can you imagine investors lining up to buy a bond which is paying 10% when new bonds are being issued at 9% or below? Of course. In fact, they will pay a premium to buy the bond. The reverse is that when interest rates increase, the bond's price must be discounted. The result creates a total return for the buyer equal to that of new issues. This is a simplistic explanation, but it serves to illustrate interest rate risk. All corporate, municipal, government, mortgage backed securities, and convertible bonds react in a similar fashion to interest rates.

The following example clarifies this further:

> "The mathematics of bond investing. Here's a perspective on how interest rate movements affect the price of bonds. We'll use as an example a bond with a 9% yield and a maturity of 7 years.
>
> "One year from today...
>
> - If interest rates are still at 9%, you'd have a total return of 9% (actually a bit higher with semi-annual compounding).
> - If interest rates are 2% higher, you'd be about even. That's because at this level in yield and maturity, for every 2% increase in rates, prices decline by roughly 9%.
> - If interest rates are 2% lower, you'd have a total return of about 18% — a yield of 9% plus price appreciation of about 9%. (For every 2% decline in rates, prices rise by roughly 9%).
>
> "Thus, if interest rates move approximately 2% over the course of a year, your potential total return would be about zero on the downside or around 18% on the upside, depending on whether rates rose or declined."
>
> *Source: Winter/Spring 1990 edition of* **The American Funds Investor,** *a publication of Capital Research and Management Company.*

One way to cope with the risks associated with interest rate changes is to stagger the maturity of a bond portfolio. For example, if you want to commit $100,000 to six to ten-year duration bonds, you could place $20,000 in a ten year bond and then work backwards with bond durations of nine, eight, and so forth down to six years. The result would be a bond maturing every year after the fifth year. If you did not need the cash from the maturing bond, you would purchase a new five-year bond and would have achieved a rolling average of five-year rates. This immunizing of your fixed income portfolio protects it against interest changes. This strategy can be used with any fixed-income investment such as bonds or CDs.

Treasury Bonds

T-Bonds are available in 10-year to 30-year maturities. Like T-Notes, the bonds pay interest semi-annually. You can spend as little as $1,000 for a Treasury Bond and purchase directly from a brokerage firm or through the Federal Reserve Bank (FRB). If direct purchasing is of interest, call the closest FRB for a pamphlet on how to establish an account with them. Keep in mind that when you purchase a 30 year T-Bond, you are speculating on interest rate trends.

All of the government securities described above are exempt from local and state taxation but subject to federal income tax. This makes them an attractive investment for taxpayers who are subject to taxation from sources other than the IRS. Of course, each of the above government bonds is also backed by the full faith and credit of the U.S. Government. There is no other investment as safe from default since the government has the power to either raise taxes to make good their debts or print more money.

Mortgage Securities

Government National Mortgage Association securities (GNMAs) are 30-year, fully taxable government guaranteed mortgages. The initial investment is $25,000 and can be increased in $10,000 increments. They are the bellwether interest rate for the housing industry. The high yields help compensate for the uncertain duration of the investment. The average life of a mortgage security is about 12 years as homeowners sell, refinance or default on loans for reasons such as death, divorce, disability, job transfers, or personal preference. This takes the timing of the payback away from the lender and places it with the borrower. If you purchase a GNMA, you are the lender and as such will receive monthly principal and interest payments. If you spend the payment, you will be spending away your principal. A convenient way to own GNMAs is in mutual funds where the principal is automatically reinvested and the initial investment can be as low as $1,000. Investors with less than $25,000 can also purchase GNMAs in other formats such as mutual funds, unit trusts and collateralized mortgage obligations.

Similar government agency bonds, Federal National Mortgage Association (FNMAs) and Federal Home Loan Mortgage Corporation (Freddie Macs), pay slightly higher returns than GNMAs. The higher rate is paid due to an absence of the rock solid guarantee. In line with the widespread view that the government would never let a federal agency fail, FNMAs and Freddie Macs bonds are categorized as safe investments.

Collateralized Mortgage Obligation (CMO)

This investment is a repackaging of the above GNMA/FNMA/Freddie Mac mortgage securities. Rather than subject investors to the duration uncertainty of holding a share in 30-year mortgage pools which may or may not pay off within the average life specified, creative minds on Wall Street created a new configuration of this security — the CMO.

Collateralized with underlying securities of government mortgages, this investment is sold to investors in slices — officially labeled as tranches (french for slice). You can purchase a tranche with the maturity you wish from quick pay to slow pay. These investments are synthetic bonds with expected, but not guaranteed, durations. The quick pay investors will receive all their principal back before tranche #2 starts. The second investor will receive all his/her principal before the next in line. In the meantime, all investors are receiving the stated interest.

For instance, John wanted the higher interest of a government mortgage security without the accompanying immediate principal payback characteristic of mortgage backed securities. He also wanted to count on interest only payments for a period of eight years and then have interest and principal returned within the next four years. With the CMO, he can be fairly certain his expectation will be fulfilled. The biggest risk with this bond position is volatility and the potential for the principal to be returned earlier or later than projected.

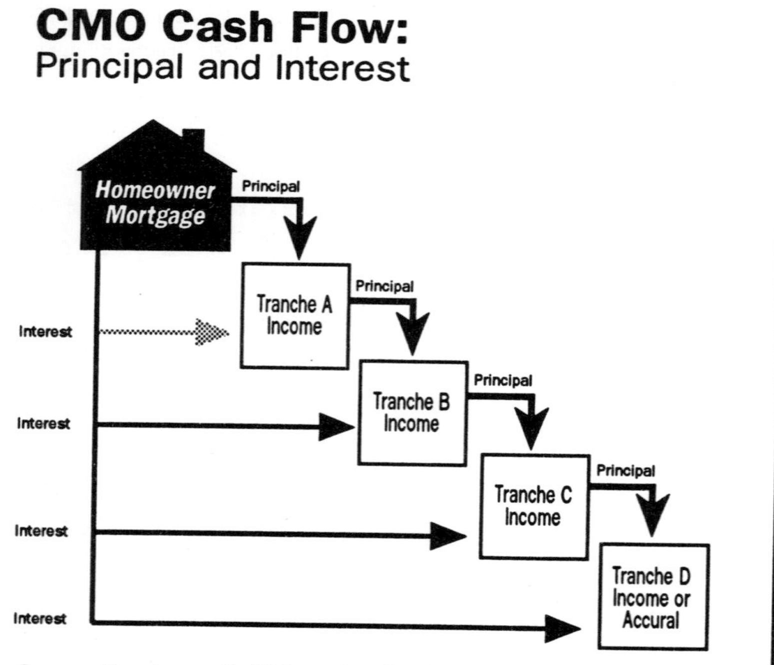

Source: Renaissance Publishing, Seattle, WA.

Municipal Bonds

What's better than rain in August? The prospect of completely avoiding taxes on investment earnings. That is the role of most tax-free bonds. Be aware, however, that some states impose taxes on federally tax-exempt bonds. In order to avoid a state tax, an investor would seek to buy bonds issued in the state in which they reside or in Puerto Rico. Municipal bonds are debt obligations of cities, counties, airports, public utilities, states, and other civil entities, which can be purchased for as little $5,000. Safety conscious investors will stick with A or above rated bonds which are generally either pre-refunded or insured by FGIC, MBIA, AMBAC or other municipal insurance associations. The next safest municipal bond investment would be housing authority and state general obligation bonds.

The yields on tax free bonds always sound low until they are accurately compared to available yields on fully taxable bonds. Here's another method to compare tax-free with taxable returns:

In this example, 5% is the tax free rate. Now to compare it to a taxable rate:

$$\frac{\text{Tax Free Rate}}{(1 - \text{Your Tax Bracket})}$$

$$5\% \div .72 = 6.94\%$$

It is evident anyone in a 28% bracket or above would consider the tax-free variety if similar rating and term taxable bonds were yielding less than 6.94%. Would a 15% taxpayer benefit? Refer to the following table for instant answers.

COMPARISON OF TAX FREE RATES VERSUS EQUIVALENT FULLY TAXABLE RATES

Tax	Taxable Rates at Marginal Tax Brackets		
Free Rates	15%	28%	31%
2%	2.4%	2.8%	2.9%
3	3.5	4.2	4.4
4	4.7	5.5	5.8
5	5.9	6.9	7.3
6	7.1	8.3	8.7
7	8.2	9.7	10.2
8	9.4	11.1	11.6
9	10.6	12.5	13.0
10	11.8	13.9	14.5
11	12.9	15.3	15.3
12	14.1	16.7	17.4

Corporate Bonds

Corporate bonds are promissory notes (IOUs) of a corporation, and generally not insured against default. An exception to that statement would be a unit trust packaged by an investment institution for resale to small investors. These trusts can be found with default insurance. The cost of the insurance is minimal and simply lowers your yield a modicum. Higher yields on these taxable investments are a result of lowered safety. Even with Standard and Poors' highest AAA rating or a Moody rating of Aaa, the return still reflects a risk premium over similar duration government bonds. A prudent investor will want to determine if the additional risk is worth the marginal difference in return.

BOND RATINGS

Standard & Poor's	Quality of the Bonds		Moody's
AAA	Prime	Best	Aaa
AA	High	High	Aa
A	Upper Medium	Higher Medium	A
BBB	Medium	Good	Baa
BB	Fair to Good	Lower Medium	Ba
B	Speculative	Speculative	B
CCC	Poor	Poor	Caa
CC	Outright Speculative	Outright Speculative	Ca
C	Potential to Default	Lowest Rated	C

Ratings are used to determine eligibility of bonds for purchases by certain large investors. Bonds must have one of the top four ratings to be eligible for bank investments. As the ratings measure the risk against default or the issuer's ability to honor an obligation, the issuer's financial status and management policies are used as a gauge. If a bond is unrated, it usually infers the total debt is insignificant and too small to be considered for rating.

Corporations that want to raise cash issue these debt instruments in denominations of $1,000 (usually purchased five at a time). The interest rate will be higher on unsecured corporate debentures than on bonds secured by an asset of the corporation. Junk bonds are those bonds rated BB or lower by Standard and Poors and Ba and below by Moodys. These bonds are more safely owned through a mutual fund due to the great diversification of issues and active supervision of the portfolio.

Unit Trusts

This vehicle is not an investment at all. It is simply a format in which investments are held. The unit trust format offers diversified investments held in an unmanaged trust with a fixed term. The underlying investment choices are varied: utility stocks, corporate bonds from investment quality to junk, government bonds, and municipal bonds. Once the trust is fully funded, the door is closed to new investors. The trust then trades like stock on the stock exchange. If you want to liquidate before the trust is mature, you place a sell order just like with a stock, therefore, a willing buyer must be waiting in the wings.

OWNERSHIP ASSETS

In addition to corporate bonds, corporations issue two varieties of stock and one hybrid.

Preferred Stock

Preferred stock is aptly named. Shareholders of preferred stock are paid dividends prior to any disbursement to common stock holders. They are third in line in case of a liquidation behind secured creditors and unsecured creditors, but ahead of common stock holders. Because the dividend is fixed, preferred stock behaves similarly to bonds when interest rates fluctuate. Investors purchase this stock primarily for its higher dividend rate rather than the growth potential.

Convertible Bonds

Is it a bond or a stock? Convertible bonds appear to be the perfect investment — a bond with fixed interest payments which can be converted into a stated number of stock shares at a fixed price. The bond will be valued primarily by its stock conversion value unless the stock market is depressed. Then it is valued according to the competitiveness of the bond yield as compared to regular corporate bonds. It pays more interest than the dividend on the underlying stock it represents, but less than a straight bond of the corporation.

Common Stock

Last in the liquidation line and first to get dividends cut, common stock investments are higher risk than preferred stock or convertible bonds. Still, they are the liquid investment of choice of most investors due to their historical risk premium of 7%. The risk premium is the amount over a riskless rate that stocks have returned on the average. Combine this risk premium with the right to share in the company's growth through increased dividends and you have an investment destined to outpace inflation.

Stocks are readily marketable but can be volatile in price. Choosing individual stocks requires great skill as financial fundamentals (earnings projections, earnings per share, price to earnings ratio, book values, historical dividend trends, debt to equity, return on equity, etc.) of the corporation must be evaluated. One good place to start your research is to review a Value Line or Standard & Poor's report on a stock of interest. Both services take the labor out of calculating the various measurements, and assign stock ratings. And, in the case of the Value Line service, provides a commentary and analysis of the stock.

Stock analysts' opinions of what constitutes value varies widely. Each seasoned stock picker will have favored methods ranging from fundamental to technical analysis. The proof is, of course, revealed in the performance figures they achieve. Here are a few of the more common methodologies.

- Price/earnings ratio analysis: In ***Practicing Financial Planning***, Prentice Hall, 1990, Sid Mittra extols the virtues of relying on the PE ratio as a barometer of value. This ratio shows how much money an investor is willing to pay for each dollar of the company's earnings. The PE can be evaluated against the Standard & Poor's ratio to determine if the stock under scrutiny has potential for growth. If the market is in a decline, the average PE of the market will be about 8 to 10. When the stock market is hot, PE ratios tend to increase in the range of 13-15. On the fateful day of October 19, 1987, the S&P PE ratio was 21. A year later the PE ratio was 10. The easiest way to estimate what a stock price should be is to multiply the PE ratio times the projected future earnings. This gives you a present value figure you can use to compare against the stock's selling price.
- Historical dividend trends: Because earnings can be manipulated by clever accountants, the earnings per share figure isn't the most reliable guide of value according to information in ***Dividends Don't Lie***, Longman Financial Services Publishing, 1988 by Geraldine Weiss and Janet Lowe. Dividends are. Dividends represent real money — the kind you can put in your pocket. Weiss and Lowe look for the following: Dividend increases in at least five out of the last twelve years, increased earnings in at least seven of the last twelve years, 25 years of uninterrupted dividends; five million shares outstanding, and ownership of the stock by at least 80 institutions. Lastly, they look for a Standard and Poor's rating of "A" or higher. This leads us to consider the merits of blue chip stocks, including utilities. Years of historical dividend increases in a stock can be a real comfort when the market gets rocky.
- Dividend discount method: The dividend discount method is a quick calculation used to estimate value. It takes the expected stream of future dividends and discounts them by rate of return being sought by the investor. For example, if ABC was paying a yearly dividend of $1.50 per share, the stock was trading at $20.00 and you wished an 11% dividend, the value for the stock would be determined as follows: $1.50/ .11 = $13.63. At the present price of $20.00 the rate of return would only be 7.5%. By the above criteria, it is over valued. This is the basic approach. In practice, it is the future stream of payments (hopefully increasing) discounted at the required rate of return to a present value. Professional stock analysts impute a growth rate on the dividend (if historically evident) and look forward 3-5 years when performing this analysis.

- Price/book ratio analysis: A quick test of value is to examine the book value per share. This is the stripped down value of a company's assets less intangibles, debts, and equity issues with a prior claim divided by the shares outstanding (shareholder equity). The next ratio would be to compute the price to book value ratio. A find, according to bargain hunters, would be stocks selling for not more than 30% over book. Don't become too enamored with this method though as canny accountants can manipulate the book value or assets could have a market value greater than book value.
- Earnings per share (EPS) trends: The direction of the EPS is an important element to consider when evaluating stocks. The earnings determine the ability of the company to pay dividends or to subsidize research and development activities. Consequently, it is linked closely to price changes in the market value of stocks and one of the key factors used by analysts when formulating an opinion on a specific stock. Over time, there is a close correlation between share prices and corporate profitability.
- Price earnings growth ratio (PEG): This ratio is a tool to determine the merits of purchasing a growth stock (those with rapidly increasing earnings). Many analysts will not buy a stock unless its PE ratio is equal to or less than the estimated five year average annual growth rate for earnings. For example, if BUYME's PE ratio was 10, and the estimated annual growth of its earnings were 10%, the PEG would be 1.00. What if the growth rate anticipated on BUYME was 16%? Then the PEG (10/ .16) would equal .62. To get started on this analysis, look at the average PE and earnings growth rates for industries of interest. Then establish a lower limit on the PE ratio and a minimum growth rate. Filter that universe of contenders. Some analysts won't consider a growth stock unless the PEG is in the lower 25% of its industry sector.
- Beta volatility ratio: The beta is another useful element to consider when evaluating stocks. It is used as an indicator of volatility. The S&P 500 beta equals 1. Therefore, stocks with betas above 1 should outperform the market when it rises and decline faster when it corrects. Stocks with betas below 1, likewise will fluctuate in price less dramatically than the market as a whole. If you are a bull, you will seek to own stocks with high betas and, therefore, more potential of outperforming the S&P 500 Index. If you are a bear, you will try and cushion your portfolio volatility by selecting stocks with betas below 1.

If analyzing stock were that easy, we would all be wealthy stockholders. It's not. The economy and a myriad of economic indicators — inflation, interest rates, supply and demand, what's hot and what's not — can depress a stock price. If you're driven to drink by irrationality, don't try and buy individual stocks. But if you're an analyst who enjoys pouring over facts and figures of professional research services and annual reports and have the stomach to ride a roller coaster to the appropriate stop, you might like to give it a try. One good way for a novice investor to learn is to join an investment club before you take the plunge. And read. The two books cited on page 128 would be a good start.

I believe most investors need at least $50,000 to build a stock portfolio with adequate diversification of businesses and industries. That, however, may not be enough to purchase at least 100 each of the 30 or so stocks it takes to diversify away the business risk associated with stock ownership.

The majority of small investors fail in the stock market because they buy emotionally. They see the market rising, watch it, and finally become motivated to act as the roller coaster approaches the peak. When the market cycles down again, their fear forces them to bail out. If you decide to go forward on your own, here are some guidelines to help you:

Don't be greedy. Take profits when they are in excess of 40%
Place 15% stops to limit losses on your stock position.
Buy the unpopular.
Sell it when everyone wants it.
If you read about it in the paper, hear it from a neighbor or talk show host, it is too late.
Diversify your portfolio to cushion losses.
Don't invest money you will need within three to five years.
Get advice until you know what you are doing.
Don't become too attached to your investments.
Be willing to study the companies you want to buy.

Bernard Baruch, the brilliant financier who was the envy of investors and counselor to presidents, characterized the challenge of successful stock market investing as follows:

> "If you are ready and able to give up everything else and will study the market and every stock listed therein as carefully as a medical student studies anatomy and will glue your nose to the ticker tape at the opening of every day of the year, and never take it off till night; if you can do all that and, in addition, have the cool nerve of a gambler, the sixth sense of a clairvoyant, and the courage of a lion — you have a minimal chance."

Real Estate Investment Trusts

This investment area is not well understood by investors. Real Estate Investment Trusts (REITs) purchase diversified properties with values rarely reflected in the trading price of the shares. Since these assets trade like a stock, their price is affected by supply and demand as well as by the dividend yield and value of the assets held by the trust. If few buyers are lined up, the share price of the REIT may be severely depressed. If you are interested in a high income asset and believe in the intrinsic value of the underlying assets, this area offers some appeal.

Limited Partnerships

After the mid-1980s, this form of purchasing real estate, oil and gas, equipment, and other more creative endeavors fell into disfavor. Limited partners found their partnerships defaulting or being rolled up into master limited partnerships (MLPs). The MLP activity served to shore up marginally performing partnerships by blending them with the more successful syndications. The lack of control by investors over management decisions and limited success of public partnerships is a compelling reason to proceed with caution in this area.

If you are interested in a partnership approach to a business venture, consider local partnerships first. You can visit with the general partner, view the assets, and study the economics with your CPA, attorney, and financial advisor.

You can also go bargain hunting through the active secondary market. Organized exchanges exist which buy and sell partnership interests from disenchanted investors or simply those who wish to cash out now rather than waiting for the general partner to liquidate the partnership assets. Partnership units trade at steep discounts over original issue prices. There is room for profits in this market if the partnership is selling for less per share than the equity per share (appraised real estate values minus liabilities divided by the shares outstanding).

Precious Metals

The last of our practical ownership assets is one of the more glamorous choices. You can really enjoy the money you spend on this asset by adorning your body with it or simply jingling it in your pocket. Precious metals, namely gold, silver, platinum, are higher risk assets due to their greater volatility. Gold and silver are easy to own if you purchase coins such as Eagles, Maple Leafs, or pure silver dollars. You can also purchase precious metals in bullion form priced by the ounce.

You need to study this market if you expect to be a trader. Precious metals are a hedge against inflation and derive part of their value from a limited world supply. But as a long-term investment, gold has merely kept pace with inflation rather than outpaced it.

Most investors just purchase it as a 5-10% insurance position for their portfolios. Gloom-and-doomers (the Chicken Littles who think the sky is falling) are keen on this asset and believe if the world-wide economy were to falter, banks fail in droves, governments default on their obligations, etc., gold would be a sought after commodity with high trading value.

SUMMARY

Each of these loanership assets — money markets, certificates of deposit, bonds, mortgage securities, T-bills and ownership assets — stocks, convertible bonds, REITs, limited partnerships, and precious metals — help build wealth with time and care. But they are not the sole building blocks available. A sturdier portfolio will also contain mutual funds and tax deferred annuities. These two types of building blocks are described in Chapters 12 and 13.

CHAPTER 12

MONEY MANAGEMENT WITH MUTUAL FUNDS

"Take nothing on its looks; take everything on evidence. There's no better rule."

Charles Dickens

If you're convinced that stocks, or combinations of stocks and bonds, are the only way to stay ahead of inflation for the long term, perhaps you should take advantage of the professional money management available through mutual funds.

The stock market can be an exciting or alarming place to be invested depending on its direction, and it is definitely not a place for part-timers. As a small investor seeking to profit from good stock picks, you must meet or beat competition like Wellington Investment Management, Prudential Investments, Merrill Lynch, bank trust departments, huge pension investment managers and so forth. These institutional investors are making hundreds of phone calls every day, using computer models to make trading decisions, selling large blocks of stocks at one time which drives down prices on certain stocks — maybe one that you hold. Even if you stay up day and night, how can you hope to compete with the resources that professional full-time investment managers have access to, or with the returns they attain?

Mutual funds can be a profitable answer.

INVESTING REQUIRES TIME, TEMPERAMENT AND TALENT

MUTUAL FUNDS FACTS

Why mutual funds? Because they are ideally suited to small investors, lazy investors, smart investors, and wealthy investors. Where else can you get instant diversification and full-time professional management for pennies? Since 1980, the assets of all U.S. mutual funds have ballooned from $130 billion to over $1 trillion. Investors have been defecting to mutual funds in droves after losing ground through the negative after-tax and after-inflation returns available in bank deposits or CDs. Why? Primarily because returns in well managed growth stocks have averaged from 12% to 20% per year over the last ten years. Translated into a pure percentage change, the profits have been a breathtaking 400-600%.

Highly Structured — Highly Regulated

Mutual funds are subjected to a multitude of onerous regulations. This headache for them translates into protection for you. No one has ever lost money in a mutual fund due to insolvency or impropriety.

Here's the lowdown on why. Mutual funds are investment companies whose business it is to invest shareholders' money for the sole purpose of achieving specific investment objectives. They are organized under the rules of the Investment Company Act of 1940, and their affairs are watched over by a board of directors, a specified number of whom must be entirely independent of the fund's advisor or underwriter. Each fund contracts with an investment advisor to manage the portfolios and a principal underwriter who buys new shares for distribution through securities dealers or direct to the public.

Fund operations and financial dealings must be audited by an independent public accountant. Their securities and other investments must be held by a custodian (usually a bank) and segregated from all other accounts. Cash and securities may be delivered only for specified transactions and upon receipt of proper instructions from the fund officers.

Officers with access to fund securities must carry fidelity bond coverage, and there are stringent prohibitions against self-dealing between funds and their officers, directors, investment advisor, and other affiliates. Finally, the funds' status as separate companies helps insulate them from any financial difficulties that could befall their advisors or underwriters.

Every mutual fund is accompanied by a prospectus, which states the investment objective of the fund, financial information, and management fees. The prospectus is the official document describing the guidelines and policy by which the investment company must abide. For complete information about the fund of your choice, be sure to read it.

TYPES OF MUTUAL FUNDS

There are two types of mutual fund companies:

1. <u>Open end</u>: Most investors are familiar with these funds. They are the funds you hear more about — Safeco, Oppenheimer, American Funds, Fidelity, Twentieth

Structure of a Mutual Fund

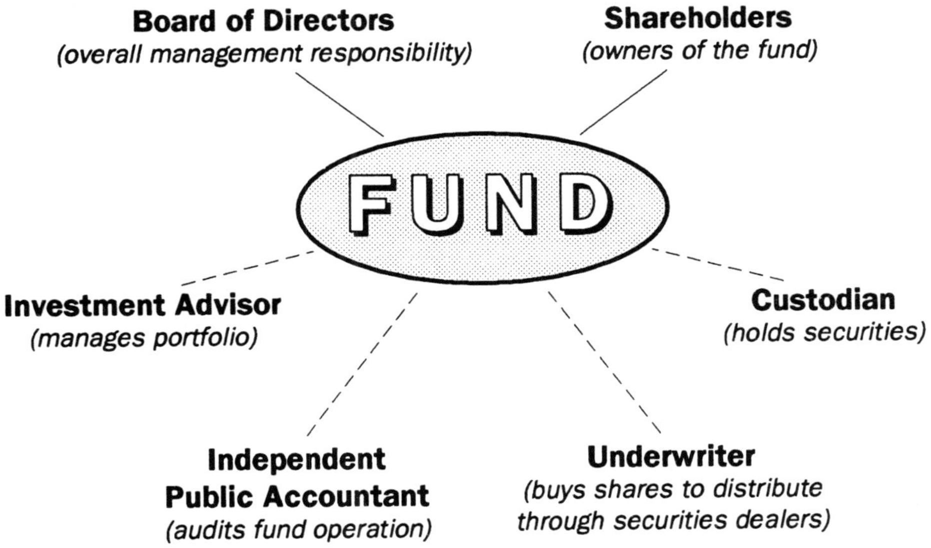

Century, Franklin, Vanguard, and many more. Open end funds are so labeled because they almost never close the door to investors. They will usually always accept new money and seek to invest that money in additional stocks and bonds. Occasionally a mutual fund will close its door in order to maintain the fund at a particular size.

2. Closed end: These funds are organized by some of the same managements that run open end funds, but they are not as well advertised. This is because once a fund is organized and a prescribed number of shares are sold, the fund management forever closes its door to new money. They will neither sell further shares nor purchase back your shares. Closed end funds will trade on stock market exchanges at prices ranging from a discount to a premium over their intrinsic value. If you want to purchase a closed end fund after the initial offering, you must deal with a brokerage firm. It is similar to purchasing a stock.

Mutual Fund Advantages

Mutual funds can safely build you a foundation of wealth. Short-term volatility and significant corrections must be expected from time to time. But if you believe in the history of this country, you can bank on the stock market rising long term. Where is the majority of institutional money invested? The stock market. The following advantages of mutual funds will allow you to run in the same race with the big boys — the institutional investment firms — and see your money double as rapidly as theirs.

- Instant diversification of stocks, bonds, or other securities: This diversification through numbers will take away the business risk of stocks and bonds discussed in Chapter 12. You get far more diversification than you could ever afford buying individual stocks. Mutual funds by law cannot invest more than 5% in any one stock. A minimum investment of as little as $25 can give you a share in as many as 30 to 100 different securities.

- Professional management by a full-time investment manager: The most brilliant minds are put to work for one sole reason — to make you money. The decision to buy certain stocks, bonds, and other securities is made by them. The manager, not you, has the headache of "number analysis, on site visitations, in-depth research of each stock held, and sorting through many megabytes of computer data. If you don't like the results of one fund, you can select another fund with different or better professional management.

- Public record: Unlike private money management, mutual fund results are published daily in major newspapers. Open-end mutual funds are regulated by the SEC and must report results uniformly. All the securities in the fund are valued on each business day and the resulting share value is published the next business day. This Net Asset Value (NAV) fluctuates each day. Two prices may be shown for some funds: the first is the price of the share value, including an entry fee, the next is the NAV of the fund. Those with just one price listed are no-load (no sales fee) funds.

  In addition, many professional rating services follow mutual fund performances and evaluate the manager's skill in achieving returns commensurate with the volatility risk they assumed. Mutual Fund Values, Lipper Analytical Service, Weisenberger, and CDA are professional services used by advisors, in addition to computerized databases. Individual investors often rely on ***Forbes, Business Week, Money, Fortune*** and other financial magazines to help them evaluate funds. These publications, however, rarely provide enough comprehensive information to make an informed choice among funds.

- Liquidity: By regulation, all open end mutual funds must allow you to redeem your shares on demand at the current net asset value. You can pick up the telephone and request a redemption, write a check, or mail the fund a letter. By owning an open end fund, the investment company purchases your shares back directly. The value you realize on the day your shares are liquidated directly reflects market conditions. The number of shares you own, multiplied by the NAV share value on the day of the transaction, will be the amount of money you receive (minus any sales fee or redemption charges — READ THE PROSPECTUS).

- Continuity of management: Your extended vacation, new business venture, or even your demise will not disrupt the continuous care that is available for your mutual fund. You can kick back and relax or spend your time and energy doing what you do best, whether that is playing golf, staying current in your occupation, or managing a business.

- Dollar cost averaging: If you want to purchase stocks on a regular periodic basis with fixed amounts of money, mutual funds are your only practical choice. You can start out with as little as $25 per month and invest systematically. If you purchase shares when the stock market is fluctuating up and down, your average cost per share will be less than the average price per share over the investment period. The validity of this concept has been proven by past studies.

  For example, if mutual fund shares are presently selling for $10.00 a share and you have $100 per month to invest, the results of investing in a fluctuating market could be as follows:

Regular Investment	Share Price	Shares Acquired
$100.00	$10.00	10
$100.00	$ 5.00	20
$100.00	$10.00	10
$300.00	$25.00	40

Results: Total invested $300.00. Total shares owned 40. Ending market value per share $10.00. 40 x $10.00 = $400.00.

If the share price recovers from the hypothetical 50% drop, you would have a $100.00 gain. The total of the share price divided by three investment periods equals an average price of $8.33. The average cost to you, because of your strategic investing, is only $7.50 ($300/40 shares). This strategy always works in a fluctuating market or declining market. It can also work in a market where the prices fluctuate as little as $2.00 per share.

If your real reason for investing is to make money, dollar-cost averaging is an infallible way to invest. Larry Loser started to buy the Dow-Jones Industrial Average in 1929 and continued to invest $1,000 at the beginning of each year for the next ten years. At the end of that time, the stock market had lost 57% of its 1929 value. Larry Loser's result through dollar cost averaging resulted in a profit to him of about 6% during one of the worst crashes in the stock market in history. His son, Larry Loser, Jr., started investing in 1971 and each year invested at the worst possible moment — the absolute market high. He continued on this program for 20 years. At the end of the 20 years, he tallied up his compound return and found it to be 14%. Just 2% less than if he had perfect market insight by investing when the market was at the low point each year. In summary, both father and son find their "losing" experiences quite profitable.

- Care and feeding: Until you've owned stocks individually, you may not appreciate this next benefit. Dividend checks end up being spent rather than reinvested, stocks are not sold or purchased at the opportune time, and stockholder rights are not fully understood. Owning stocks and bonds in mutual funds allows you to have all of this taken care of automatically. The stock certificates are held by the fund which takes care of reinvestment of dividends and other housekeeping duties.
- Excellent value: Fees for money management within mutual funds are generally lower than private money managers charge. Their volume trading results in lower brokerage charges than could be negotiated individually.
- Individual attention: This feature is one of the greatest benefits of owning mutual funds. Your money gets the same attention as all other investors. The smallest investor with his or her first $25 deposit receives the same attention as Mr. and Mrs. Big with a $100,000 deposit. Professional full-time analysts devote themselves to watching the potential of each and every stock and bond position in the portfolio.

Disadvantages

Yes, there are some, but they are insignificant when weighed against the advantages:

- Impersonal stock selection: The mutual fund manager isn't going to talk to you before purchasing stocks, bonds, or cash. In fact, they are not going to consider you at all, other than to stick to the stated objectives outlined in the prospectus. This is a good reason to be sure to match your fund purchases to the investment objectives you identified.
- Lack of tax control: Even if you have chosen growth stocks in an effort to defer capital gains, mutual funds are actively managed, and therefore, will incur portfolio turnover. Portfolio turnover will, in turn, generate capital gains or losses. Imagine how you would feel if you received a tax bill for gains realized on your mutual funds, yet the share price actually declined. This was the case in both 1987 and 1990 when portfolio managers sold some stocks at a profit in spite of the stock market's gyrations.

Here's what you can do about this second disadvantage. Most funds give advance notice of impending capital gains distributions. A shareholder could switch to the money market before the distribution, perhaps generating a loss for tax purposes. Then, after the distribution, he could switch back into a similar equity fund to await the market's eventual recovery. Don't buy the same fund back as you would violate the wash sale rule (31 days between sale and repurchase) and invalidate the tax loss.

Even if a distribution sneaks up on you, all is not lost. Switching after the distribution produces the same net effect; i.e., the distributed gain is more than offset by selling shares at the lower post-distribution price. Those who want continuous exposure to stocks could simply change from one equity fund to another in the same group.

Or you could invest your money in a tax deferred variable annuity, choosing some of the same fund management as available with open end mutual funds. As stated in Chapter 13, variable annuities defer the tax on the income and capital gain distributions which are part of owning a mutual fund.

INDIVIDUAL FUND CHOICES

All advisors have favorite funds, depending on their experience level and personal risk nature. Some good choices are:

- Growth and small growth funds: These funds are comprised of 1) stocks of companies which are reinvesting their earnings in corporate expansion rather than paying out the dividends, or 2) undervalued stocks. A value manager will seek out stocks which have a low price-to-earnings ratio (PE) reflecting the fact that there is room for the stock to appreciate in value. Growth funds rely on capital appreciation rather than steady dividend growth to fuel their total return. These funds typically offer investors a more volatile ride than funds where total return is composed of both appreciation and dividend growth.
- Blue chip funds: Equity income funds, stocked with firmly established companies, such as Pepsico, Merck, U.S. West, Boeing, GE, Con Edison, GTE, Bristol-Myers, provide a blended dividend rate of from 4-6% along with the prospects of increasing share prices. The dividends provide a steady income despite the gyrations of the stock market.
- Utility funds: High dividends of 6-7% are characteristic of income oriented utility stock funds. Primarily invested in electric, gas, and telephone utilities, these funds satisfy the needs of income dependent investors while still providing some growth. Because income oriented utility stocks have high dividends, they react like bonds when interest rates fluctuate — rising as rates drop and losing value when rates increase. Growth oriented utility funds can also be found. Their dividends will range from 2-5%. A greater percentage of the total return will come from an increase in the funds' net asset values rather than from the dividends.
- Balanced funds: A combination of stocks and bonds, generally balanced from 40-50% in either category, is a good way to poke your nose into both stock and bond markets under the professional guidance of one or more managers. Balanced funds take the edge off the volatility that can be experienced in either stocks or bonds alone. These funds also provide a dividend level of 5-7%. The bonds supply the current income and the stocks shoulder the growth. In terms of risk, a balanced fund is more conservative than an equity-income fund.

- Income funds: These funds are comprised mostly of bonds and high income stocks such as utilities. A more conservative selection than the balanced choice above, it appeals to the investor who wishes more income than growth. Dividends range around 7-8%.
- International funds: Foreign stock exchanges account for approximately 70% of the world stock capitalization. International funds can be growth oriented small stocks or international blue chip funds. Since we are in a world economy, with daily changes in the dollar's strength against other currencies, it makes sense to place a portion of one's portfolio in an international fund. Be prepared for greater share price fluctuation than in a domestic stock fund — particularly if you are invested in the Asian countries, where market drops of 10,000 points are common.
- Bond funds: This is a multiple choice category. There are high quality as well as high yield municipal and corporate bond funds in addition to the high safety of government bonds. It is important to determine the weighted maturity of the portfolio and how the price (above or below the issue value of a bond) will impact the total return. In addition, each manager will hedge their portfolio differently to take advantage of rising or falling interest rates.
- Money markets: Tax free or taxable, it's your choice. Most mutual fund companies offer a money market choice as a safe haven alternative to the volatility experienced in bond or stock funds. These funds have so many benefits, I've often wondered why everyone didn't own at least one. Why turn down a free gift. They are free: free check writing, free quarterly statements, free from volatility, free service, and free from taxes if that is what you wish.

Keep in mind that with all mutual funds there are degrees of risk. A money market has minute risk. A loss is not likely but you can lose money with other types of funds; it is generally a matter of timing. Don't get panicky and sell your investment after a market drop if you are not in need of the money. This is the time to buy more shares. Human nature, however, is to spend in this area when momentum has already built in the stock market, and sell when the market starts to crumble. Fear rears its ugly head and leaves a mark on the pocketbook.

A wiser strategy is to select a well managed mutual fund which fits your personal income or growth objective and stay invested for the duration. Enough other liquidity can be maintained in order to provide for instant cash needs and allow you to sit through market corrections.

SELECTION CRITERIA

Everyone has his or her own method for evaluating mutual funds, but most professional advisors take their research beyond the obvious performance related numbers. As an example, consider the following question.

If you had a choice between these two mutual funds, which would you choose: Fund A returning 14%, or Fund B at 17%? Most investors would choose Fund B if they knew nothing more than performance. When researching these funds, it was found that Fund B had a beta of 1.5 while Fund A had a beta of .80. The beta is a volatility measurement; how volatile the fund is expected to be in comparison to the Standard and Poor's 500 (S&P 500) Index. In other words, it measures how a stock or mutual fund will react to the daily swings of the market as gauged by the S&P 500 Index. The Index has a beta of "1" and all domestic common stocks have a beta which measures their volatility. This little bit of information may be meaningless unless you understand the significance of the above facts.

Hypothetically, assume that the S&P 500 Index of common stocks returned 14% in the same year that Fund A achieved 14% and Fund B 17%. Here's a rudimentary method of determining which fund achieved the best return. Start by multiplying the beta of each fund times the S&P market return of 14%:

Fund A: 0.80 x 14% = 11.2%
Fund B: 1.50 x 14% = 21.0%

The result is the expected return for each fund given the level of risk it assumed. Now you can clearly see which fund was the better performer. Fund A overachieved its expected return. In fact, it achieved the same result as the unmanaged S&P 500 Index with 20% less volatility (risk). Fund B delivered subpar performance for a fund with a beta of 1.5. It was expected to gain 50% more than the S&P 500 Index when the S&P Index returns are positive and lose 50% more when the Index is negative.

The beta is just one of the ratios used to evaluate and compare funds. There are more. Before going any further, a set of definitions is in order. Investment managers tend to use words that have been called technobabble. Three terms in particular are carelessly tossed around in conversation: alpha, beta, and R-square. These statistics, if understood, can provide a great deal of insight into mutual fund performance and the level of the manager's skill.

Alpha, beta, and R-square provide information regarding the performance of a portfolio relative to the performance of another portfolio or the stock market itself. The first step in comparing a portfolio to the market, for example, is to graph the performance of both. A line chart is one way to compare pure performance, but in order to evaluate whether it was good or bad in comparison to the S&P Index, you must go farther. The following definitions will be useful to you in the evaluation process:

- R-square: This statistic measures the percentage of a fund's movements that are explained by movements in the S&P 500 for equity funds and a bond index, such as the Lehman Brother's Govt/Corp Bond Index, for bond funds. In other words, if you plotted the performance of the portfolio and the S&P 500 and placed the graphs on top of each other, would the graphs be substantially the same or substantially different? R-square is expressed as a number between 0 and 100%. The lower the R-square, the lower the relationship between the performance of the portfolio and the performance of the market. R-square is important because of the relationship of this ratio to the alpha and beta statistics. An R-square over 90 indicates that some significance can be placed on the alpha and beta statistics. R-squares less than 90 mean that the alpha and beta statistics should not be relied upon. This statistic can also be used to add diversity to mutual fund portfolios.

- Alpha: This measurement exhibits the manager's skill or lack of skill. According to Morningstar's publication, ***Mutual Fund Values:***

  > "Alpha represents the difference between a fund's actual returns and its expected performance, given its level of risk as measured by beta (see definition). The difference is expressed as an annualized percentage. For example, suppose risk-free Treasury bills returned 7%, the S&P 500 returned 12%, and a mutual fund with a beta of 1.2 returned 15%. The market excess return is 5% (12%-7%) and the expected return of the fund is 13% ((1.2 x 5%)+7%). Since the fund actually returned 15%, its alpha is 2% (15%-13%), meaning that the fund performed two percentage points better than expected considering its beta. In contract, a negative alpha indicates underperformance by the given percentage."

- Beta: The beta is a measure of relative risk. A beta statistic of 1.0 means that the portfolio has just as much volatility (risk) as the market.

These statistics can be used together to estimate future performance. Assume a manager's R-square statistic is 96, his alpha is 1.2, and his beta is .90. Given an expected market return of 10% over the next year, the manager's return is estimated to be 10.2%. This is calculated as follows: Expected return = alpha + (beta x market return). In this case, the calculation equals 1.2% + (.90 x 10%) or 10.2%.

- Sharpe ratio: This measurement tool was briefly introduced in Chapter 11. It is one of the easiest ways to compare one money manager against another while adjusting his or her performance by the standard deviation — volatility away from the average (explained in detail in Chapter 11). This ratio gives you a method to measure the benefit in assuming volatility risk in order to achieve a return greater than available in a totally risk-free asset. The risk-free rate used is usually the 90-day Treasury Bill.

$$\frac{\text{Expected Return — Risk-free Rate}}{\text{Standard Deviation}} = \text{Sharpe Ratio}$$

- Treynor ratio: A variation of this theme is the Treynor statistic. It is calculated identically to the Sharpe, but the beta is substituted for the standard deviation. Some analysts prefer the Treynor using the beta, rather than the Sharpe using the standard deviation as a risk measurement tool because all movements from the norm — losses as well as gains — are seen as added risk when computing the standard deviation.

No single statistic should be the determining factor in hiring any one manager or determining the benefit of combining a group of funds. However, understanding alpha, beta, R-square, standard deviation, and the Sharpe and Treynor ratios can add to your understanding of a manager's performance.

More Selection Criteria

While performance is only part of the picture when determining fund suitability, it is important to examine fund performance during particular periods, such as bear markets like the crash of 1987 or the market drop of 500 points from July through December of 1990. You should also compare your pending fund's twelve-month, three- and five-year performance against the competition. Don't perform this analysis in isolation, though. Remember, those useful characters: alpha, beta, standard deviation, R-square, Sharpe, and Treynor!

One of my cardinal rules is never to buy into a brand new fund. If you're interested, put it on the sidelines and watch it perform for a few years. In three- to five-years, it will have a record which may be worthy to consider. Until then, as Charles Dickens said, "Take nothing on its looks; take everything on evidence. There's no better rule."

Find out if the manager is a value oriented manager or a growth manager. Or is the fund a blue chip fund? What is the portfolio composed of: small stocks, blue chips, special interest stocks, utilities, international stocks, short- or long-term bonds, quality or junk, corporate or government? What percentage of the assets are in stocks, bonds, cash, and other? How many and which industries are represented through stocks and bonds?

Is the portfolio managed by one individual or by committee rule? Is the present manager the same one who achieved the fine returns you are drooling over? It is important that the fund has had the same manager for the previous five years. If you're counting on a repeat performance, you want the same captain at the helm.

How large is the fund? This is nice to know, but often does not have a lot to do with performance, as was exhibited for years by Peter Lynch's management of the mega-large Magellan Fund. Large funds can be impacted negatively when the market drops because they tend to be less manageable than their smaller counterparts when reacting to changing market conditions. In fact, they may not be able to dump all of a position in a particular stock in a timely manner without impacting the price of the stock by their actions. Large funds may provide better customer service than small funds due to their ability to hire the necessary staff to do the job. If it comes to a choice between performance and service, most individual investors will choose performance first. Professional advisors, understandably, are concerned about service in addition to risk-adjusted performance.

How much cash does the fund typically hold? The importance of this position was made clear when the 1987 crash forced some funds to sell stocks prematurely in order to meet the redemption requests of the shareholders. The end result of these liquidations was lowered net asset values borne by those shareholders who chose to buy and hold throughout the market volatility.

THE COST OF INVESTING IN MUTUAL FUNDS

Cost is a consideration. It shouldn't be the first consideration when purchasing a fund, but it often is. There are many ways to pay for the selection effort that takes place when evaluating mutual funds:

- Front-end commissions: These sales charges can range from 3 to 8.5% of each dollar you invest. The average entry charge assessed by load funds has moderated in the last several years. You can expect to find many fund choices in the 4-6% range. Front-end loaded products are represented by financial advisors and stockbrokers. Even with a front-end commission, if you buy a proven fund and stick with it, your commission cost will be less than if you had purchased the same stocks and bonds and traded them as actively as a mutual fund portfolio manager does. Much less.
- Quasi no-load: Many brokerage firms sell proprietary products which appear to be no-loads but actually have back-end penalties, known as surrender charges. Investors exiting prior to a predetermined schedule will be assessed "x" percent penalty against their beginning capital value or ending capital value depending on the fund's structure. The percentage normally declines over several years and disappears around years five to six. There are a few good funds to be found among the brokerage pickings, but most investors are not informed enough to find those cherries. Another way funds take a piece of your money is with the addition of 12b-1 fees. These fees are a yearly expense paid by all shareholders. Some back-end and front-end load mutual funds as well as no-load funds have these fees. My suggestion is to look at the total expenses of the fund — yearly management fee plus the 12b-1 fee — to determine if the fees are in line with industry averages.
- No-loads: If you want to find a true no-load, you're going to have to be astute. These funds are available direct or through advisors. You can open the ***Wall Street Journal*** and select a fund from one of the many advertisements. You pay nothing other than your time, that is, if you've selected well. If you haven't, the cost in disappointing performance or inappropriate objectives, can be an expensive lesson. If you deal with an advisor who recommends no-loads, you will pay also. Most advisors who recommend no-load funds insist on monitoring those choices, hiring and firing funds as necessary, and rebalancing funds on a periodic basis for a percentage of the asset base.

How should you pay? Do you want a professional advisor? If so, you'll pay either a monitoring fee or a commission fee. Are you a do-it-yourselfer? If you're confident of your expertise, there is nothing to stop you from dealing direct with mutual fund investment companies.

FILTERING THE UNIVERSE OF MUTUAL FUNDS

How important is it to select your funds carefully? Very! There are over 3,000 mutual fund choices. How will you know if the one you select is the best of its type? I use a computer program stocked with performance returns over the past 10 years, technobabble statistics, and miscellaneous information about the major funds. In order to find the superior fund choices, the universe of funds can be filtered by objective, performance, alpha, beta, Sharpe and Treynor ratios, and so forth. Then, the funds that rise to the top are compared and analyzed using further research services and by reviewing other analysts' opinions of the same funds.

How do you know if the fund you choose will continue to outperform other funds of its type with less risk? You won't unless ongoing filtering of the universe takes place. There are many bad investment choices available as well as a few good ones. In reality, only a few funds qualify for my buy list at one time, though we have a farm team of funds which are potential contenders for future buy recommendations. The remainder are discarded because they expose the investor to too much risk for each increment of return achieved, lost their ace of a portfolio manager, are brand new, are proprietary (only sold by the company which runs the fund), available only to institutions, or have too high of a minimum initial investment.

It is always an interesting experience to evaluate clients' existing portfolios of mutual funds. Investors are never aware of how their fund choices stack up against the competition. They focus on performance without any regard for the volatility risk they may incur. Unfortunately, by the time they are alerted to better fund choices, they have either sacrificed returns or taken more risk than was necessary.

BUILDING A PORTFOLIO OF FUNDS

Here is the profit promise mentioned earlier in the chapter — diversified managers and diversified securities. There is no shortage of mutual funds from which to choose, and one or more are always gaining on the leaders. Funds are available in all sizes, risk levels, objectives, and track records. Once you begin to understand how to analyze mutual funds, it is hard to decide which ones to select. This leads directly to the next point. Create diversified holdings by purchasing into only one fund and instant asset allocation by selecting more than one type of fund:

- Instant diversification: Own a single mutual fund rather than a single stock or bond.
- Instant asset allocation: Own several funds.

Building a multi-fund portfolio has several advantages. Perhaps the most important is the fact that you can have from five to ten portfolio managers employed to manage your money. Each of those managers will not perform 100% as well in subsequent years as they did in preceding years. An off year will occasionally be the norm for any manager. By holding multiple funds, overall consistency is enhanced and management risk reduced.

THE SIMPLICITY OF MUTUAL FUNDS

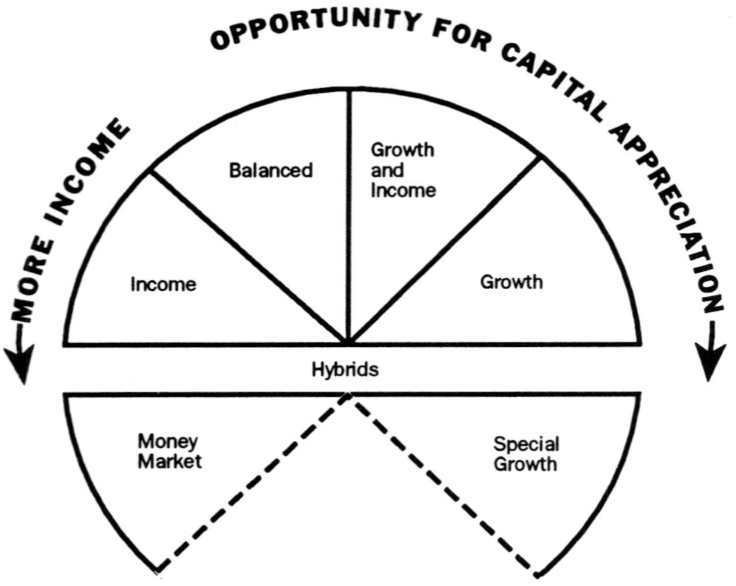

A portfolio of multiple funds can 1) dramatically lower risk (volatility) by the blending effect of stocks and bonds, 2) add measurable benefits from skilled management, 3) potentially outperform the S&P 500 Index, and 4) straddle several different equity markets — emerging growth, growth, blue chip, utility, international, sector, and so forth. You can use balanced or income funds to add short and long bond positions. Aggressive, moderate, or conservative or defensive growth portfolios can be created by varying the percentage of your portfolio allocated to types of equity mutual funds versus types of fixed income funds.

In other words, mutual funds can be used as a creative money management tool. Diversification of stock and bond holdings, management diversification, risk reduction, and above average returns are all within reach for the knowledgeable.

Should you do it yourself? I believe that with the number of funds in the marketplace and the complexity involved in evaluating appropriate choices, the average investor only has a minimal chance of selecting a superior fund. Even if he or she does select well, how can confidence in the fund be maintained unless continual evaluation of the selected fund against the universe of choices is performed? Seek professional help.

CHAPTER 13

TAX DEFERRED WEALTH

"A penny saved is a penny earned."
Benjamin Franklin

John and Clara Elden had discussed the same topic as the above quote about five years before their targeted retirement date:

"Do you realize, Clara, that we are giving the government 31% of our investment earnings each year?" John had recently become aware of the large toll that taxes were taking of their investment returns when reviewing the results of their last year's tax return.

"You bet. I've wondered what we can do about our high taxes yet still keep the majority of our investments guaranteed," replied Clara. Like many of her generation, she was concerned about investment characteristics such as safety and liquidity for their loaned assets.

At that time, the Eldens were still building assets for their pending retirement. The sole reason they were accumulating was to increase their retirement income. And they felt they were not making much progress after they had adjusted their investment earnings for both taxes and the effects of inflation. They were finally fed up with the continuing saga of new tax legislation and the resulting impact on their personal tax situation. Just since 1950, they could recall about 15 major tax changes Congress had enacted — raising and lowering brackets, taking and giving capital gains exclusion, adding and subtracting from their Schedule A, and so forth.

John was aware of the benefits of investing pre-tax and he was taking full advantage of his corporate 401(k) retirement program. He wondered, though, if it would still be beneficial to defer taxes when the money he would invest was already taxed. What would happen if, in the future, the government decided to raise tax brackets again? If that were the case, the Eldens would have to pay a higher rate on the interest earned than they would pay currently.

THE IMPORTANCE OF TAX DEFERRAL

For John and Clara and other investors who are seeking to draw income from their investments during retirement, tax deferred growth can be extremely beneficial even with rapidly escalating tax brackets. The following two examples clarify which investment strategy results in the highest income after ten years. In both cases, $100,000 was invested at 12% in a rising tax environment.

TAXABLE EXAMPLE

Year	Marginal Tax Rate	After Tax Balance	Net Yield
1	30%	$108,400	8.4%
2	30%	$117,506	8.4%
3	35%	$126,671	7.8%
4	40%	$135,791	7.2%
5	45%	$144,754	6.6%
6	50%	$153,439	6.0%
7	50%	$162,645	6.0%
8	50%	$172,404	6.0%
9	50%	$182,748	6.0%
10	50%	$193,713	6.0%

After-Tax Spendable	
Ending Balance	$193,713
Net Spendable	$193,713

Income Production	
Investment Yield	12%
Pre-Tax Income	$ 23,246
Tax Rate	50%
Less Taxes Due	($ 11,623)
Spendable Income	$ 11,623

TAX DEFERRED EXAMPLE

Year	Balance	Net Yield	Difference
1	$112,000	12.0%	$ 3,600
2	$125,440	12.0%	$ 7,934
3	$140,493	12.0%	$ 13,822
4	$157,352	12.0%	$ 21,561
5	$176,234	12.0%	$ 31,481
6	$197,382	12.0%	$ 43,934
7	$221,068	12.0%	$ 58,423
8	$247,596	12.0%	$ 75,192
9	$277,308	12.0%	$ 94,560
10	$310,585	12.0%	$116,872

After-Tax Spendable	
Ending Balance	$310,585
Less Initial Investment	($100,000)
Taxable Portion	$210,585
Tax Rate	50%
Less Taxes Due	($105,292)
Spendable Cash	105,292
Add Initial Investment	$100,000
Net Spendable	$205,292

5.92% Greater Balance

Income Production	
Investment Yield	12%
Pre-Tax Income	$ 37,270
Tax Rate	50%
Less Taxes Due	($ 18,635)
Spendable Income	$ 18,635

60.33% Greater Income

What investor wouldn't like to achieve a 60% greater income potential for retirement? The longer the tax deferral, the greater the results over a fully taxable account. Naturally, all investors won't achieve a 12% return in a tax deferred annuity. Those that invest for safety and security will attain returns slightly greater than comparable length certificates of deposit. Those unafraid of day-to-day volatility and who wish to reach out for the greater growth potential of the stock market may.

IS AN ANNUITY RIGHT FOR YOU?

This investment is not for everyone. Some investors, like the Youngs who are in their mid-30s, aren't old enough for a tax deferred annuity because of the 10% pre-59-1/2 penalty. They could, though, use an annuity if the money targeted for the annuity is dedicated retirement money or used to fund an IRA. Others may want greater access to their money. Annuities should not be purchased if the funds will be needed before the investment is mature — usually about five to six years. Purchase annuities when:

You want to have a greater capital base in retirement to produce income.
You are 10-15 years away from age 59-1/2.
Your tax bracket during retirement may be lower.
You want investment guarantees without taxation.
You want professional stock and bond portfolio management without taxes.

Take the following quiz to determine if annuities make sense for your retirement plan. If you answer yes to most of the following questions, you will want to consider purchasing a tax deferred fixed and guaranteed or variable annuity.

YES	NO	
___	___	I don't need the money in my annuity before I am age 59-1/2.
___	___	I'm in the 28% or greater tax bracket or simply want to pay taxes due later.
___	___	I am willing to invest the money for at least five years to seek a meaningful potential return.
___	___	I'm looking to invest more than I can in an IRA.

THE INSIDE SCOOP ON ANNUITIES

The tax deferred annuity, while a clever investment invention, is quite complicated. An easy way to conceptualize it is to compare the annuity to a certificate of deposit (CD), or a mutual fund holding a tax umbrella. The similarities to a CD are guaranteed principal, competitive interest rates, and a withdrawal penalty. The benefits which attract investors are interest rates, the ability to defer federal income tax, and safety.

The managed accounts are similar to a mutual fund with account choices ranging from bonds to stocks and combinations of those securities. You can find name brand portfolio managers running clone funds of popular mutual funds packaged in the variable annuity.

The illustration on the next page provides a visual example of how $10,000 in a tax deferred annuity earning 8% for nine years would double:

When the spigot is turned on, interest is taken first and principal last. That is the LIFO accounting method — last in, first out. It allows the IRS to receive the unpaid taxes on the interest before any principal is withdrawn. The IRS will wait patiently until the spigot is opened but no longer. In addition, if you are under 59-1/2, get ready for a 10% excise tax penalty for early withdrawal. The good news is that it is applied only against the interest.

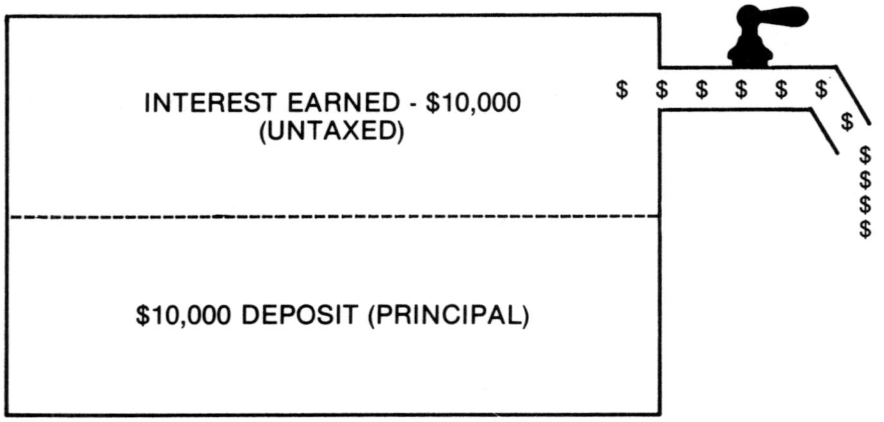

You can spread the principal and interest payments over a period of years by annuitizing your accumulated capital. If you are under 59-1/2, you must annuitize payments as if they were taken over your lifetime in order to escape the 10% penalty. Due to an exception in the tax law, you can withdraw via this method for five years and until you are 59-1/2 and then decrease, increase or stop your mandatory withdrawals. Because you could change the payments, insurance companies will require you to sign a statement that you agree this election is irrevocable until the above test is met. If you are past 59-1/2, you can simply withdraw money from this investment.

An investor of any age can purchase an immediate annuity of five plus years and take payments without the IRS 10% penalty. The immediate annuity is simply a convenient way of spreading interest and principal payments over five years or up to a lifetime.

How do insurance companies make a profit on these investments? As do banks — they invest their funds at a slightly higher rate than they pay you. And, if you remove the money before they are prepared to let it go, you pay. Doesn't that sound similar to the penalty the banker imposes if you break into a CD before its time? Since investors do not pay a sales charge when purchasing this product, they will pay a penalty if premature withdrawal takes place. This declining exit fee usually disappears somewhere between year five and year seven.

You should know about the 10% window of liquidity that is allowed on the majority of annuity contracts. The insurance company provides access to 10% of the money on deposit each year. A few companies will allow you to accumulate the 10% withdrawal privilege from year-to-year and withdraw 20%, 30%, 40%, or more later.

Enterprising insurance companies have introduced CD annuities which function much like a 12-month certificate of deposit. They have a 30- to 60-day window each year when all funds can be withdrawn without any insurance company penalties. But the IRS still insists on watching over you until you are 59-1/2.

Annuities have three important players: the owner, annuitant, and beneficiary. And they can be complicated depending on who plays which part. John Elden, our pending retiree, has decided to buy an annuity and be the annuitant also. His wife, Clara is the beneficiary. If John dies, Clara will receive the investment proceeds outside of probate or can become the new owner and continue the deferral process. There are several other configurations of owner, beneficiary, and annuitant which, if explained, would serve as an antidote for insomnia. That explanation is best left to your insurance agent or financial advisor.

To summarize, annuities come in two varieties — fixed guaranteed accounts or variable investment accounts. Both types can be purchased as an immediate income version with monthly payments or as a tax deferral device.

1. Fixed annuities: Select the insurance company well because your money is deposited in their general account when you elect to invest in a fixed annuity.

   A. Fixed immediate annuities are offered with fixed income payments beginning 30 days after the contract purchase. Various payout options are offered as discussed above.

   B. Fixed deferred annuities are offered for a fixed term. It is a good idea to keep the term not more than six years. Interest withdrawals can be deferred to the future or taken as current income.

   The good news on a fixed guaranteed annuity is the insurance company assumes mortality expenses and investment risk.

2. Variable annuities: As above, choose your insurance company carefully. In addition, review the performance of the investment management team. If the investments provide a healthy return, you win; if not, you lose. Remember, market value fluctuation is a side effect of growth investing. The investment choices are separate accounts, managed and structured like mutual funds. Many insurance companies have retained name brand investment advisory firms, such as Fidelity, Oppenheimer, American Funds, T. Rowe Price, Drefus, Templeton, Vanguard, and so forth, to manage these separate accounts.

   Strive only to invest in variable annuities where proven mutual fund investment advisors are managing the money. Total returns for variable annuities are tracked by Lipper Analytical Services, Variable Annuity Research and Data Service (VARDS), and Morningstar, Inc. To locate these services, check with your local library or with a financial advisor.

   Inside each variable annuity, several investment choices are offered, including stocks (domestic and international, large and small), bonds (corporate, convertible, government), and money markets. It is not unusual to find from six to 12 different investment combinations.

A. Like the fixed annuity above, variable immediate annuity payments can begin 30 days after purchase and the payment fluctuation will mirror the underlying investment performance.

B. Also, like the fixed annuity, variable deferred annuity returns are determined by performance of the underlying investments.

With this version, the insurance company assumes only the mortality and expense risks. You pay approximately 1.25% per year to the insurance company for the death benefit, and an investment management expense is levied against the capital invested. It is worth mentioning that the mortality charge is intended to pay for the insurance company's guaranteed death benefit. What death benefit?

That is what Mary wondered as she and Tom invested $50,000 in a variable annuity stock equity account on August 1, 1990. By December, the stock market had dropped to a low of 2,400 and their account balance was off by $7,642. Then Tom died. Mary was distraught and proceeded to contact the insurance company because she needed to withdraw money. What she found was that the mortality charge they had been paying served to restore the account balance back to the amount of the original deposit. What a relief to Mary. The unfortunate part is the policy owner must die to trigger the benefit.

Protection of assets from creditors is another side benefit of investing in variable annuities. These investments, in some states, can not be attached by creditors.

SPLIT ANNUITIES

Split up your money — part to compound and the remainder to return principal and interest yearly — and put tax free income in your pocket. Split annuities do the job for Gladys and Verne, who were looking for a way to reduce their yearly tax bill without a decrease in their cash flow. The following example was computed assuming a 9% interest rate on the deferred annuities. Different interest rate assumptions would result in either shorter or longer deferral periods and some variance in the level of income payments. Here's how it works:

1. $50,000 starting capital

   A. Immediate annuity funded with $25,000 paid back over eight years = monthly payments of $350, of which 75% is income tax free.

   B. One deferred annuity of $12,500, A, and two of $6,250 each, B and C into separate annuities, which are left to defer at a hypothetical 9%.

In eight years, Gladys and Verne's deferred annuities have doubled and their initial capital of $50,000 is intact again. The immediate annuity has been spent with minimal tax impact. Now they start again:

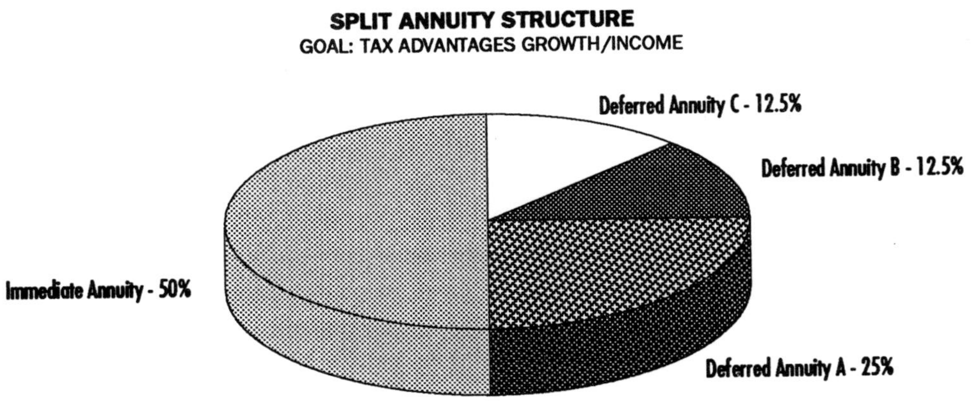

2. $50,000 starting capital
   A. Immediate annuity funded with $25,000 from deferred annuity A. Monthly payments of $350 for eight years, of which 45% is tax free.
   B. Deferred annuities B and C are left to compound tax free until the end of eight years.

It has now been 16 years and the original $6,250 placed in deferred annuities B and C has doubled twice and compounded to equal the starting capital of $50,000. Verne is now 76, spending has slowed, but income continues at the same level. This may be the last monthly payment go-round.

3. $50,000 starting capital
   A. Immediate annuity funded with $25,000 from deferred annuity B. Monthly payments of $350 for eight years, of which 25% is tax free.
   B. Deferred annuity C is left to compound tax free until the end of eight years.

Twenty-four years later, Gladys and Verne's original $50,000 capital is still intact in deferred annuity C. True, most of that $50,000, about $43,650, is untaxed interest. At this point, they can draw interest from the account just as they would if it were a certificate of deposit in a bank.

Since Verne started this program when he was 60, he is now 84. If both he and Gladys die before this asset is exhausted, they will have pushed the untaxed interest in annuity C beyond their lifetime. In fact, their heirs would have to pay Uncle Sam the taxes due on this inheritance. Do they care? Not likely. Do their children care? They might, but then who would turn down money — even if it does come with tax obligations? They'll smile all the way to the bank.

The results make sense. First, these two retirees established a simple to administer method of putting a monthly check in their pocket. Secondly, they reduced federal income taxes for years with the effect of lowering the risk that up to one-half of their Social Security would have been subject to tax. (More about this in Chapter 19.)

DO YOUR HOMEWORK

The investment guarantee is the key difference between other guaranteed investments and a tax deferred annuity. Insurance assets are protected either through state guarantee associations or by the financial prowess of the insurance company. Look for a firm that is rated by A.M. Best as A+. Ratings by other rating services, such as Standard and Poor's, Moody's, and Duff and Phelp's, are a plus. To review the significance of the ratings, refer back to Chapter 8, page 76. It is vital that you choose your insurance company carefully.

Not only are the above ratings important, but you should review the structure of the insurance company's investment portfolio. What is the percent of government bonds and/or corporate bonds rated BBB or above? How much do they have invested in high yield, lower rated bonds? How about real estate or real estate mortgages? Remember that you are investing as they have when you give them your money. Also, before you invest, request information on their interest rate renewal history. Insurance companies vary dramatically in how they credit interest. For example:

Company A credits interest rate changes to 100% of your investment.

Company B credits your the original interest rate on the invested sum and credits new interest rates on the compounding interest pool.

Company C guarantees you can get out without penalties if they drop interest rates below a predetermined level.

Company D ties interest rate changes to an index such as the long term utility bond index and guarantees never to be more than "x" percent below that index.

If the interest rates promised you are higher than current conditions warrant, you can place bets that 1) junk bonds are in the portfolio, or 2) punitive backend fees (such as 9, 9, 8, 7, 6, 5, 4, 3, 3, 3) will be accessed for early withdrawals.

Since there are hundreds of insurance companies, you must filter potential choices by the methods described above. Only invest when you have all the answers necessary to have a full understanding of the strength of the company and attractiveness of the product offered.

GOOD RETIREMENT MONEY

Annuities are wonderful retirement funding vehicles. Investors with enough foresight to dedicate certain pools of capital to retirement can win big with this investment's ability to defer taxes. Unlike the IRA, money in an annuity can be deferred even longer than age 70-1/2. Most insurance companies will not force the withdrawals until age 80 or so.

If you've chosen to invest in annuities, you can only get hurt in three ways:

1. You surrender your annuity before you attain age 59-1/2, incurring the government's 10% excise tax penalty.
2. You surrender the annuity before it is mature (usually about five to six years) and incur the insurance company's exit penalty.
3. You fail to choose a rock solid insurance company and are disappointed in either investment performance or stability of the company.

If you wish to transfer your money to another insurance company and continue the tax deferral process, you can. Investors might wish to switch companies for several reasons: to secure a different type of annuity with another company; if the investment results are disappointing; if the insurance company itself gets into financial difficulties.

SUBSTANTIAL PENALTY FOR EARLY WITHDRAWL

You can transfer your money to another company and still defer taxes. This is called a 1035 transfer and must be initiated by the insurance company, not you. You apply for a new annuity with insurance company A but do not give them any money. They in turn send a transfer request to insurance company B — the one with which you hold the annuity. Company B then sends the proceeds direct to company A via a 1035 exchange, and because you personally never took receipt of the money, it does not get taxed.

Understand this investment and you have a powerful tool to stave off the IRS's greedy tolls. Unpaid taxes earning interest with enough time can catapult your wealth potential.

CHAPTER 14

TAX REDUCTION WITHOUT JAIL

"Wealth is the product of man's capacity to think."
Ayn Rand

Why pay the IRS money you can keep in your own pocket — permanently or for a brief period of time? As illustrated in Chapter 9 and Chapter 13, tax sheltering and tax deferral are powerful tools with which to build wealth. But there is more.

TAX FACTS

You really need to know the tax deferral, tax sheltering, tax reduction and tax free income rules to completely understand the IRS tag game. The objective is not to get tagged by the IRS. Winning this game can be a challenge since many previously used avoidance techniques have been written out of the rules in recent years by Congress. Tax reduction has become difficult due to the government's simplification of taxes. Just since 1950, the following tax acts have changed the way Americans calculate their debts to the IRS:

1950 Review Act of 1950
1954 Tax Reform Act
1964 Revenue Act of 1964
1975 Tax Reduction Act
1976 Tax Reform Act
1977 Tax Reduction and Simplification Act
1978 Revenue and Energy Tax Act of 1978
1980 Installment Sales Revision Act
1981 Economic Recovery Tax Act
1982 Tax Equity and Fiscal Responsibility Act
1984 Deficit Reduction Act; Tax Reform Act
1986 Tax Reform Act of 1986
1987 Revenue Act of 1987
1988 Technical & Miscellaneous Revenue Act of 1988
1988 Medicare Catastrophic Coverage Act of 1988
1989 Revenue Reconciliation Act of 1989
1990 Revenue Reconciliation Act

It is no wonder taxpayers throw up their hands in frustration. While the intent of the recent tax reforms has been to simplify the tax system, Congress has not been successful. The system is still too complex. Modifications, grandfathering, lack of grandfathering, phase outs, exclusions, changes ad nauseam confuse and complicate taxpayers so they feel compelled to have even the most basic of tax returns prepared by professionals.

The forerunner of our present system of taxation began with the July 1, 1862 tax act. This act, which was later declared unconstitutional, taxed personal income to help finance the Civil War. The 16th Amendment of the Constitution, enacted in 1913, provided the start of annual federal taxation of income. The maximum bracket was a huge one percent.

Since we started paying taxes, taxes have increased many times faster than income. Bit by bit, incomes have been eroded by taxes. An organization in Washington, D.C., devoted to tracking when the average taxpayer is through paying his or her annual taxes each year, estimates that it takes about four months of full-time effort each year to pay taxes before wage earners can move on to earning income they can keep.

Think of the many ways taxes bite into your dollars: state income tax, federal/state/city/county sales taxes, property tax, gas tax, excise tax, and cigarette and liquor taxes. Social Security tax must be added to the growing pile — it is now 7.65% for an employee. Self-employed people pay 15.3% but can deduct one half of it as a business expense thus, if they are in the 28% bracket, the effective rate is 13.15%.

Some have likened paying taxes to bleeding. Others say we have caused these wounds ourselves by falling prey to the consumption tax — spending it all. Clearly, reducing taxes has a lot to do with financial strategies involving money.

AXE YOUR TAXES

Thankfully, there are still a few tools and strategies left with which you can defer, avoid, or shelter income. Many of these have been given in-depth coverage in other chapters and so will be mentioned just briefly here. Most are not complex or exotic but do require pre-planning.

Tax Freebies

- Municipal Bonds — covered in Chapter 11 — are still viable options for the highly taxed. Federal income tax free bonds are issued by municipalities when the proceeds are intended to be used exclusively for traditional governmental purposes. Residents in states where a state income tax is present can avoid paying it on municipal bond interest if they purchase a bond issued within their own state. There are a couple of exceptions to be aware of: 1) private activity municipal bonds are not tax exempt, and 2) certain non-essential bonds are subject to the alternative minimum tax. Your broker can alert you to the tax nature of a municipal bond you may be considering.

- Child Support has always been tax free income to the receiver, but it has never been tax deductible to the payor. Don't divorce to increase your tax free income. The economic burdens that come with divorce far outweigh any advantages to this income's receipt.
- Series EE bonds are tax free if used for your child's tuition expense. There are a number of qualifying rules which are detailed in Chapter 16. Be sure and read them.
- Gifts and inheritances are federal income tax free to the receiver. In certain states, there is an inheritance tax levied. Check with your tax advisor.
- Foreign earnings up to $70,000 can be excluded from your gross income, provided certain rules are met.
- If you are 55 and have lived in your home three out of the last five years, you can exclude gain of up to $125,000 upon sale. See Chapter 9 for a fuller explanation.
- Income from taking out a loan has never been taxable. You can borrow from a relative, bank, qualifying insurance policies, your home, investment securities, or 401(k) retirement plan without having to include that income on your Form 1040.
- Social Security income is all or partially tax free depending on whether or not your modified adjusted gross income exceeds certain levels. This is covered in detail in Chapter 19.
- Death benefits from a life insurance policy, as discussed in Chapter 8, are 100% income tax free. Unfortunately, someone has to die to trigger this benefit unless your policy has tax free borrowing privileges. If so, you may as well enjoy some of the tax free death benefit before you die and pass it on to your survivors.
- Any dollars earned up to the combined total of your standard deduction and qualifying personal exemptions are free from federal taxation. Presently, this number is being indexed yearly by the Consumer Price Index and will keep increasing at a rate to match inflation. However, the standard deduction and personal exemption will be phased out for upper income individuals. Low-income taxpayers will benefit from this provision of the tax law.

Tax Shelters

- Rental income is partially or fully tax sheltered depending on the equity/debt ratios of the rental real estate. This subject was discussed in Chapter 9. Actively managed real estate is subject to more favorable tax provisions than other investments. You can deduct tax losses of up to $25,000 against other income until your adjusted gross income exceeds $100,000, provided management and ownership tests are met. These excess deductions are phased out when income is between $100,000 and $150,000 and completely disallowed when total adjusted gross income exceeds $150,000. Unusable passive losses are carried forward and used when the property is sold to offset capital gains.

- A college condo may make sense if your children are going to college, need a place to live, and plan to complete their education at one campus. In this instance, your purchase of a residence or apartment close to your child's school has the potential to create a tax-deductible college expense for you. You could buy a residence large enough to support several renters (something like a boarding house) and install your preppie landlord as the on-site manager. The salary you pay him or her is an expense you can offset against the income produced by the investment. Keep in mind that the salary must be based on fair market wages. What the IRS calls an arm's length transaction — no special benefits for family members — is required in order to keep this family operation qualified as a tax shelter.
- Purchasing your elderly parents' home can also be a great shelter. It has several benefits: 1) it allows your parents to use the $125,000 exclusion and stay in their home, 2) it establishes a steady cash flow for them, 3) they are the best renters in the world for you, 4) it removes the home from their estate, 5) you have a rental with all the associated benefits, such as deductible expenses and depreciation, 6) it gives you the ability to hire your children or parents to manicure the lawn and perform repairs — one more tax deductible expense, and 7) it adds an asset with appreciation potential to your investment holdings. Be sure to review the IRS's guidelines for establishing a fair market rent to extend to your parents.
- Tax deferred income always makes sense if you are in the upper tax brackets and, if you can defer long enough, even the lower brackets. Chapters 13 and 18 contain all the details. Tax deferral is easy to find — look for tax deductible retirement plans such as IRAs, 401(k) retirement programs, profit sharing, and pensions. Annuities, non-qualified deferred compensation plans, life insurance, growth stocks, and Series EE bonds are other choices.
- Repurchase of a residence within 24 months before or after the sale of an old residence defers tax on the profits if you meet the rules. The price of the new home must be more than the adjusted sales price of the old. This allows you to tax shelter the gain on a personal real estate sale until you reach age 55, when you qualify for the $125,000 exclusion mentioned above.
- Installment sales will work to defer gain if you take a portion of the value of the asset plus interest as a monthly payment over a period of years. Only the fraction of capital gain received yearly, plus interest on the loan, is subject to current tax. Taxes are

deferred on the remaining portion of the gain not yet received. This doesn't change the amount of taxes owed, but it is to your benefit because 1) inflation reduces the buying power (taxes can be paid with cheaper dollars) and 2) it may keep you from crossing into a higher tax bracket.

- Like-kind exchanges of real estate are an opportunity to further defer taxes. The difference between the cost basis and the market value can remain sheltered when real estate is properly traded. This area is tricky and an expert in Section 1031 exchanges should be consulted.

Tax Shifts

- Transferring income into your child's or parent's name can make sense. Historically, this strategy has been used to shift the taxes on income into another family member's name, one who is in a lower tax bracket. The result is that wealth is kept within the family and total taxes are reduced. The tax law penalizes shifting more than $1,200 of income to minors under age 14. After this point the strategy backfires. If you couple the negative aspects of loss of ownership and control over the asset along with the fact that income in excess of a yearly adjusted maximum (1992 — $1,200) is still taxable to the parents, you can see why it may be just as wise to consider other tax reduction tactics.

  If you comply with the rules, you can shift about $15,000 earning 8% to a child under 14 without adverse tax consequences.

- Annual gifting of $10,000 per person to any number of recipients is a good strategy for shifting tax. You can transfer assets and lower immediate taxation by transferring appreciated securities to your offspring. When they sell the assets, they pay the taxes at their tax bracket which is, hopefully, lower. If you're responsible for supporting your parents and you plan to give them money for support, you might want to shift income to them to reduce taxes on investment earnings.

TAX TRICKS

- If charitable contributions are part of your planned gift strategy, consider giving appreciated securities rather than cash to your favorite charity. This tactic allows you to deduct the stock or bond at fair market value and avoid incurring taxes on the appreciation of the stock. The charity liquidates the securities and pays the taxes due. Be aware that the gift of appreciated securities is a preferential item included in the calculation of alternative minimum tax and you are limited to a deduction not exceeding 30% of your adjusted gross income. If this strategy sounds appealing, give only securities which are eligible for long term capital gains tax treatment. Securities which have not been held long enough to qualify can only be deducted at their cost or the market value, whichever is less.

- Bunch expenses such as contributions, medical/dental expenses, miscellaneous deductions, property taxes, etc., into one year if you believe your tax rates will be higher or lower in the future than currently. This strategy will make the most of your deductible dollars.

  It makes sense to group related expenses which are subject to a floor — a stipulated percentage of adjusted gross income — before calculating the deductions. Medical costs are one kind of expense that must exceed 7.5% of the adjusted gross income before any deduction is realized. For most people, this means non-reimbursed medical expenses are not tax deductible because the total isn't high enough.
- Timing of income is important. Short-term deferral of taxes can be achieved several ways: 1) purchasing Treasury Bills at a discount to avoid taxes on the growth until the T-bill matures in a future tax year, 2) shifting of earned income by cash basis business owners into another tax year by billing so that payments will not be received until after New Year's Eve, 3) delaying collection of a note receivable payment or rent from your rental property. Methods two and three can be reversed to accelerate income into the current year if you expect future taxes to be higher.
- If you need to borrow for such things as medical bills, a new car, debt consolidation, home improvements, and college tuition, borrow first from the equity in your home for a tax deductible interest expense.
- Realize a loss on stock without giving up your position by doubling up on your position. Buy the same or similar securities 31 days prior to your sale of the original stock. Thirty-one is the magic number. If you miscount and hold the securities only 30 days, you incur the wash sale rule. The unrealized loss is still just that and deferred until you sell the new securities.

TAX TRAPS

- An extension to your filing date does not mean an extension of time to pay taxes. Unless 90% of your estimated tax burden is paid by April 15, you will have late penalties of 1/2% per month up to a maximum of 25%.
- While long- or short-term capital gains are taxed as ordinary income subject to a maximum tax rate of 28%, excess losses can only be written off up to $3,000 against income other than capital gains. Losses exceeding $3,000 must be carried forward to the next tax year.
- The IRS has taken a lesson from the banks and will pay you 1% less on tax refunds than you will pay them for your underpayment of taxes.
- Being subject to the alternative minimum tax (AMT) is a tax trap which can work for you or against you. The AMT kicks into effect when certain events take place and qualifying criteria have been met. The flat 24% tax is activated when enough

preference items have been triggered (such as tax exempt interest on industrial development bonds issued after August 7, 1986, untaxed appreciation on property contributed to charity, deferred income from use of certain installment sale transactions, and the list goes on).

The only good news in this computation is that these preference items must exceed certain exemption amounts ($40,000 for married people, $30,000 for single people) before the flat rate of 24% is applied. But if you think you will exceed the limitations, it is wise to take advantage of the 24% rate rather than save the preference items for another year where they would be taxed at higher rates.

KEEPING GOOD RECORDS

Record keeping has been and always will be important. Good records can be dollars in your pockets. Additionally, once an expense is deducted, the IRS expects to see receipts for 100% of the deduction. Nothing is worse than trying to resurrect records for a full year — what you paid the sitter, donated to charity, paid for investment advice. It is a brain-racking activity guaranteed to cost you money. Track your tax deductible expenses by setting up a system to record expenses as they are incurred. You don't want to pay the IRS a penny more in taxes than necessary. There's another good reason, for keeping good records — the IRS audit. Reconstructing carelessly kept records can be a nightmare.

The best paper trail is receipts and cancelled checks. Put into a shoebox several legal-size envelopes, each marked with a deduction category. You can start by looking at last year's income tax return for ideas on categories. As receipts are collected, file them in the appropriate envelope. Go a step further recording expenses in a bookkeeping ledger under appropriate columns and watch your tax preparer smile. If you own a personal computer, there are several good software programs available for this type of record keeping.

Other reasons to keep good records:

- If you have both deductible and non-deductible IRAs, keep detailed records of all contributions. When you start to withdraw money, you will have to factor the withdrawals between both tax free and taxable dollars according to the size of the IRA accounts.
- When you have to calculate how much profit from the sale of real estate is reportable to the IRS, good records prove the basis. These records should be kept as long as you own the property and at least three years after the sale of the property.
- Keep all receipts pertaining to business meals and entertainment. These expenses, incurred in the course of conducting business, are only 80% deductible. The IRS is sticky about this area. The primary reason for the function must be business and you must prove it. Keep a diary to annotate activities such as who you entertained, when, where, how much you spent, and what you talked about.

Taxing matters aren't simple, and neither is complying with the IRS's multitude of mandatory rules.

TAX RETURN "SMUGITIS"

If you've been one of those people who give themselves a sound slap on the back when tax refunds are calculated, don't feel too smug. You've just successfully lent money to the IRS for up to one year without receiving any interest. If this has happened to you, take steps to increase the number of exemptions you are claiming on your W-4 form. This will decrease the tax withheld with the intent of more closely matching withholding to actual taxes due.

If you've been diligent in reading this chapter and others, taking note of tax reduction strategies, you may have better reasons to reduce the taxes withheld from your wages or estimated quarterly taxes than described in the previous paragraph.

There are numerous other strategies which, in their uniqueness, are only applicable to certain taxpayers. To ensure that you have taken advantage of all tax avoidance methods for which you are eligible and side-stepped all tax traps, check with a qualified tax practitioner at least once a year and always before you make major changes in your asset positions.

CHAPTER 15

LEAVING A LEGACY

"True, you can't take it with you, but then that's not the place where it comes in handy."

Brendan Francis

Estate planning is an act of love. It is something that you do now to make life easier for your loved ones after you're gone. Planning your estate involves more than just drafting a will. It encompasses reviewing your assets, how they are titled, methods of current management, and ultimate destination after your demise. Poor estate planning results in unnecessary taxes — both income and estate. Good estate planning, then, is usually only accomplished after a concerted effort to study the various methods of transferring assets to your heirs.

Your first goal should be to transfer the estate to your beneficiaries as easily and cost effectively as possible. The emotional trauma of dealing with the death of a dear friend or close family member can cause even the most organized survivor to fall apart. Whatever steps you can take to detail exactly what you want done with your assets will help ease the trauma for those you leave behind.

If I were an estate attorney and financial planner both, I could probably retire early since the majority of the people I see do not have wills. And, if they don't have a will, they also are without such items as a durable power of attorney or living will. This is one area where it seems difficult to take action. Now, there would be nothing wrong with procrastination in this area if we could just predict when we were going to die. But death is never on time.

I recall a family who retained my services several years back. Their finances were in fairly good shape. Minor tune-ups to their financial picture were all that were required. We carefully laid out a plan of action to cover various financial issues with estate planning at the top of the list. About a year later, I received a call from the husband telling me his wife had been killed in an automobile accident. My first question was, "Did you and Marilyn complete your wills?" The long silence answered the question. Marilyn had died intestate. Her will was the one size fits all, state mandated distribution system.

Scott found out first hand why having a will is advisable. Marilyn and Scott had three children — all minors. All the children had to have trusts established to hold their share of Marilyn's assets. Those funds would be unavailable to help sustain the family until each child reached the age of majority. This was a hardship for Scott because he had the unenviable chore of accounting for the fiduciary care of those assets and restrictions on use.

It is unlikely that Marilyn would have chosen this plan of action if she had realized the consequences of not having a will.

The following quiz may be the first and most important step you take in safeguarding your loved ones after you are gone.

ESTATE PROTECTION QUIZ

	Yes	No
Do you have a will which still distributes your assets in the manner you wish?	___	___
If you have minor children, is there a trust established by the will to hold assets for the children in case both parents die?	___	___
Have you nominated a guardian and contingent guardian for your minor children?	___	___
Is consideration of a trust for the benefit of your spouse appropriate?	___	___
If your estate is over $600,000, is your will coordinated with the latest legislation concerning the unlimited marital deduction, unified credit trust, or qualified terminable interest trust? If your will addresses any trusts and was created prior to 1982, it may be outdated.	___	___
Do you understand the value of having a living will?	___	___
Do you have a durable power of attorney?	___	___
If you live in a community property state, do you have a community property agreement?	___	___
If you have assets held in joint tenancy with rights of survivorship, are you aware these assets will be transferred outside of your will?	___	___
Have you made a bequest list for tangible personal property and attached it to your will?	___	___

If you answered any of the above questions No, a visit with an attorney specializing in estate planning will be beneficial.

YOUR WILL SHALL BE DONE

Everyone needs a will. And, yes, you probably do have enough assets to make one worthwhile. What kinds of assets can be controlled by your will? All assets that are individually owned, and your share of those titled as tenants in common or which are community property can be distributed via a will. Assets that are titled as joint tenants with rights of survivorship are not impacted by your will. Instead they are transferred outside of probate to the surviving joint owner. Life insurance, tax deferred annuities, and retirement benefits are passed by contract direct to the named beneficiary. In some cases, you may want the beneficiary to be your estate or trustee under the will.

In the will, you can decide who will inherit your estate, how much each individual will receive, how the estate will be administered, and when it is to be distributed. You name a personal representative and an alternate (also known as executor/executrix); someone you know and trust. I often jokingly suggest appointing someone you dislike as the personal representative because it is not an enviable job.

The will is the place to name a guardian for your minor child(ren). You can even go so far as to leave specific instructions for their care. You may include in your will details regarding any trusts you wish established for your children or spouse. If you establish a trust for asset management, estate tax reduction, or for the benefit of minor children, you must name a trustee. The trustee's position is to manage the trust assets and comply with tax and reporting regulations and terms of the trust. You should also consider naming an alternate trustee in case the initial trustee can't serve.

You may want to leave specific assets or belongings to particular people or charities. Document those desires in your will. But you don't want a laundry list of all personal keepsakes written in the will, "My toothpick holder collection to my niece, Pam"; "My tool and die set to my son, Tom". Attorneys may recommend, depending on state law, that you make a list of personal property and attach it to the will. If the list is referenced in the will, you can change it as many times as you wish without incurring the legal fees necessary to add the amendment, known as a codicil.

You can also attach a Personal Instruction letter to your will (be sure and reference it in the will). For a sample of what it might look like, refer to Worksheet 15B at the end of this chapter.

Here are eight things you should consider when drafting your will:

1. Get your spouse involved and, of course, seek professional assistance. If you develop your wills together, you'll be doubly protected. Family objectives will be met regardless of whether you or your spouse dies first.
2. As a general rule, use percentages rather than fixed dollar amounts in designating inheritances. If you leave $10,000 to each of your three brothers and the rest to your children, guess who doesn't receive anything if your asset base should drop

to $30,000 before your death. It may be appropriate, however, to leave a dollar sum when you want to recognize an heir with a gift but do not want to leave him or her more than a stated figure.

3. Don't be so controlling as to insist that certain assets be preserved in the hands of your heirs as you held them. Your loved ones will suffer if economic conditions later demand that they liquidate or redistribute these investments.
4. If you have chosen a beneficiary as a witness to the will and that individual is asked to validate the will, dire consequences could result, such as the loss of his/her inheritance.
5. Always amend a will by adding a codicil. You can't make handwritten changes on your original will and expect it to hold up in court.
6. You and your beneficiary may wish to incorporate a simultaneous death clause in each of your wills. The Uniform Simultaneous Death Act provides that in the case of a common disaster, double administration of the estates will be avoided. But two probates will still occur.
7. Handwritten wills (holographs) are not legal in some states. Check your state laws.
8. Designate the guardian for your minor children. If you don't, the court will. Nominate an alternate guardian, too, if possible.

Fundamental estate documents such as the will and the following durable power of attorney are often loss leaders for attorneys. As such, they may be the most cost-effective services provided by the legal profession.

A DURABLE POWER OF ATTORNEY

Many people, mystified by the durable power of attorney, don't have one. The durable power of attorney is merely a means by which you transfer to someone else the ability to make legally binding decisions. Should your mental or physical capacities drop below stated levels, you can be declared incompetent and have your financial and legal matters handled by your named representative.

This transfer of the right to make legal decisions regarding financial affairs can be so broad as to encompass everything you own, or so narrow as to give someone the right to control only a specific asset. In this same or a separate document, you can delegate health care decisions to your named representative also.

You can see that this powerful document belongs only in the hands of someone you trust implicitly. Your attorney-in-fact must be aware of the document in order to exhibit it to the appropriate authorities when transacting business on your behalf.

Here's a story illustrating unfortunate circumstances that could have been avoided. In the mid-80s, an elderly woman sat in my office discussing her financial affairs. During this conversation, I discovered her husband was ill and that most of their money was in his name in a bank in Colorado. Two issues jumped out at me: 1) if he were to die, there would be possible probate in both Washington and Colorado; and 2) if he became mentally or physically incompetent, she would not be able to get at his out-of-state funds. To make a long story short, I recommended that the woman immediately secure a durable power of attorney from her husband. This document would give her the right to liquidate or move those assets in the event her husband became incompetent. Before she took action, her husband was placed in a nursing home and declared mentally incompetent.

The distraught wife had to go to court to be named her husband's legal guardian. This action cost her $1,000. It all could have been avoided had she heeded my recommendations. Shortly after that, her husband died.

COMMUNITY PROPERTY AGREEMENT

This document only affects those individuals living in one of eight community property states; nine if you count Wisconsin, a quasi-community property state. State laws may differ, but since I practice financial planning in the state of Washington, I can comment only on the laws that apply in that state. If you live in a community property state other than Washington, check with an attorney in your state to see if the following discussion is applicable to you.

The community property agreement, when signed, can be used by married individuals instead of a will for distribution of part or all of their assets. Don't record this document. Let that be a choice for the survivor. The reason for its popularity is that the most commonly used form, the community property agreement with survivorship, completely avoids the probate process. However, it is not always wise to avoid probate because it is the process that limits creditors from filing claims against the estate after a specified time period. If assets are transferred outside of probate, creditors can file their claims anytime within the statute of limitations.

If you still wish to use a community property agreement, but don't want to avoid the probate process for a variety of reasons (such as limiting creditors, making use of a testamentary trust, distributing your half of the community property to several beneficiaries), you can. It is a community property agreement without survivorship. The document confirms that one-half of all the marital assets belong to each party unless specifically noted by exception. By directive, it points to the will for asset distribution directions.

This brings up an important issue relating to the community property agreement. When signed, both husband and wife have agreed that all current assets and future inheritances shall belong to each of them equally, unless noted by exception. Don't sign this agreement in haste. Consider the strength of your marriage.

And if you're considering a second marriage be sure and have a premarital agreement. If you direct your community property agreement to distribute to a trust with children as beneficiaries, be sure and clearly state that all current property is community property and all future inheritances are separate, and exclude separate property brought into the marriage.

LIVING TRUSTS

Here is another vehicle which will avoid probate. It can be used by anyone who wishes to establish a revocable trust to manage assets during one's lifetime. Revocable means you can change your mind and "untrust" your assets at any time. A living trust does not reduce taxes — estate or income. The sole purpose is to organize and manage your assets in such a manner that they can be passed to your beneficiaries outside of probate. Your living trust will protect your financial affairs should you become incapacitated. Should that occur, you would no longer be the trustee. Instead, a successor trustee, named by you in the trust documents, would take over the management of the assets.

The issue of whether or not a living trust makes sense is hotly debated in some states such as Washington, where non-intervention wills are the norm and probate fees are based on the hourly rates of, usually, a paralegal. Most attorneys, with whom I have discussed this issue, claim that probate is not that onerous or costly. But if you live in a state where probate fees are based on a percent of the estate, a living trust is a sensible way to avoid the high cost of probate. For individuals owning property in more than one state, a living trust is a great solution to multiple probates.

Privacy is the last benefit of a living trust. Probated estates are a matter of record. Anyone can go to the county courthouse and review those records. A living trust, which passes outside of probate, keeps your affairs out of the public limelight. Whether or not that is important will depend on your position in the community and level of assets accumulated.

The downside of having a living trust is the great amount of paperwork to be completed. All the assets you own must be retitled in the name of the trust: autos, property, investments, retirement plans, etc. Usually the attorney who drafts the living trust will also take care of retitling your assets — for an extra fee, of course. Or to limit costs, you can do it. Structuring a living trust and activating it is rarely a problem. What can be difficult is the continuing maintenance of it — remembering to title your next car in the name of the trust, to sign all sales papers as trustee, to provide proof of the trust whenever you change assets, and so on. Regardless of the housekeeping duties associated with them, living trusts are very popular with both the wealthy and the not-so-wealthy, alike.

PROBATE BENEFITS

There are some very good reasons to have your estate probated. It limits creditors, e.g., malpractice claims for professionals, unpaid lenders, to making a claim against the estate until a specified time period has passed. For non-probated estates, creditors have until the statue of limitations to file a claim. Whether or not you want to deal with probate will depend on the state in which you reside. If you live in a state that charges a percent fee against the estate for probate, you will want to consider avoiding probate. If you live in a state where non-intervention wills are the norm, probate costs may not even be a factor in your decision.

LIVING WILL

This document provides a record of your wishes regarding life support systems. With more and more people living longer and science keeping bodies ticking mechanically, the living will is becoming a popular option. It is legally valid in most states and in some is recognized officially as a Directive to Physicians.

THE FINAL WEALTH TAX

In 1981, Congress passed a tax act that made significant improvement in the regulations governing federal estate taxation. There are two main items you need to be aware of:

1. Married individuals, regardless of wealth, can pass all qualified marital deduction assets to the remaining spouse with no immediate taxation. This is the Unlimited Marital Deduction. With this provision, Congress gave the green light to tax deferral until the death of the surviving widow or widower.
2. Net estates up to $600,000 are not subject to any federal estate tax. Be forewarned, though, that some states do impose inheritance taxes.

The result of that legislation was to allow about 90% of Americans to breathe easier. They are the not-too-wealthy — those single individuals with net estates of less than $600,000 and married folks with under $1,200,000. If estate distribution documents are properly structured, both categories will avoid estate taxes. The following example clarifies the result of a lack of foresight:

NET ESTATE
$1,000,000

Husband		Wife
~~$500,000~~	⟶	$ 500,000
		+ 500,000
		$1,000,000

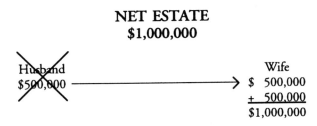

This couple had a sizable estate. But because each owned less than $600,000, they thought their estate would escape the impact of estate tax. The husband died and transferred his estate to his widow outright. She lived another five years and managed to keep the estate value level. At her death, only $600,000 was excluded from taxation, the remaining $400,000 was subject to federal estate taxes. Of the amount eligible for tax, roughly one-third to one-half was donated to the federal government. How do you think that made the heirs feel?

This problem could have been eliminated by the establishment, in the will, of a testamentary disclaimer Unified Credit Trust, or bypass trust. Upon the death of the first party, the trust can be utilized or disclaimed if the beneficiary has changed his/her mind about utilizing this strategy. The Unified Credit Trust, if structured properly is used to shelter the free $600,000 exemption from being taxed in a surviving spouse's estate. It can save thousands of dollars of needless taxation. Visually, this is how it operates:

NET ESTATE
$1,000,000

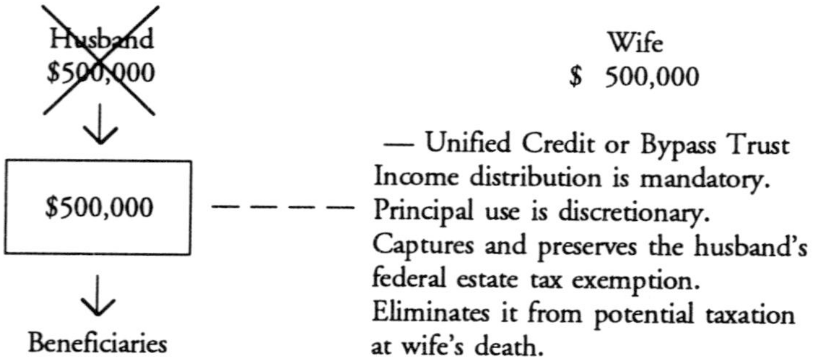

It would be wise to put the highest growth assets in trust at the first death. These assets are forever protected from estate tax even if they double or triple before the survivor passes on. If the spouse lives another 12 years, just a 6% growth rate on the assets will double their value.

I recently consulted with a widower. Ted and Esther were financial planning clients I had not seen for several years. I had recommended in their financial plan that a unified credit trust be established to protect their rapidly growing estate. But of all my recommendations, this one probably had the least sizzle and was easily delayed. Neither expected to die. Esther fell ill and died within a relatively short time. Prior to her death, I begged their estate attorney to visit them and draft that document. Much to my chagrin, it didn't get done. As a result, the widower and his children faced a future estate shrinkage problem. And the only way to solve it was by systematically reducing the size of the estate by either making gifts or by employing other more complex strategies. Ted was not enamored with the complexity facing him nor was it practical for him to reduce the size of his estate by gifting. His solution was to establish a irrevocable wealth replacement trust for the sole purpose of owning a life insurance policy on his life. Ted now must give considerable dollars each year to the trust. The trust then pays for a million-dollar life insurance benefit to replace the part of his estate to be forfeited to the government at his death.

For the wealthy, estate planning is complex. It involves consideration of many strategies, such as family partnerships, private annuities, irrevocable trusts, life insurance, charitable giving, and more. The financial advisor's role is to educate clients in these strategies, but it is up to the client to see an attorney and take action.

PROPERTY OWNERSHIP TRAPS

How your assets are titled is an important estate planning issue. Incorrect titling of assets can create complex problems after your death. For example, if John and Clara Elden's assets were held as joint tenants with rights of survivorship (JTWROS) with their daughter, upon their deaths, they would have inadvertently disinherited their two boys. The daughter would have instant ownership of the assets. John and Clara's will and the plans contained within it would be totally ignored. This simple illustration points out the need to seriously consider the end result of each property titling decision. Coordination with your will is a must.

And if they were millionaires who had drafted an exotic estate plan including a unified credit trust to preserve their $600,000 asset exemption from federal estate taxation, owning property as JTWROS would bypass the will and sabotage their estate tax avoidance plans.

If you are lucky enough to live in a community property state, another form of property titling exists between husband and wife: community property. This is the recommended method of holding titled property in all cases where a potential for growth exists or has already occurred. This type of titling allows all assets so held to assume a step-up in basis on both halves — the decedent's and the survivor's — for income tax purposes. The question to ask here is do you want to convert separate property for the advantage of a step-up in tax basis?

Property held as joint tenancy only takes a step-up on one-half of the value — the part owned by the decedent — at the date of death. Note that some states may have adopted a state law which makes the presumption that JTWROS property is community property for purposes of the step-up in basis for both halves.

It is very important to ensure you have your property titled correctly, not just for estate distribution reasons but also for tax planning purposes. If you give appreciated assets to your heirs prior to your death, the cost basis of the asset follows the gift. That $80 stock which you purchased for $20 will still have the same amount of gain regardless of whether you own it or you gave it away. Good tax planners will evaluate assets and determine which ones to make a gift of and which ones to retain in the estate in order to take advantage of legal tax avoidance. Your heirs then can liquidate your assets at the stepped-up basis valuation.

What does the term, Stepped-Up Basis mean? Here is an illustration:

John and Clara own a piece of property which cost them $60,000 in 1975 and is now worth $200,000. According to their will, their son, James, will inherit the property. If James were to sell the property immediately, he would pay no federal income tax. This is because the original cost basis would go with the Eldens to their grave and James would be assigned a new cost basis equal to the market value of the property at the time of John and Clara's deaths.

Property titling can be confusing but this is a very important area to understand. Exhibit 15A shows the effects of different property titling on estate plans.

ILL-LEGAL ADVICE

As a financial advisor, I cannot dispense legal advice. My role is confined to educating clients about potential estate problems or opportunities available. This area is complex. A mistake can be very expensive in terms of both finances and emotions. Take charge of the ultimate disposition of your estate by creating a distribution program that fits your family's needs. Don't let state laws, inappropriate documents, or property ownership traps do your planning — by default. This is one area where professional counsel is invaluable.

EXHIBIT 15A

PROPERTY OWNERSHIP RULES

	TENANCY IN COMMON "TIC"	JOINT TENANCY "JT/WROS"	SEPARATE PROPERTY	COMMUNITY PROPERTY "CP"
DEFINITION	Each tenant owns specified percentage as undivided interest.	Automatic Right of survivorship, so survivor owns 100% at moment of first owner's . death.	Property owned by married per - son before marriage or acquired dur- ing marriage by gift or inheritance.	All property acquired by by a married person during marriage which is not separate property.
HOW TO TITLE	John Jones, as to a 37.5% undi- vided "TIC" interest.	A and B, as joint tenants.	John Jones, as his sole and separate property.	John and Mary Jones, husband and wife, as community property.
EFFECT, WILLS & OTHER	Owner has full lifetime and death time control, over his/her percentage ownership.	Cannot be willed by any- one except final survivor, so is a quasi- inheritance.	Owner has full lifetime and death time control over 100%.	Spouses have equal management and control. Each can will their own half to anyone.
PROBATE	Yes; undivided interest is probated.	No; avoids pro- bate costs and delays.	Yes, 100% goes through probate.	Decedent's half goes through pro- bate (see Community Property Agreement discussion).
DEATH TAXES	Undivided interest is part of own- er's taxable estate.	Portion equal to decedent's contribution is part of his/ her taxable estate if be- tween spouses. Otherwise 100% taxable in estate of 1st to die un- less survivor can prove con- tributions or unlimited marital deduction used.	100% taxable, though sub- ject marital deduction of 100% if it goes to spouse.	Only dece- dent's half is taxable. Subject to marital de- duction.
STEPPED-UP BASIS FOR INCOME TAX	Yes, 100% .	Only that portion taxable in estate gets new basis.	Yes, 100%.	Yes, 100%, even including surviving spouse's half.
NOTES:				Title must be this and not joint tenancy for tax sav- ing trust or estate plan to work.

WORKSHEET 15A

SURVIVOR'S TO DO LIST

1. Find will. Immediately visit the safety deposit box (if used) and inventory contents.

2. Contact a lawyer and notify them of the death. Arrange for them to notify the necessary beneficiaries and witnesses to the will to start the estate settlement process.

3. Contact a clergy man and/or a funeral home to arrange for the funeral. Notify friends and relatives.

4. Assemble papers: Ten certified death certificates (from the funeral director). Deceased birth certificate, insurance policies, statement of assets and liabilities, marriage certificates, spouse's social security number, children's social security numbers, proof of widows age, proof of age for minor children or children in college, and tax returns for the last three years.

5. With certified death certificate, proof of marriage, and social security number, visit the nearest Social Security office and immediately apply for the death benefit and survivor's benefits.

6. Check to see if VA benefits or other military service benefits are available.

7. Send in death claim statements along with certified death certificates to life insurance companies.

8. If deceased was employed, notify employer and request a list of benefits: insurance, vested retirement benefits, salary savings plans, stock programs.

9. Notify any organizations of which the deceased was a member. He/she may be eligible for benefits.

10. Notify all financial institutions, stock brokerage firms, insurance carriers, and investment companies. Request that account or ownership registrations be modified as necessary. Change beneficiaries on insurance policies, annuities, and retirement plans.

11. Ask an attorney or accountant about filing the federal estate tax return, inheritance tax report, federal income tax returns (individual and fiduciary) for state of death and other states where property is held.

12. Lastly, remake your will.

WORKSHEET 15B

PERSONAL WISHES AND DIRECTIONS TO FAMILY

I am writing this supplement to my estate plan (location: ______________________________
____)
to serve as a guide for my family. It is an attempt to help handle the family finances and investments accumulated to date. While my suggestions should be evaluated in light of current circumstances, I believe these thoughts will lighten the load for my survivors.

1. Family Goals which I feel are important: ______________________________
____
____

2. Suggestions for dealing with current investments and review of the investment policy ascribed to in the past:
____
____
____

3. Family advisors who should be consulted:
Attorney: ______________________________
Accountant: ______________________________
Investment Advisor: ______________________________
Clergy: ______________________________
Physicians: ______________________________

4. If I should need extended nursing home care and indefinite medical care and am unable to communicate my wishes: ______________________________
____
____

5. Regarding donating organs or body parts, my preference is: ______________________________
____

6. Right to die preferences (living will or Directive to Physicians location: ______________________):
____
____

7. Regarding last rites, wake, graveside services, open/closed casket, cremation, pallbearers, etc. my preference would be: ______________________________
____
____
____

Attached to this document is a listing of my personal bequests. I have signed this document, in sound mind and body, this ______________________ of ______________.
(Month/Day) (Year)

____
Signature

CHAPTER 16
MANAGING COLLEGE COSTS

"He who does not teach his son a trade teaches him to be a robber."
Hebrew Proverb

You've been a good parent. You have provided your child or children with at least the necessities of life: food, shelter, clothing, and the ability to attend 12 years of schooling. Perhaps you have indulged your children with an assortment of toys. But, how many of you arrived at the day of reckoning with a full pocketbook for higher education? And how many of you were in shock?

A college education is an important issue if you want to give your child a competitive edge. I am not inferring that wealth can't be achieved without college preparation, but it may make the road to wealth shorter. It's been reported that the average high school graduate earns about one-half as much as the average college graduate. Over a forty-year career, the difference could be astounding.

EDUCATION PLANNING

Beyond buying your first home and funding retirement, one of life's biggest expenditures is supporting a child's higher education. This predictable expense, which sneaks up on some parents, contains an expensive and unpleasant lesson — pay-as-you-go education funding.

I know this well. I was a self-employed single parent, developing a new career in 1982, when my oldest child took advantage of four full years on campus at a state university. I simply wasn't prepared for the economic impact college costs would have on the next four years of my life. Stress became my daily companion.

Pre-planning for this expense can eliminate the pain of pay-as-you-go funding or, at the very least, relieve it. How expensive is college in the 90s? It depends on what type of school your child attends. The costs can range from affordable to out-of-sight:

AVERAGE ANNUAL COLLEGE COSTS (1992)	
Community College	$ 2,300
State University	$ 7,584
Private University	$ 16,292

The above costs include room, board, tuition, fees, books, supplies, and miscellaneous expenses, including transportation, at the university level. Community college costs exclude room and board.

In the last ten years, these costs have doubled, which means the average increase was 7%. In another ten years, doubling will most likely take place again. Children of parents who have not prepared for this impact on their pocketbook will have to make sacrifices. Those who can live at home and commute to campus will do so. Those who can't may have to modify their choice of educational institutions. The parents will not only have a college funding problem, but also a retirement problem. Dollars will be spent for college costs at a time when parents are also becoming concerned about their ability to fund pending retirements.

START NOW TO FUND YOUR CHILD'S COLLEGE EDUCATION

Planning as early as possible for your child's education is the easiest way to be fully prepared to give your child the best start you can educationally. For instance, using Worksheet 5A, found in Chapter 5, Susan and Larry Young calculated how much they will need to save to put three-year-old Thomas through four years of state university. Next, they calculated the college expenses for Stephen, their 11-year-old whiz kid, and Laura, who is 13. The answers are somewhat shocking in that the difference in the effort required for each child is considerable:

COLLEGE SAVINGS	
Thomas	$176/month
Stephen	$368/month
Laura	$497/month

While the Youngs may not be able to fully fund their children's college years as shown above or take advantage of all the strategies listed below, they will be able to make good education funding decisions based on their available opportunities.

COLLEGE FUNDING STRATEGIES

Income shifting, or tax sheltering, is a great tactic if it works for you. The strategies which follow are unique and won't be available to the majority of parents. Those who can use them, should.

- Creating tax deductible college costs: Buy a piece of rental real estate and employ your children at bona fide jobs (such as maintenance of the grounds). Pay them a reasonable wage for the work performed and deduct their wages as an investment expense. Check with a tax accountant to ensure you are aware of employment taxes you may be required to pay on your new employees.

- Developing a college condo: Locate a large residence in close proximity to the college campus your child(ren) will attend. Make sure it has several bedrooms and is suitable to convert into a rooming house. Install your fledging student as the on-site landlord. This strategy works well if you want to invest in real estate close to a campus and your children are of college age. The strategy is similar to the previous suggestion except that you will be able to pay your student a higher wage. The result is tax deductible tuition, a place for your student to roost, depreciation write offs, and hopefully, enough income from the roomers to pay the mortgage payments.
- Keeping it in the family: As any accountant will testify, hiring children in your business is one of the best ways to keep money in the family circle. Unfortunately, this strategy is hard to implement in the real world because hiring one's own children can make reluctant employees.
- Uniform Gift to Minors Account (UGMA): This strategy works well if money is available. You can give your child up to $10,000 a year without any gift taxes. This money would be placed in your child's name and be taxed at his/her bracket. Most parents would rather make a series of monthly gifts, than give $10,000 all at once, into a UGMA. A child is the owner, and one of the parents is the custodian. Shifting assets from you to your children results in potentially lower taxes on the growth of the investment. There are, however, a few disadvantages to making gifts into a UGMA, such as:

1. <u>The kiddie tax trap</u>: This limits the amount of unearned income which can be taxed at your child's tax bracket if the child is under age 14. Once the child's income exceeds the greater of $1,200 or $600 plus certain itemized expenses (1992 limitation — indexed to the CPI), the excess is taxed at the parent's tax bracket rather than at the child's 15% bracket. If your child is 14 plus, any amount of unearned income will be taxed at his/her rate.
2. <u>The coming of age syndrome</u>: You lose control over the money in your child's account when your child reaches age 18 or 21 (age varies according to state). He or she can withdraw the entire proceeds for any purpose. As I like to say, college has the potential of going up in a cloud of exhaust fumes as your child zooms off in his or her new sports coupe.
3. <u>Financial aid disqualification</u>: If your family income is under certain levels which depend on whether you are married or single, your children could qualify for limited financial aid. Having money in their names could disqualify them from consideration. Under present guidelines, 35% of a child's asset base is deemed available for college expenses, while 5.6% of the parent's assets are considered available. The student is also disqualified from receiving financial aid if the parent claims them as a tax deduction.

- Utilize a 2503(c) minority trust: This strategy is complicated and can be expensive, but it allows you greater control over money intended for a college education. This revokable living trust is a vehicle for holding money that is solely for the benefit of a minor. A major feature is the trust pays its own income tax. Further, the trustee has control of the money until the child's age 21 when his or her aptitude for college should be evident. An attorney should draft this trust to include provisions which will qualify it for the annual $10,000 gift tax exclusion.
- Establish a Crummy Trust: This trust allows the beneficiary of the trust (your child) to withdraw the current year's contributions. If the child does not withdraw that sum, it is added to the principal of the trust. A key advantage of the Crummy Trust is its unlimited life. You can continue it as long as you, the trustee, wish.
- Borrowing: If all else fails, borrow. The following may be logical sources of lower cost education loans.

  1. Life insurance policies: Older policies may be the best source of "cheap" money. Often the interest charged is 6% or less, and the loan never has to be paid back. Newer universal life policies charge rates which approximate the interest rate credited to the cash account.
  2. 401(k) accounts: Check out the interest charges to borrow against your 401(k) retirement account. The higher the better since all the interest you pay is deposited directly back into your account. Interest is not tax deductible but it really is not an expense to you anyway.
  3. Margin accounts: You can borrow against securities in a brokerage account and, if you use the money to purchase investments, you can deduct the interest up to the investment income produced. In order to qualify for this provision, you should sell enough positions to pay the college costs and then borrow on margin to purchase more securities. Be careful as to what you buy as borrowing to buy tax free municipal securities does not qualify for an interest deduction.
  4. Loan programs for students: The Perkins Loans will make available up to $4,500 at 5% interest to students who have completed less than two years of undergraduate study. Third-year students are eligible for higher amounts. Loan amounts again are based on financial need. Another loan program, the Robert Stafford Loan Program, is also based on need. Undergraduates can borrow up to $2,625 in their first two years and $4,000 for the third through fifth years. Again, need must be demonstrated.
  5. Parent Loans for Undergraduate Students (PLUS): Financial need is not a prerequisite for PLUS, but you must be able to make the payments. Parents are limited to borrowing $4,000 a year at an interest rate approximating the 52-week T-bill rate. Other loans designated for solving family college funding problems

may be available through federally chartered agencies, such as the Student Loan Marketing Association or the Supplemental Loans for Students (SLS) program. For details, call 1-800-831-5626. The college of your child's choice may also offer loans to parents who do not qualify for financial aid.

6. Home Equity Loans: Fully deductible up to $100,000, this source of money is available to anyone with a home and the ability to carry more monthly debt payments.

- Seeking Financial Aid: If you feel there is even a remote chance your child may be eligible for financial aid, apply. The completion of the Financial Aid Form (FAF) is a trying exercise in itself. These forms, which can be obtained from high school guidance counselors, are to be mailed in as soon as possible after January 1, to the College Scholarship Service (CSS), P.O. Box 6364, Princeton, N.J. 08541. Most families get delayed as they wait for completion of their previous year's tax returns, but early application is crucial to full consideration for all available programs. CSS performs a preliminary analysis of eligibility and sends each school a statement acknowledging the student's financial aid status. At that point, the school steps in and determines the level of awards. When students apply for financial aid on time, they are considered automatically for all programs for which they are eligible, including the following:

  1. Pell Grants: Based on need, this program of college funding has been cut in recent years. Those eligible must be enrolled at least half-time as students. More information is available by calling the Federal Student Financial Information Center at 1-800-433-3243.

  2. Supplemental Educational Opportunity Grants (SEOG): This campus-based program is designed to help those students demonstrating the greatest need. Priority is given to students with Pell Grants and the lowest family contributions. Check with the financial aid office at your campus of choice.

  3. College Work Study Program (CWSP): These programs put students who demonstrate need to work on campus, earning money to offset their expenses. Again, no less than half-time enrollment is required. The best source for learning if the college your child plans to attend participates in the program is the school's financial aid office.

INVESTING OPPORTUNITIES

Investment choices are broad. You can invest in your name, or in your child's through the Uniform Gift to Minors Account (UGMA), in a variety of areas. These include certificates of deposit, Series EE bonds, municipal, corporate or government bonds, money market, stock and bond mutual funds, unit investment trusts, and zero coupon bonds. For parents desiring more flexibility, the Uniform Transfers to Minors Act (UTMA) will allow real estate, collectibles, art, antiques, and so forth, to be transferred into an account in your child's name while you continue to control the asset until the child is age 21 or 25 in some states. Not all states use both the UGMA and UTMA. Check with a financial advisor. Or trusts, such as the 2503(c) Minority Trust or the Crummy Trust, could be utilized.

How do you know which way to invest and how much risk to take when investing on behalf of your children? According to information published by the Oppenheimer Funds in their brochure, ***Getting Your Financial House in Order***, the following guidelines can help:

> "Experts suggest that you consider investing college savings in growth oriented stocks or mutual funds until the child turns age 14. When the child is between 14 and 16, you might want to moderate your investment plan slightly by moving towards income oriented investments. Once the child reaches 16, your primary goal should be safeguarding the funds you've already accumulated. At this point you should consider shifting your savings into a conservative investment vehicle such as a money market fund."

Systematic savings work best if enough time is allowed for compounding. Mutual funds are the easiest and most convenient way to save in investments targeted to outpace inflation. One mutual fund company, Twentieth Century Investors, has established a program to make it downright simple. With no minimum initial investment limitations, and as little as $25 per month, you can get started. They will even deduct the contribution from your checkbook. You can choose to have the accounts rebalanced starting four, five, or six years before college. Dollars will be incrementally shifted from one of their growth funds to a money market. Aggressive individuals may wish to hold out longer before shifting to a conservative stance. Nervous parents will probably start shifting from stocks to cash six years before college. This is an interesting program which I believe other mutual fund families will adopt by offering similar packages.

Since investments have been covered thoroughly in the preceding chapters, only brief descriptions of investments with characteristics unique to college funding follow.

- Series EE Bonds. Easy to purchase with as little as $25 per bond, Series EE grow at a rate approximately equal to certificates of deposit, yet are tax-deferred during the growth phase. If purchased for your child's college, university, or qualified technical school, Series EE bonds can be tax free. There are some qualifying rules to be aware of, such as:

  1. The bonds must be titled in the name of the parent(s) rather than the child.
  2. The parent must be age 24 or older when purchasing the bonds.
  3. If the proceeds are used 100% for tuition and the following income limitations are met, the redemption proceeds are tax free. If tuition is less than the redemption amount, only the amount of the Series EE redemption equal to the tuition is tax free. The remainder of the deferred interest is taxable.

4. Parental income must be below certain levels in the year of the redemption. Income limitations for 1992 are: Single parents, $44,150 for 100% tax free proceeds; up to $59,150, only a portion is tax free. For those who are married and filing jointly, the limitation is $66,200 for tax free proceeds, and up to $96,200 for a partial tax free redemption. When income exceeds the upper limits, none of the Series EE redemption proceeds qualify for tax free treatment. Income limitations are adjusted annually based on changes in the Consumer Price Index (CPI).

5. These provisions applies only to purchases made in 1990 and beyond.

For complete details, send 50 cents to Consumer Information Center, Dept. 474 W, Pueblo, CO 81009. You will receive the pamphlet, ***U.S. Savings Bonds: Now Tax Free for Education.***

- Baccalaureate bonds: About 22 states offer these general obligation municipal college bonds, which may pay a slightly higher interest rate than other municipal bond issues. They are popular due to their perceived safety and non-callable feature. They are also issued in varying maturities, which make it easy to match bond redemptions to funding needs.
- Prepaid tuition programs: A handful of educational institutions offer parents the ability to guarantee a future four-year education for a one-time current payment. This essentially insures your child will be able to attend regardless of how rapidly tuition costs escalate. The disadvantage is that your child may change his or her mind about the college of choice. If so, you may only receive back the original investment and perhaps not until the child reaches college age, except in the event of the child's death or disability. Further, if the tuition exceeds 25% of the funds invested in the program, the IRS will consider the tuition a gift of a future interest not eligible for the $10,000 annual gift tax exclusion. Consider this strategy as an insurance policy rather than an investment program.
- College Sure CDs: This certificate of deposit is offered by the College Savings Bank in Princeton, New Jersey. The annual return on the CD is tied to an index tracking the cost of full college funding for freshmen at 500 private four-year colleges and universities. For parents depositing from $1,000 up to $9,999, a rate equal to the index less 1.5% is credited. Parents who establish accounts in excess of $10,000 will be credited just 1% less than the index. FDIC insurance, the ability to keep up with college inflation, and the pure safety of the investment will probably make this a popular investment choice. Additional deposits can be made for as little as $250.

The above are just a few of the innovative investments creative minds have formulated. In the years to come, I predict many more unique investments and special programs will be made available to help ease the burden of educating America.

DISPELLING THE MYTHS

Many parents float along without much concern over this looming financial need. Common myths regarding college funding are:

- "My income will be large enough for us to pay all college expenses from my salary." It would be nice if this were true for the majority of the population. But it is not. Less than 6% of potential students have parents who can meet the test of pay-as-you-go.
- "Johnny or Susie can go to work and pay their own way." This sounds good, but it would be very difficult for a student to make enough money and have time left over after work to keep grades up in today's competitive college environments.
- "Not to worry, we have lots of time left to save for college." If this is your attitude, review the different levels of savings required by the Youngs for their three children. Wouldn't you rather be spending a smaller amount now than making a larger payment later?
- "My child will qualify for a scholarship, financial aid, or government loans." Betting on this occurrence is like gambling in Reno. The chances that your child will be able to snare a scholarship are no better than 50%. In addition, government restrictions on subsidy programs have tightened up considerably in the last 10-15 years; only about 20% can get subsidized loans, and financial aid packages are not available to middle-income parents (income more than $60,000, assets greater than $80,000).

Funding mounting college costs will be difficult to all but the most affluent. However, with enough time and preparation, your child(ren) will have a much greater chance of attending the college of his or her choice.

For more information on resources and opportunities available to your student, read: ***Don't Miss Out: The Ambitious Student's Guide to Financial Aid,*** published by Octameron Press, P.O. Box 2748, Alexandria, VA 22301; ***Paying for College: A Step by Step College Planning Guide,*** free from T.R. Price Mutual Funds, 1-800-638-5660; ***Meeting College Costs,*** The College Board, (408) 288-6800; ***Planning Now for College Costs: A Guide for Families,*** send $3.00 to Early Planning, P.O. Box 2155, Washington, D.C. 20013.

CHAPTER 17

PLANNING FOR FINANCIAL INDEPENDENCE

"Even though work stops, expenses run on."
Cato the Elder

Financial independence is a term that is often used to denote retirement. It doesn't necessarily have to mean retirement, though. Some people define it as having the ability to quit working or simply change direction without risking life-style. Whatever financial independence means to you, it can be one of the most important times of your life. If it is to be so, you will need to plan for it — not just let it happen. Without planning, your future life-style may not match your dreams, leaving you stressed, depressed, and unable to enjoy financial independence or retirement at any age.

The following information was reported in ***Financial Services Week***, June 21, 1991:

> "A majority of consumers (61%) say retirement is the most important reason for individuals to add to their savings, according to a survey conducted by Phoenix-Hecht/Gallup, a market research firm.
>
> "'When we asked consumers to rank the importance of saving for their retirement on a 1 (low) to 5 (high) point scale, 45% rated it a 5, with an additional 26% scoring it as 4,' said Larry A. Marks, president of Phoenix Hecht/Gallup.
>
> "The firm, based in North Carolina, interviewed more than 1,000 financial decision makers between the ages of 35 and 64 with household incomes of at least $25,000.
>
> "'It is very interesting to note that the majority (60%) of all respondents expect to be able to maintain (52%) or even to improve (8%) their life-style after they have retired. Those respondents under the age of 45 were the most optimistic about their ability to live better than they do now,' Marks said."

This survey was weighted in favor of upper income households and clearly illustrates that this group is both concerned and confident about future financial prospects.

The most successful retirees are those who planned as many details as possible well in advance of their target independence date. Concern over retirement becomes most evident in the early 40s because, for some, that is when children are almost finished with college or other educational pursuits, and retirement looms on the horizon as the next major life transition. For others, due to the current trend of having children later in life, retirement pushes right on the heels of the tremendous, rising expense of college education.

I have had clients say, "I didn't expect an early retirement offer. We're not ready — we're still paying for college." What a shame not to be able to take advantage of an attractive incentive retirement opportunity. This not so subtle message is: plan ahead. If you want your financial independence planning to be as easy as possible, start investing with that in mind as soon as you start working. It is never too early. The following example shows how much easier it was for Keith to accumulate more money than his brother, Wayne:

COMPOUND INTEREST EXAMPLE

10% Rate of Return

Year	Keith	Wayne
1	$3,000	Procrastination
2	3,000	Procrastination
3	3,000	Procrastination
4	3,000	Procrastination
5	3,000	Procrastination
6	3,000	Procrastination
7	3,000	Procrastination
8	0	$3,000
9	0	3,000
10	0	3,000
11	0	3,000
12	0	3,000
13	0	3,000
14	0	3,000
15	0	3,000
16	0	3,000
17	0	3,000
18	0	3,000
19	0	3,000
20	0	3,000
21	0	3,000
22	0	3,000
23	0	3,000
24	0	3,000
25	0	3,000
26	0	3,000
27	0	3,000
28	0	3,000
29	0	3,000
30	0	3,000
Total Contributions	$ 21,000	$ 69,000
Value at Year End 30	$254,853	$238,629

Procrastination can be detrimental to retirement plans. Start early to evaluate your retirement readiness. Do you know enough about retirement to design the kind of future you want for yourself? Spend a few moments with the following quiz to see how knowledgeable you are:

DESIGNING YOUR RETIREMENT FUTURE

1. What percentage of your pre-retirement income do you think you'll need to live comfortably during retirement?
   a. 50% b. 60% c. 70-80% d. 90%

2. At what age should you begin to save for retirement?
   a. 35 b. 40 c. 55 d. As soon as you enter the work force.

3. If you retire at 62, your monthly Social Security benefit will be less than if you retire at age 65 by how much?
   a. 10% b. 15% c. 20% d. 25%

4. Employer sponsored benefit plans such as 401(k)s and 403(b)s allow employees to build up retirement savings tax deferred.
   a. True b. False

5. To build a retirement nest egg of $1 million, a 25-year-old person needs to save how much money each month at a 12% tax deferred interest rate, until age 65?
   a. $85 b. $115 c. $200 d. $325

6. A 30-year-old who is starting to save for retirement should save what percent of before tax income each year?
   a. 2% b. 5% c. 15%

7. If you are employed by someone else and also have income from a self-employment activity, you are eligible to open a Keogh account.
   a. True b. False

8. Most pension plans have a built-in protection against inflation.
   a. True b. False

Answers:

1.c. According to the Institute of Certified Financial Planners, the average person will need 70-80% of annual preretirement income each year of retirement.

2.d. Many people don't begin saving for retirement until age 50 or later, but the sooner you start, the more time you're allowing for your savings to accumulate and compound.

3.c. 20%. However, you may retire at 62 and wait until 65 before starting to collect. Deciding whether to retire early is a financially complicated question. Don't make this decision without carefully evaluating your assets and sources of income, preferably with the assistance of an accountant or financial advisor.

4.a. True. But many people overlook the benefits of these tax-deferred vehicles. Financial advisors recommend you make the maximum allowable contribution.

5.a. $85. But at age 35, you need to save $286 a month, and at 45, it rises steeply to $1,011 a month.

6.b. Financial advisors suggest 5% as a good rule of thumb for those between 30 and 40. After 40, you should aim to add one percentage point a year. And after 45, try to save 10%.

7.a. True. You shelter up to 20% of your self-employment income (up to $30,000) annually, in a tax-deferred Keogh account, even if you also work for someone else.

8.b. False. Most are not, which means that inflation will eat into the purchasing power of your pension income. That's why it is important to consider other means of savings for retirement, such as IRAs and Keogh plans, in addition to your employer's pension plan.

*Source: Quest for Value Mutual Funds, (*Retirement and Investment Planning Update, *Volume 1, No. 1)*

How did you do? If you answered every question correctly, congratulations! If you got more than four wrong, you may need to chat with an accountant, financial advisor, or a benefits specialist where you work.

ESTABLISHING INVESTMENT SPENDING GOALS

To live comfortably, you need at least 70-80% of your preretirement income. Here's what a typical working couple should be putting aside each year, assuming a 5% wage inflation and retirement at age 65.

NEEDED TO INVEST ANNUALLY[1]

Current Salary	Current Age	With Pension	With Double IRA No Pension
$35,000	30	$ 3,600	$ 4,000
	40	$ 4,360	$ 5,900
	50	$ 6,000	$ 9,970
$50,000	30	$ 7,590	$ 8,350
	40	$ 8,940	$11,790
	50	$12,280	$17,925
$75,000	30	$15,270	$18,050
	40	$17,890	$23,220
	50	$24,730	$33,700

1. At 8% interest taxed in a combined state and federal tax bracket of 35% after a $4,000 deduction for the IRAs.

Source: **Ernst & Young,** *Certified Public Accountants*

Articles like the one that follows lead me to believe that a good percentage of those now retired could have started sooner and planned better.

> "Income Cut in Half at Retirement. Bryn Mawr, Pa. - A joint project of the American Association of Retired Persons and the Administration on Aging, U.S. Department of Health and Human Services revealed that the median income for older men was $11,854 while for women it was $6,734, according to an American Society newsletter, '**Query**,' designed for society members to send to their clients.
>
> "Most Americans' income is cut in half at retirement, according to the report. And while most elderly will say planning is important to them, few have comprehensive financial plans and only 7% have long term care insurance.
>
> "The '**Query**' report on the senior boom also noted that nearly half of all women 65 or older are widows. The ratio of widows to widowers is almost five to one. Only 10% of families headed by a senior citizen have a household income of $50,000 or more. Twenty percent of individuals in this age bracket are at or below the poverty level. In 1987, 12.3% of Americans had reached age 65, as compared to 4.1% in 1900."

Source: **Financial Services Week,** *February 5, 1990*

So you can see from the above samples of media reporting that consumers have more confidence in their ability to retire well than the actual results appear to prove. Planning is the secret to developing a successful retirement.

There are four main fears that confront middle-age adults when contemplating their ultimate retirement. Those fears are:

Having too much spare time
Living too long
Lack of adequate health insurance
Poor health

These are real fears. In the ***Wall Street Journal***, June 23, 1989, an article cited why many retirees go back to work. According to a mid-1980s study by the Travelers Corporation on 1,400 of their retirees, one out of four had returned to work. And two out of three had returned within a year of retiring. Why? Some cited the social and emotional benefits of work, but the majority said they went back to meet living expenses or pay for large special outlays.

HOW LONG WILL YOU LIVE?

Longer than your parents perhaps, and maybe much longer than your grandparents. But how long is that? Life expectancy tables offer an average at any given age, but are you average? Exhibit 17A on page 198 gives the life expectancy of either a male or female of the same age. It can be used to establish the minimum distribution of an IRA at any particular age or to estimate how many more years the average American will live. For example, the life expectancy of a male or female, age 60, is 24.2 years; age 65, 20 years. With this IRS table, the longer you live, the longer you are expected to live. The table recalculates your life expectancy each year based on your current age.

You may be the proud owner of strong genes, healthy habits, and a low stress environment. In that case, you may outlive the averages cited above. Retirees should plan on an income stream at least through their 90th year. If the investment coffer is empty at that time, it would be appropriate to liquidate the residence and live off the proceeds. This would be the optimum solution. The following exercise will help you assess your life expectancy based on your personal answers to the test. This quiz is based on a study developed by Robert Allen, Ph.D., and Shirley Linde in their 1985 book, ***Lifegain: The Exciting Program That Will Change Your Health and Your Life***, Human Resources Institute.

HOW LONG WILL YOU LIVE?

START WITH THE NUMBER 72

Personal Facts

____ If you are male, SUBTRACT 3.
____ If you are female, ADD 4
____ If you live in an urban area with a population over 2 million, SUBTRACT 2.
____ If you live in a town under 10,000 or on a farm, ADD 2.
____ If any grandparent lived to 85, ADD 2.
____ If all four grandparents lived to 80, ADD 6.
____ If either parent died of a stroke or heart attack before age 50, SUBTRACT 4.
____ If any parent, brother, or sister under 50 has (or had) cancer or a heart condition, or has had diabetes since childhood, SUBTRACT 3.
____ Do you earn over $70,000[1] a year? SUBTRACT 2.
____ If you finished college, ADD 1. If you have a graduate or professional degree, ADD 2 more.
____ If you are 65 or over and still working, ADD 3.
____ If you live with a spouse or friend, ADD 5. If not, SUBTRACT 1 for every ten years alone since age 25.

Life-Style Status

____ If you work behind a desk, SUBTRACT 3.
____ If your work requires regular, heavy physical labor, ADD 3. If you exercise strenuously (tennis, running, swimming, etc.) five times a week for at least a half-hour, ADD 4. Two or three times a week, ADD 2.
____ Do you sleep more than ten hours each night? SUBTRACT 4.
____ Are you intense, aggressive, easily angered? SUBTRACT 3.
____ Are you easy going and relaxed? ADD 3.
____ Are you happy? ADD 1. Unhappy? SUBTRACT 2.
____ Have you had a speeding ticket in the past year? SUBTRACT 1.
____ Do you smoke more than two packs a day? SUBTRACT 8. One to two packs? SUBTRACT 6. One-half to one? SUBTRACT 3.
____ Do you drink the equivalent of 1-1/2 oz. of liquor a day? SUBTRACT 1.
____ Are you overweight by 50 lbs. or more? SUBTRACT 8. By 30-50 lbs.? SUBTRACT 4. By 10-30 lbs.? SUBTRACT 2.
____ If you are a man over 40 and have an annual checkup, ADD 2. If you are a woman and see a gynecologist once a year, ADD 2.

Age Adjustment

____ If you are between 30 and 50, ADD 2.
____ If you are between 40 and 50, ADD 3.
____ If you are between 50 and 70, ADD 4.
____ If you are over 70, ADD 5.

Add up your score. Remember, you started with the number 72.

Score __________ = Personal Life Expectancy

---

1. Original version $50,000. $70,000 represents 1992 dollars inflated at 5%.

SADLY HE OUTLIVED HIS RETIREMENT BY TEN YEARS

Many individuals who have taken this test have scored in the mid-80s. How did you score? An exercise like this may be a little more valid than letting the life expectancy tables dictate how many years of investment funding you will require. It could also provide the necessary motivation to begin the process of evaluating your potential to build an adequate capital base for your retirement.

PRE-RETIREMENT PLANNING STEPS

The first step in retirement planning is to determine when you want to be financially independent. While identifying a target date is important, it is just as important that your plans encompass where you might live and what activities you will participate in.

Estimating Future Expenses

With your target date set and a good idea of what life-style you want to replicate, you can start to address the problem of determining how much money you'll need. Retirees can live quite well on about 70-80% of their pre-retirement income and maintain the same standards. Expenses will drop as commuting costs are decreased, office attire is traded in for casual clothes, and so forth. On the other hand, some old expenses will be replaced by new ones. Travel and medical insurance coverages are the common ones.

For assistance with estimating your future retirement expenses, use Worksheet 17A found at the end of the chapter. This is essentially the same form you may have completed in Chapter 7. When you fill it out this time, you will want to change some expense levels, eliminate others and, perhaps, add expense estimates for special activities planned for retirement years. Be sure to state expenses in current dollars. Once you know the bottom line dollar estimate of how much you would need if you were retired currently, you can calculate how much to save each year to meet your future inflation-adjusted, financially independent income need.

Income Need: $______________
(in today's dollars)

Rounding up Your Retirement Money

How will your retirement income need be met? The vast majority will depend on pensions and Social Security. But that won't be enough. Unless you are in the military or a federal employee, your pension will most likely be a fixed sum for life. At 5% inflation, in 10 years your buying power on a fixed pension will be cut by 39%. In 14 years, the buying power is cut by 50%. If you want the ability to give yourself a cost-of-living raise throughout retirement, you will have to accumulate an investment base to make up the difference.

Most financial advisors have access to sophisticated computer programs which can evaluate the many financial variables impacting retirement, such as: inflation, regular and sporadic expenses or income streams, Social Security, investment earnings, mortgage payoffs, vacation funding, or extraordinary expenses. These programs can also create "what if" models to help you make better decisions.

SOURCES OF RETIREMENT INCOME

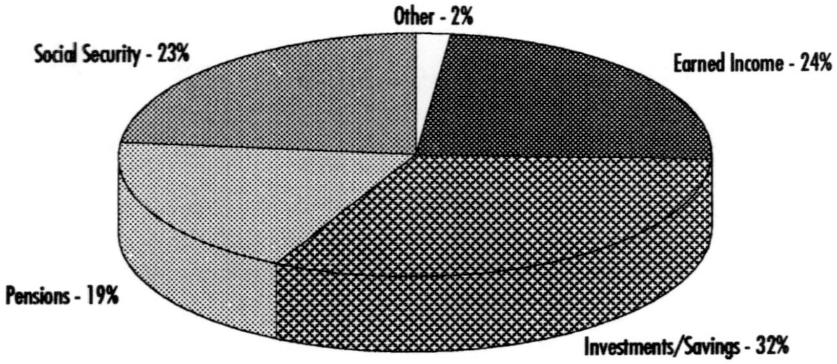

Source: Social Security Administration

The following steps will help you calculate a close enough to the truth estimate for now. If a more in-depth analysis is desired, a professional consultation may be in order.

1. Pensions: The best method for assessing this income stream is to ask your employer to give you the value of your today's vested pension (ie., what you have now). If you are unable to secure it, you may calculate it yourself with the appropriate formula — usually a percent factor (such as .02) multiplied by present years of service and again multiplied by your current annual salary averaged over the past 2-5 years. Many companies will also provide a future estimated pension. Be sure you have a today's dollar pension estimate for the following worksheet.

   Pension: $______________

2. Social Security: It is much easier to analyze retirement needs since Social Security benefit estimates are available. If you send in a request on Form SSA 7004, Request for Earnings and Benefit Estimate Statement, you will receive in 4-6 weeks an estimate of your future Social Security benefits in today's dollars. You may send in multiple requests citing different retirement ages on each. For instance,

you may wish estimates based on retirement at age 55, 60, 62, and 65. Individual benefits will vary depending on your salary levels during earning years, how many years you worked and paid FICA taxes, and when you retire. The process is simple: call 1-800-234-5772 or walk into your local Social Security office and request a copy. Easier yet, copy Exhibit 17B included at the end of this chapter and mail it in.

I routinely advise clients to request this information to help project future income resources as accurately as possible.

Social Security
Source #1: $______________
Source #2: $______________

3. Investment effort required: This next exercise can be a bit daunting, but if you completed the similar worksheet found in Chapter 5, you may be able to breeze through it. Using Worksheet 17B, Larry and Susan Young, our 35-year-old couple, are going to determine whether they need to increase assets dedicated to retirement if they retire by their age 60.

DETERMINING RETIREMENT SAVINGS QUOTIENT

Assumptions:

	Inflation rate:		5%
	Average after-tax investment return:		7%
	Years until retirement:		25
	Life expectancy at retirement age:		24
A.	Estimated annual retirement income need in today's dollar:		$ 40,000
B.	Estimated annual fixed income sources:		
	Pensions (today's vested value)	$1,000/month	
	Social Security (today's dollar)	$1,500/month	
	Total		$ 30,000
C.	Current annual deficit (A - B):		$ 10,000
D.	Years to retirement:		25
E.	Future value of income deficit using inflation factor from Table I (3.386 x C):		$ 33,860
F.	Real return, i.e., estimated after-tax investment returns minus expected average inflation rate (7% - 5%):		2%
G.	Deficit from (E) x Table III present value factor, ($33,860 x 19.523), reflecting real return (F) over 24 years of retirement = amount required at retirement to provide an inflation adjusted income equal to the projected annual deficit:		$ 661,048
H.	Dollars already dedicated to the goal x Table I factor, ($50,000 x 5.427), reflecting after-tax investment return (7%) and number of years (25) until retirement:		$ 271,350
I.	Total remaining dollars required to accumulate (G - H):		$ 389,698
J.	Annual investment amount necessary to accumulate remaining dollars. Divide (I) by Table II factor, ($389,698 ÷ 63.249), reflecting anticipated after-tax investment return (7%) and number of years (25) until retirement:		$ 6,161

Larry and Susan are somewhat comforted by completing this exercise. But they realize that a more sophisticated approach to analyzing this important area would be beneficial because 1) the above analysis fails to calculate the impact of a fixed pension on retirement spending or the fact that Social Security is not available until their age 62, 2) it does not adjust for retirement program dollars that are compounding tax deferred, 3) they are planning major vacations during the first years of their retirement, and 4) they feel their spending will slow down after age 75 or so.

Turn to Worksheet 17B and work through your retirement numbers. How do you feel about the annual investment necessary to make your retirement a timely event? If you question your ability to meet that requirement, here are three potential solutions:

Work longer and save more.
Lower your retirement standard of living.
Strive for higher returns on your investment assets.

Working longer and lowering your retirement income goal are the least desirable choices to solve the problem. Increasing potential investment returns by selective asset repositioning may be the easiest way to meet a retirement deadline. But don't take more risks than you can handle by becoming overly aggressive instantly. Take it easy and live with a new investment position for a few months before making a second or third change. With some adjustments either in investment positions or in rate of accumulation, you can probably reach a satisfactory retirement goal. Once this financial goal has been solved, the way will be smoothed to concentrate on other, perhaps more immediate, gratifications.

Do not cross your fingers and hope that everything will turn out all right. Make it happen. Remember, it is not what you know but what you do that creates success. Once you have identified your financial problem (i.e., the difference between where you are and where you want to be), take action. Then, when you see the result of your systematic investment purchases, it will be easy to make yearly commitments to the goal.

EXHIBIT 17A

TABLE V — ORDINARY LIFE ANNUITIES ONE LIFE-EXPECTED RETURN MULTIPLES

Age	Multiple	Age	Multiple	Age	Multiple
5	76.6	42	40.6	79	10.0
6	75.6	43	39.6	80	9.5
7	74.7	44	38.7	81	8.9
8	73.7	45	37.7	82	8.4
9	72.7	46	36.8	83	7.9
10	71.7	47	35.9	84	7.4
11	70.7	48	34.9	85	6.9
12	69.7	49	34.0	86	6.5
13	68.8	50	33.1	87	6.1
14	67.8	51	32.2	88	5.7
15	66.8	52	31.3	89	5.3
16	65.8	53	30.4	90	5.0
17	64.8	54	29.5	91	4.7
18	63.9	55	28.6	92	4.4
19	62.9	56	27.7	93	4.1
20	61.9	57	26.8	94	3.9
21	60.9	58	25.9	95	3.7
22	59.9	59	25.0	96	3.4
23	59.0	60	24.2	97	3.2
24	58.0	61	23.3	98	3.0
25	57.0	62	22.5	99	2.8
26	56.0	63	21.6	100	2.7
27	55.1	64	20.8	101	2.5
28	54.1	65	20.0	102	2.3
29	53.1	66	19.2	103	2.1
30	52.2	67	18.4	104	1.9
31	51.2	68	17.6	105	1.8
32	50.2	69	16.8	106	1.6
33	49.3	70	16.0	107	1.4
34	48.3	71	15.3	108	1.3
35	47.3	72	14.6	109	1.1
36	46.4	73	13.9	110	1.0
37	45.4	74	13.2	111	.9
38	44.4	75	12.5	112	.8
39	43.5	76	11.9	113	.7
40	42.5	77	11.2	114	.6
41	41.5	78	10.6	115	.5

Source: **Federal Tax Coordinator 2d,** *Research Institute of America*

EXHIBIT 17B

SOCIAL SECURITY
ADMINISTRATION

Request for Earnings and Benefit Estimate Statement

The Social Security program belongs to you and you can count on it to be there for you. Social Security can protect you in many ways. It can help support your family in the event of your death and provide monthly payments and health insurance when you retire or if you become disabled.

To help you learn how Social Security is a part of your life, we are pleased to offer you a free Personal Earnings and Benefit Estimate Statement.

The Personal Earnings and Benefit Estimate Statement shows your Social Security earnings history and estimates how much you have paid in Social Security taxes. It also estimates your future benefits and tells you how you can qualify for benefits. When you receive your earnings statement, we hope you will use it to start planning for a strong financial future.

To receive your statement, please fill out the form on the reverse and mail it to us. You should receive your statement in 6 weeks or less. We look forward to sending it to you.

GWENDOLYN S. KING
Commissioner of Social Security

First
Class
Postage
Required

SOCIAL SECURITY ADMINISTRATION
ALBUQUERQUE DATA OPERATIONS CENTER
P.O. BOX 4429 STATION A
ALBUQUERQUE, NM 87196-4429

SOCIAL SECURITY . . . It never stops working!

Form Approved
OMB No. 0960-0466 ☐ SP

SOCIAL SECURITY ADMINISTRATION

Request for Earnings and Benefit Estimate Statement

To receive a free statement of your earnings covered by Social Security and your estimated future benefits, all you need to do is fill out this form. Please print or type your answers. When you have completed the form, fold it and mail it to us.

1. Name shown on your Social Security card:

   First ______ Middle Initial ______ Last ______

2. Your Social Security number as shown on your card:

   ☐☐☐-☐☐-☐☐☐☐

3. Your date of birth: ______ Month ______ Day ______ Year

4. Other Social Security numbers you have used:

   ☐☐☐-☐☐-☐☐☐☐

   ☐☐☐-☐☐-☐☐☐☐

5. Your Sex: ☐ Male ☐ Female

6. Other names you have used (including a maiden name):

   ______

   ______

7. Show your actual earnings for last year and your estimated earnings for this year. Include only wages and/or net self-employment income covered by Social Security.

   A. Last year's actual earnings:

   $☐☐☐,☐☐☐.0 0 (Dollars only)

   B. This year's estimated earnings:

   $☐☐☐,☐☐☐.0 0 (Dollars only)

8. Show the age at which you plan to retire: ☐☐ (Show only one age)

9. Below, show the average yearly amount that you think you will earn between now and when you plan to retire. Your estimate of future earnings will be added to those earnings already on our records to give you the best possible estimate.

   Enter a yearly average, not your total future lifetime earnings. Only show earnings covered by Social Security. Do not add cost-of-living, performance or scheduled pay increases or bonuses. The reason for this is that we estimate retirement benefits in today's dollars, but adjust them to account for average wage growth in the national economy.

   However, if you expect to earn significantly more or less in the future due to promotions, job changes, part-time work, or an absence from the work force, enter the amount in today's dollars that most closely reflects your future average yearly earnings.

   Most people should enter the same amount that they are earning now (the amount shown in 7B).

   Your future average yearly earnings:

   $☐☐☐,☐☐☐.0 0 (Dollars only)

10. Address where you want us to send the statement:

    Name ______

    Street Address (Include Apt. No., P.O. Box, or Rural Route) ______

    City ______ State ______ Zip Code ______

I am asking for information about my own Social Security record or the record of a person I am authorized to represent. I understand that if I deliberately request information under false pretenses I may be guilty of a federal crime and could be fined and/or imprisoned. I authorize you to send the statement of earnings and benefit estimates to the person named in item 10 through a contractor.

▶ ______

Please sign your name (Do not print)

Date ______ (Area Code) Daytime Telephone No. ______

ABOUT THE PRIVACY ACT

Social Security is allowed to collect the facts on this form under Section 205 of the Social Security Act. We need them to quickly identify your record and prepare the earnings statement you asked us for. Giving us these facts is voluntary. However, without them we may not be able to give you an earnings and benefit estimate statement. Neither the Social Security Administration nor its contractor will use the information for any other purpose.

Form SSA-7004-PC-OP3 (9-89) Destroy prior editions

Moisten, fold, and seal before mailing.

We estimate that it will take you about 5 minutes to complete this form. This includes the time it will take to read the instructions, gather the necessary facts and fill out the form. If you have comments or suggestions on this estimate, or on any other aspect of this form, write to the Social Security Administration, ATTN: Reports Clearance Officer, 1-A-21 Operations Bldg., Baltimore, MD 21235, and to the Office of Management and Budget, Paperwork Reduction Project (0960-0466), Washington, D.C. 20503. **Do not send completed forms or information concerning your claim to these offices.**

WORKSHEET 17A

RETIREMENT LIFE-STYLE EXPENSES

Monthly Average Outgo			Notes
Federal income tax	____________	F, V, D	____________
State/local income tax	____________	F, V, D	____________
Housing			
Mortgage payments	____________	F, V, D	____________
Monthly rent	____________	F, V, D	____________
Utilities			
Electricity	____________	F, V, D	____________
Oil or gas	____________	F, V, D	____________
Water	____________	F, V, D	____________
Telephone	____________	F, V, D	____________
Maintenance/repairs	____________	F, V, D	____________
Insurance			
Homeowners	____________	F, V, D	____________
Renters	____________	F, V, D	____________
Property tax	____________	F, V, D	____________
Groceries	____________	F, V, D	____________
Restaurant meals	____________	F, V, D	____________
Clothing			
Purchases			
Husband	____________	F, V, D	____________
Wife	____________	F, V, D	____________
Laundry	____________	F, V, D	____________
Dry cleaning	____________	F, V, D	____________
Repairs	____________	F, V, D	____________
Transportation			
Auto payments	____________	F, V, D	____________
Auto insurance	____________	F, V, D	____________
Gasoline	____________	F, V, D	____________
Repairs/maintenance	____________	F, V, D	____________
Auto licenses	____________	F, V, D	____________
Medical			
Health insurance	____________	F, V, D	____________
Uncovered medical	____________	F, V, D	____________
Prescriptions	____________	F, V, D	____________
Life insurance prems.	____________	F, V, D	____________
Major purchases			
Appliances	____________	F, V, D	____________
Furniture	____________	F, V, D	____________
Other	____________	F, V, D	____________
Vacations	____________	F, V, D	____________
Entertainment	____________	F, V, D	____________
Gifts			
Holidays	____________	F, V, D	____________
Birthdays	____________	F, V, D	____________
Other	____________	F, V, D	____________
Charitable contributions	____________	F, V, D	____________

Miscellaneous

Newspapers	____________F, V, D	____________
Magazine subscriptions	____________F, V, D	____________
Toiletries, cosmetics	____________F, V, D	____________
Personal care	____________F, V, D	____________
Allowances	____________F, V, D	____________
Other	____________F, V, D	____________
Other	____________F, V, D	____________
Other	____________F, V, D	____________
Other	____________F, V, D	____________
	Total Expenses	____________
	Total Income Less Total Expenses (+ or (-) Result)	____________

KEY: **F = Fixed Expense**
V = Variable
D = Discretionary

WORKSHEET 17B

DETERMINING RETIREMENT SAVINGS QUOTIENT

Assumptions:
- Inflation rate: ________
- Average after-tax investment return: ________
- Years until retirement: ________
- Life expectancy at retirement age: ________
  (Exhibit 17A page 198)

A. Estimated annual retirement income need in today's dollar: $____________

B. Estimated annual fixed income sources:
   - Pensions (today's vested value) $__________
   - Social Security (today's dollar) $__________
   - Total $____________

C. Current annual deficit (A - B): $____________

D. Years to retirement: ____________

E. Future value of income deficit (inflation factor from Table I x C): $____________

F. Real return (estimated after-tax investment returns minus expected average inflation rate): ____________

G. Deficit from (E) x Table III present value factor reflecting real return (F) over term of retirement = amount needed at retirement to provide an inflation adjusted income equal to the projected annual deficit: $____________

H. Dollars already dedicated to the goal ($__________) x Table I factor reflecting desired after-tax investment returns and number of years until retirement: $____________

I. Total remaining dollars required to accumulate (G - H): $____________

J. Annual investment amount necessary to accumulate remaining dollars, assuming an after-tax growth rate of ______ for ______ years. Divide (I) by the factor found in Table II reflecting anticipated after-tax investment returns and number of years until retirement: $____________

CHAPTER 18
RETIREMENT PROGRAM CHOICES

"If small sums do not go out, large sums will not come in."
Chinese Proverb

There is not another place in this book where you can spend your way to wealth so easily. Throughout the book I have referred to investment savings as investment spending. And it is. Just as you spend dollars on a mortgage payment to purchase real estate equity — a program which results, after 15 or 30 years, in your owning a debt-free residence — you can spend a predetermined sum and buy equity with interest in a retirement fund. You can't usually buy a house without making years of monthly deposits. Nor can you build a retirement fund overnight.

Your selection of retirement programs will have much to do with your successful accumulation of adequate funds to satisfy your expectation of a retirement life-style. Starting with Individual Retirement Accounts, here is a review of the best programs in which you can spend money today for spending money tomorrow.

INDIVIDUAL RETIREMENT ACCOUNTS (IRAs)

This account, around now for about 15 years, was designed to reward individuals for investing with an eye toward retirement. Millions of Americans have utilized the before-tax IRA program to accumulate billions of dollars.

One of the reasons the IRA has been so popular is that it allows you to reduce taxable income now and defer taxes on interest earned until the future. The result is a free loan from the government which you can use to compound your retirement dollars. When you arrive at retirement, anytime from age 59-1/2 forward, you can draw those funds out. The government will then have its hand out to collect the tax you owed in years past on your initial deposits plus tax on the interest earned. And, by that time, you will be paying those taxes with cheaper dollars because of inflation's devaluation of money over time. Furthermore, you only have to pay taxes on the amount of your yearly withdrawal. The rest continues to compound, tax deferred.

THIS MAY HAVE SOME EFFECT ON YOUR RETIREMENT SCORE

Look at the difference between investing $2,000 before-tax or $2,000 less 28% tax:

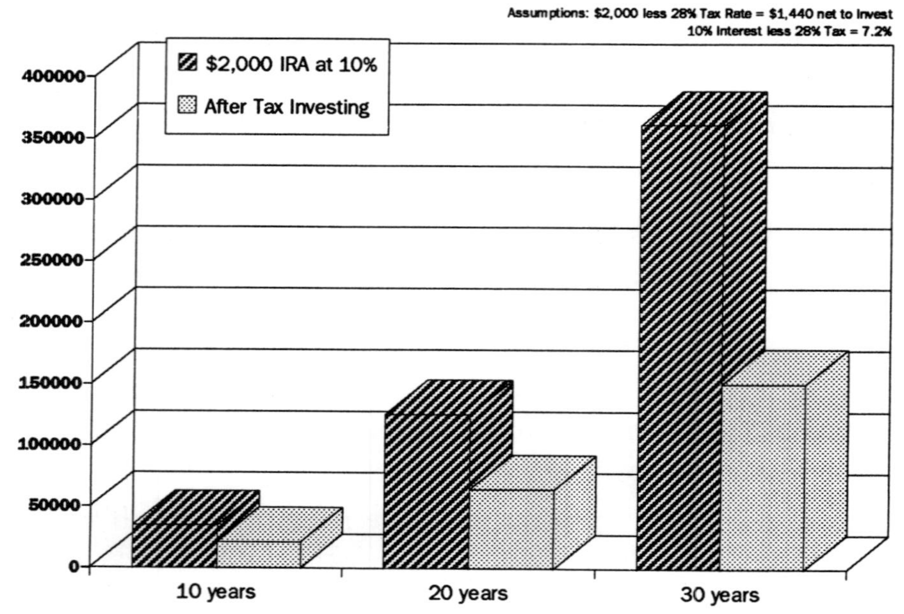

The rewards are clear. From the 20th year forward, it is at least twice as beneficial to defer taxes. An easy method of illustrating this is to compare these two income streams using 20 years as a yardstick.

Before tax:	$126,004 x 10%	=	$12,600 less 28% tax	=	$9,072
After tax:	$ 64,683 x 10%	=	$ 6,468 less 28% tax	=	$4,656

Regardless of future tax rates, the before-tax IRA figure, offers the greater reward.

Tax Cracks in Your IRA

The IRA message is familiar to most Americans. But what started as a retirement program available to everyone was converted in 1987 to a program just for individuals who meet certain criteria, that is, if one wants to continue to deduct IRA deposits. Current legislation governing the deductibility of IRAs states that individuals who are active participants in a qualified program through their employers — such as pensions, profit sharing, stock bonus plans, tax sheltered annuities, 401(k) programs, or simplified employee pensions — must have income that falls under certain limits in order to be eligible for a tax deductible IRA.

IRA DEDUCTION PHASE OUT

Single Income	Married Income	Deductible Contribution
$25,000	$40,000	$2,000
26,000	41,000	1,800
27,000	42,000	1,600
28,000	43,000	1,400
29,000	44,000	1,200
30,000	45,000	1,000
31,000	46,000	800
32,000	47,000	600
33,000	48,000	400
34,000	49,000	200
35,000	50,000	-0-

The smallest amount you can put into a deductible IRA is $200 and the largest is $2,000, according to current rules. One of my favorite quips regarding this table is that the government appears to encourage divorce. Notice that the lower limit for two single individuals is $50,000 combined while the lower limit for a married couple is only $40,000. And, if you are married and don't have a pension, you still may not be able to use a deductible IRA. Why? If your spouse and you earn over the limit, $50,000 adjusted gross income before an IRA deduction, and your spouse is an active participant in a retirement plan at work, you are disqualified from deducting your contribution.

Here is a formula which will help you calculate to the penny how much you can contribute to a tax deductible IRA account:

PARTIAL DEDUCTION FORMULA

$$\text{Contribution} \times \frac{\text{Adjusted Gross Income (AGI) Minus Deductible Limit}}{\$10{,}000} = \text{Reduction Amount}$$

Following is an illustration of the impact on Patrick, a single tax payer, with an AGI of $32,500.

$$\$2{,}000 \times \frac{\$32{,}500 - \$25{,}000}{\$10{,}000} = \$1{,}500 \text{ Reduction}$$

Patrick is limited to a $500 deductible IRA ($2,000 minus $1,500). He can contribute up to $2,000, but the difference will not be tax deductible against the current year's income.

In 1986, legislation was passed which affixed a 10% penalty to all retirement plan withdrawals made prior to age 59-1/2, with certain exceptions such as death or disability or to pay for medical expenses which exceed 7.5% of your adjusted gross income. In 1987, along with the partial deduction IRA rules, constraints were placed on the taxation of withdrawals from non-deductible IRAs. The tax on withdrawals from all your IRAs is computed by combining the accounts and weighing one against the other. The formula is as follows:

$$\frac{\text{Total Non-deductible Contributions to all IRAs}}{\text{Fair Market Value of all IRAs}} \times \text{Total Distributions for Year} = \text{Non-taxable Income}$$

Patrick has $50,000 in his deductible IRA and $10,000 in a non-deductible IRA. The total contributions to his non-deductible IRA was $8,000. At his age 59-1/2, he withdraws all $10,000 from the non-deductible IRA expecting only a small amount of interest to be taxable. Here is the result:

$$\frac{\$8{,}000}{\$60{,}000} = 13.33\% \times \$10{,}000 = \$1{,}333$$

Only $1,333 is returned of his non-taxable contribution. The remainder of the withdrawal must be reported as fully taxable income to the IRS. This is a tax trap for those who have not fully explored these rules. The major reason to avoid a non-deductible IRA is the disproportionate tax on withdrawals. To make matters worse, when the time arrives to withdraw, the government will expect you to keep records documenting withdrawals from each account. If Patrick withdrew pre 59-1/2, he would only incur a 10% penalty on the pre-tax IRA dollars. The after-tax IRA withdrawal is exempt from both penalty and tax. The one certainty on which we can count will be future changes. Congress seems to be forever tinkering with the existing rules.

Under 59-1/2 Penalty-Free IRA Withdrawals

It is true. There is an escape hatch to the 10% penalty on withdrawals taken under age 59-1/2. The following information illustrates an attractive alternative to avoid the 10% penalty:

MILKING THE SACRED PENSION COW BEFORE AGE 59-1/2

by Kathleen L. Cotton.

"Are you an early retiree with pension receipts which must be rolled into an IRA to avoid taxes and penalties? Or a divorcee who has received a large pension distribution and rolled it into an IRA to avoid immediate taxation? Maybe you're neither of those two, but an investor who has IRAs and wants to create an additional income stream.

"Assuming that you are under 59-1/2, how do you withdraw these pre-tax dollars without a penalty imposed by Uncle Sam? The answer is Substantially Equal Periodic Payments (SEPPs) with-drawn according to some rather complex criteria, but sanctioned by the IRS. If you play by the rules, there won't be a 10% penalty regardless of your age. Nor is there a requirement that you be retired in order to access IRA funds. This makes the SEPP exception the most flexible method to access funds prior to achieving 59-1/2.

"Other requirements of the SEPP exception are quite rigid. You must maintain a 'qualified' withdrawal program for at least 5 years and until you are 59-1/2. That means if you started with-drawing at 57, you will continue withdrawing using the same method until you are 62 unless you wish the IRS to knock on your door to collect retroactive penalties.

"There are three methods that have been blessed by the IRS. The first the minimum distribution method where the account balance is divided by life expectancy. One can choose to recalculate life expectancy based on IRS Tables V or VI. The second method is to amortize the account balance using interest rates and life expectancy factors. This works much like a mortgage in reverse and, conceptually, the account would be consumed by the end of life expectancy.

"In actuality, the IRS has not rejected interest rate withdrawal assumptions as low as 5% or as high as 120% of the applicable long term federal rate regardless of the earnings of the account. The last approved method uses annuity factors and is not illustrated below. It is similar to the amortization method when the withdrawal rate is the same as the earnings rate.

"These concepts are easier to understand when actually calculated. In the following example, three 54 year old individuals with $300,000 IRAs earning at 8% have decided to take advantage of this exception with the following results:

"Early Retiree, who needs the maximum withdrawal until he can collect Social Security, is going to use the amortization method, no recalculation of life expectancy, and the highest possible interest rate assumption to withdraw his funds. Thus Early decides to use 120% of the monthly long-term Applicable Federal Rate.

"Just Divorced is working, but not making enough money to maintain her standard of living. She has decided to withdraw her funds using a recalculated life expectancy and an interest rate assumption of 6%. Just is concerned that she might withdraw too much now and be short during her 65 plus years. Just also knows that if her salary increases and she doesn't need the money later, she can reinvest the distributions rather than consuming the funds.

"High Earner doesn't need additional income for his life-style; rather he needs it to help him purchase an investment in raw land as a real estate speculation. He's decided that a minimum distribution with recalculated life expectancies will be adequate or his needs.

"The following results then are achieved:

Year	Age	Early	Just	High
1	54	$29,305	$20,690	$10,169
2	55	$29,305	$20,690	$10,973
3	56	$29,305	$20,690	$11,840
4	57	$29,305	$20,690	$12,775
5	58	$29,305	$20,690	$13,783
6	59	$29,305	$20,690	$14,870
7	60	$29,305	$20,690	$15,976

"As illustrated, Early and Just elected to take level distributions while High chose minimum distributions. At their age 60, Early, Just, and High can all change their methods of taking distributions. They can then take as much or as little as desired until they reach age 70-1/2 where each will be required to withdraw at least the minimum distribution based on life expectancies. The smallest possible withdrawal can be achieved if life expectancy is recalculated yearly.

"If a spouse is younger, distributions will be further reduced by electing a joint life expectancy. For example, Early Retiree could use the joint life expectancy table and recalculate annually. Since his wife is 10 years younger, their distribution would be reduced to 28,901."

Source: **Puget Sound Business Journal,** *November 12, 1990*

The Rest of the IRA Story

IRA rules and regulations continue to confuse people. Retirees wonder if they can have multiple IRA accounts or contribute after they are no longer working. Transfers and rollovers are not understood. And so it goes.

- How do I put an assortment of assets in my IRA? When you have a self-directed retirement account, you make the choice on what investment to put inside the IRA. Within just one account, you can have several different assets contributing to your IRA's growth potential. An example would be an IRA account worth $20,000 of which $3,000 is an income producing real estate investment trust (REIT), $9,000 is in stock mutual funds, $5,000 is in a government bond mutual fund, and $3,000 is in a certificate of deposit.
- What is a self-directed IRA? The self-directed IRA is a stand-alone trust which is not affiliated with any particular investment. You pay one fee and receive quarterly reporting on all of your IRA accounts. It enables you to achieve diversification in your IRA by selecting investments from a variety of suppliers. Other choices are to go to different institutions and investment firms and set up multiple accounts, each of which would assess a service fee of from $10.00 to $30.00.
- How much can I contribute? The law allows you to contribute up to 100% of the first $2,000 of your compensation each year.
- My spouse is not employed; can he/she participate? Spousal IRAs are allowed for the purpose of placing a maximum of $2,250 into two accounts. It can be divided any way you wish provided you do not place more than $2,000 in either account. A spouse can earn up to $250 and still be able to participate in a spousal IRA of up to $1,125.
- What type of investments can I use in my IRA? Just about anything except stamps, art, municipal bonds, and life insurance contracts. This includes stocks, bonds, mutual fund shares, real estate investment trusts, limited partnerships, annuities, gold Eagle coins, and promissory notes.
- Can I put some existing stock I hold in my IRA? No. Tax law stipulates that only cash contributions can be placed in a contributory IRA. The IRA is just an empty box until funded with an investment which is purchased with cash.
- May I make IRA contributions of investment income? No, only earned income from employment. But the IRS does not concern itself over which pocket you take the IRA deposit from as long as earnings requirements are met during the year.
- Do I have to make a contribution each year? IRA contributions are entirely voluntary, so the answer is no. But, in future years, you can't make up for contributions you did not make when you were eligible.

- What if my IRA contribution comes out to more than the amount I can deduct? This can happen, particularly if you are having your contributions withheld from your paycheck by an employer, credit union, or investment company. Should you over contribute, remove the excess before the due date of your federal taxes. If you fail to do this, there will be a tax penalty until the situation is corrected.
- When can I start receiving benefits from my IRA? Normally, at age 59-1/2 or older. Distributions can start earlier if you become disabled, die, or withdraw under the Systematic Early Periodic Payment method described above.
- Can I contribute after I am 59-1/2? Yes, right up to the time you are 70-1/2 as long as you have earned income. At that time, you can no longer contribute and must start taking distributions.
- How will the benefits be distributed to me? You may elect to receive benefits in a lump sum or as periodic withdrawals spread over your life expectancy. The rules state that the longer you live, the longer you are expected to live. Potentially, your IRA money could last until you are a centenarian.
- How will the benefits be taxed? All withdrawals are taxed as ordinary income. No preferential treatment allowed. If you die, your beneficiaries will pay the tax on undistributed IRA dollars.
- How long will my beneficiaries have to withdraw my IRA? Generally speaking, beneficiaries have up to five years after December 31 of the full, post-death year. Using the same starting date, a beneficiary can also annuitize. Spouses have two other options: 1) wait to begin withdrawals until the year the deceased would have reached 70-1/2, or 2) roll your IRA into his or her own IRA.
- What is the difference between an IRA rollover and a transfer? These terms are used interchangeably, but they are different in their restrictions. A rollover is a once-a-year, per account activity. You can take each and every IRA you hold out of the IRA for a period not to exceed 60 days. A transfer is when one trustee requests the other trustee to send the IRA direct to them. You never touch the money. Each IRA account you own can be subjected to unlimited transfers every year.

EMPLOYER SPONSORED RETIREMENT PLANS

Major corporations and many small companies provide some type of retirement program for employees. These range from the popular 401(k) to the not as popular profit sharing plans. The degree of popularity of a plan with employees is directly related to how much control they can exercise over the funding choices and the predictability of annual contributions.

401(k) Plans

In a 401(k) plan, an indexed maximum contribution ceiling is imposed. Yearly, the ceiling is raised according to the consumer price index. In 1992, it was $8,728. Total contributions may be larger than this amount if the employer contributes a matching percentage. These programs are one of the best ways to invest for retirement since each dollar you contribute is a direct reduction from your gross income. The contribution escapes federal income taxation but not Social Security (FICA) taxes. Even so, it is a good idea to use a 401(k) program before worrying about an IRA, especially if you like the investment choices available. Most employer plans are structured as follows:

Fund #1	Fund #2	Fund #3	Fund #4
Common Stock of Employer	Equity-Inc. Stock Fund	Corporate Bond Fund	Guaranteed Income Choice

You can diversify your contribution over two to four choices in increments of 10%. If the employer contributes, they will usually put their contribution in company stock. It creates an ongoing market for their stock, and employees are comfortable holding stock of their employer. Be sure you have evaluated the choices carefully. One major disadvantage of investing in a 401(k) is the delay time in transferring money between accounts. You can't pick up the phone and instantaneously move money from one fund to another. It may take up to a month for a change to take place, making it impossible to time the market.

You may be able to borrow from your 401(k) plan. The interest is not deductible, but it is interest you pay back to your own account. The disadvantage when you borrow, of course, is that the money is removed from the investment. If that was the year your stock fund did 30%, you would have second thoughts about the advisability of this action. You may only borrow the lesser of $50,000 or 50% of the balance over $10,000, whichever is greater.

Upon your early retirement after age 55, 401(k) funds are available without the 10% tax penalty. If you are eligible for ten-year tax averaging (born before 1/1/36) you have a choice of tax averaging or rolling your 401(k) distributions into an IRA. Tax averaging is discussed further in the following chapter.

403(b) Plans

This plan is more commonly known as a Tax Sheltered Annuity (TSA) and is offered by non-profit organizations such as hospitals, school districts, and charities. The contribution ceiling is higher than for the 401(k) plan above: lesser of $9,500 or 16-2/3% of salary (adjusted for amount of the deferral). The contribution limit is fixed at $9,500 until the 401(k) indexed ceiling reaches $9,500. At that point, the TSA ceiling will be adjusted yearly to the CPI index.

The TSA has some favorable aspects not available in IRAs. The catch up provision is one of the most favorable. If you have been contributing at less than your full allowance, you can "catch up" prior to the end of a year. Funds accumulated up to 12/31/86 are not subject to minimum distribution rules at age 70. These dollars can stay in the account until approximately age 75. Tax sheltered annuities allow loans with a payback period of five years unless used to purchase a primary residence. Like the 401(k), retirees who separate from service after their age 55 can withdraw TSA funds without a 10% penalty. And, like IRAs, all income withdrawn from a TSA is taxed at full and ordinary federal income tax rates.

SEP and SARSEPS

Simplified Employee Pension Plans (SEPS) and their sidekick, the Salary Reduction SEP (SARSEP), are easy-to-administer retirement programs favored by smaller corporations. The SARSEP, a mini-401(k), allows employees to contribute on a before-tax basis. This program is limited to firms with 25 or less employees of which 50% must participate. The straight SEP plan is easier yet. A contribution is not required annually, but when one does take place, it must not discriminate if employees qualify. In other words, the employer contribution is the same percentage for all eligible employees. The contribution for both plans was limited to $8,728 for 1992 or 15% of compensation, whichever is lesser. This ceiling is adjusted annually for inflation. The combined employer/employee contributions cannot exceed the lesser of $30,000 or 25% of an individual's compensation.

Other Choices

The above represent prevalent retirement programs where the employee is in control of his or her contributions. Each of these programs can have a percent matching contribution made by the employer.

In addition, many corporations have pension plans targeted toward providing a defined benefit annuity at retirement age, profit sharing programs spreading the wealth of the company to its employees, employee stock ownership programs, stock discount programs, and stock options. It is difficult to envision resistance to this type of investment spending. Tax breaks, matching funds, discounts, free stocks and more, are the side benefits of good retirement programs.

WORKSHEET 18A

IRA INVENTORY
DEDUCTIBLE VS. NONDEDUCTIBLE

Contribution Year	IRA Description/ Location	Total Deposit	Deductible Amount

CHAPTER 19

KNOCKING ON RETIREMENT'S DOOR

"Money gives a man thirty more years of dignity."
Chinese Proverb

The long awaited goal, retirement, has materialized for John and Clara. Having arrived at the doorstep, they hope, of leisure living, John has started to have second thoughts. Both he and Clara wonder if they are really ready. Will retirement be good for them, or will their days stretch into long lonely hours?

There are various opinions voiced by those who study the greying of America. Some say retirement is not good for you; those who continue to work live longer. Boredom, inactivity, and sometimes even depression can surface when motivation is left behind in the workplace. Experts from Miami University's Scripps Gerontology Center in Ohio challenged that school of thought in the mid-80s, claiming there is no evidence to support it.

ARE YOU RETIREMENT COMPATIBLE?

If you, like John, wonder if you're emotionally ready for retirement, ask yourself the following questions. Delve deep into your psyche to find definitive answers that you can retire with:

- Did you prepare financially? I hope Chapters 17 and 18 were sufficient to motivate you to consider the benefits of early preparation. Now that you're here, plan on spending 70-80% of your pre-retirement income to maintain the same life-style. If your Social Security and other sources of income are not sufficient, you can consider part-time work.
- Are you sick and tired of your present job? Some retirees dislike their work so much that even retirement at a reduced standard of living holds more appeal. Examine your feelings to determine if leaving your job would be good for your mental health. You may shudder at the thought of disconnecting, but your ulcer may breathe a sigh of relief.
- What other activities excite you? Many retirees just can't wait to quit paid employment to take up their consuming passions. Golf, woodworking, travel, gardening, volunteering — activities that could only be dabbled in before can be enthusiastically embraced in retirement. Consider this area long and hard. Some say the golf course is only good, at the most, for several months.

- Is your health in good order? Sadly, we read every day about those that worked long and hard for 30-40 years, just to die shortly after retiring. Perhaps that is a compelling reason for you to plan for retirement as early as possible. On the other hand, it is not unusual for those in poor health to experience a reprieve once daily work routines have been shelved.
- Do you have the support of your significant other? Many a spouse has been driven crazy by his or her newly retired spouse. Did you marry for better or for worse, but not for lunch? I can't think of anything worse than having to entertain a bored husband or wife. Both parties must have a clear, mutually understood expectation of their new roles and an agreement that previous schedules will be respected or new ones negotiated.
- Have you been put on the corporate shelf? This is all too common as more and more corporations bring in young blood at lower salaries than those paid to the seasoned worker. Corporate reorganizations and mergers may result in some bloodletting — otherwise known as early retirement. Giving special assignments is another delicate way to diplomatically inch seasoned workers toward an early retirement offer. Before you throw in the towel, be sure it is the right move for your future.
- Is your life wrapped up in your career? Will you be able to adjust? Type "A" personalities often thrive on the strokes and achievements they chalk up in the workplace. If running a shipshape department, beating last year's sales campaign, or snaring that big sale puts the color in your cheeks, adrenaline in your blood, and sparkle in your eye, slow down and think. Overachievers of the world need to consider their retirement decision very carefully.
- Will retirement rust your job skills? If you have plans of future employment, part- or full-time, you need to stay up-to-date in your field of interest. When you peddle your expertise, remember the slogan, "Old age and treachery will overcome youth and skill." Don't be apologetic and self-demeaning if you find yourself back in the job market. Your skills, finely honed by irreplaceable experience; your wisdom, polished by time; and your level-headed maturity will speak for you.
- Will time plus ideas create new opportunities? This may be the time in your life that you can start the next Microsoft in your garage or basement. Ideas you never had time to fully develop while employed now beg for attention and may put money in your pocket. Explore this area carefully, however. Overcommitment of precious retirement capital could also be dangerous to your wealth.

If you sailed through those questions with nary a care, get ready. You're closer to retirement than you may think. If your responses have been "Hmm, let me think about that...," it's time to explore the issue in depth with a retired friend or two, a retirement counselor, and perhaps an eligible retiree who has opted to continue working. If the majority of your answers were Nos, the jury's in and the decision is made. You are convicted as a workaholic and sentenced to continue doing what you enjoy.

Retirement can be one of the best times in your life. As one of my clients once said, "We're having as much fun this year as we had the first year we were married." A renewal, revitalization, whatever you may call it — retirement does not have to be retiring.

MONEY TALKS

As a financial advisor who works primarily with the over 50 crowd, I have been privileged to be a part of hundreds of retirement decisions. A few clients have been on the edge and backed away, others have inched their way to the edge very carefully, but most have sailed over the edge full speed ahead. The last group was already mentally adventuring in some far away place or tackling their favorite golf course even before financial considerations were fully discussed.

There are many financial questions most retirees need to answer before making a binding retirement decision. The most common are:

How long will the money last?
What level of after tax income will be adequate to maintain my life-style?
What types of major expenses can I anticipate during retirement?
How do I manage my cash flow?
Will I need to work part-time?
When should I draw Social Security?
Will Social Security income be taxed?

Determining Your Spending Speed

At this point, you have arrived at your destination. It is hoped, the years of dedicated investment spending have resulted in enough money to fund your extraordinary expenses plus provide income to help keep your standard of living one step ahead of inflation. The tricky part of managing retirement savings is deciding just how fast to utilize investment capital. To start the analysis, list your expected income sources on the 12-month Cash Flow, Worksheet 7B from Chapter 7.

Now, on the same form, tally up your expected expenditures for a complete year. Don't forget new expenses, such as medical insurance, estimated tax payments, increased travel; and those items which also will decrease, such as clothing, FICA, reduced insurance expenses, restaurant meals, gifts (more time to shop sales), charitable giving, etc. Personal spending needs will vary from individual to individual, depending on the goals aspired to during retirement years.

Is there an excess of income over expenses? Which months? If the answer is all, congratulations, you have planned well. If not, does the total monthly inflow divided by 12 equal your total monthly expenses divided by 12? Or do you have too much month and not enough money? Now is the time to take a macro look at your expected income need over your remaining lifespan to see if it will last as long as you do. You need to know whether underspending your income at the onset of retirement is necessary to put money aside for future cost-of-living increases, or if you can spend your entire pension, interest income, and Social Security from the start.

Cash Flow Tactics

Too much month and not enough money can be dealt with if you have an adequate accumulation of retirement investments. The ideas listed below are designed to simplify your inflow/outgo by utilizing tried and true cash flow techniques:

- Review Chapter 7 for this technique: Deposit your interest and dividend income in a money market fund with check writing privileges and write yourself a monthly expense check.
- Rather than reinvesting dividends and interest, have your bank, brokerage, or mutual fund company send them directly to you.
- If you are using one or more mutual funds from a family of funds, have all the dividends and interest sent to their money market fund. Request that a fixed amount be distributed automatically each month from the money market to you.
- Match your expenses against the expected interest and dividends generated from your investments. Try to tie mandatory expenses, such as property taxes, auto licenses, and insurance premiums, to predictable income streams such as semi-annual bond interest payments or quarterly stock dividends.

Look at the table below to calculate how long your investment money will last at various spending levels.

YEARS OF WITHDRAWAL AT SPECIFIC EARNING RATES

If Principal Is Earning	And You Are Withdrawing At This Rate										
At This Rate	16%	15%	14%	13%	12%	11%	10%	9%	8%	7%	6%
12%	12	14	17	23	—	—	—	# of Years Your		—	—
11	11	13	15	18	24	—	—	Money Will Last		—	—
10	10	12	13	15	19	25	—	—	—	—	—
9	10	11	12	14	16	20	27	—	—	—	—
8	9	10	11	12	14	17	21	28	—	—	—
7	9	9	10	11	13	15	18	22	31	—	—
6	8	9	10	11	12	13	16	19	24	33	—
5	8	8	9	10	11	12	14	17	20	26	37

Source: Dow Jones Guide to Interest

This is a best estimate guide only. Years shown are approximate and assume constant earning and withdrawal rates. In reality, total returns on investment portfolios will vary from year to year.

The table is easy to use. The number of years money will last is listed across from the earnings under the specified percentage you want to withdraw. As an example, John and Clara have saved $200,000 on which they expect to earn 9% by investing in a mixture of stocks and bonds. If they withdraw 10% of the account value yearly, the money will run out 27 years later, at John's age 89. A withdrawal of 9% or less will never deplete their capital.

Perhaps, you will be one of the fortunate few who can delay using investment earnings for a period of time until inflation's toll on spending power forces you to increase your spendable income.

WHEN TO DRAW SOCIAL SECURITY

There are a number of viewpoints on this issue. My theory is that drawing as soon as possible makes the most financial sense. For instance, if you retire at age 62 and delay drawing your Social Security until your age 65, it will take you 12 years to break even. John had that choice and this is how he worked it out:

Age 62 Social Security $ 800 x 180 months (to age 77) = $144,000
Age 65 Social Security $1,000 x 144 months (to age 77) = $144,000

If he waits until he is 65 to draw Social Security, John will have said no to $28,800. Dividing $28,800 by the increase in his Social Security, $200, he calculates he will be 77 before he benefits from the increased income of having waited three years.

Theoretically, if John could afford to wait until age 65 to draw, then he could go ahead and draw $800/month at age 62, but invest that money each month until his age 65. Investment results of 7% (after taxes) on the invested money, would provide John with $31,944. At this point, a couple of income options could be explored:

1. He could withdraw a fixed monthly payment of $228. The money would last until his age 90 if the account earned 7%.
2. He could withdraw interest from the fund and preserve the capital base for an emergency fund or special expenditures.

Here is the percentage of your age 65 benefit you will draw if you start at the following ages:

Age	Percent Available
65	100.00%
64-1/2	96.66
64	93.33
63-1/2	90.00
63	86.66
62-1/2	83.33
62	80.00

SPOUSAL BENEFITS

Spouses have two options at their retirement: drawing Social Security on their own earnings record or drawing one-half of their spouse's Social Security, whichever is greater. This recognizes to some degree the unpaid efforts of non-working spouses, but still penalizes them for making the decision to work in the home and for the family rather than at a paying job. The unspoken message is that their activities in the home are less worthy than their employed spouse's.

Spousal Benefit at age 62: 37.5% of the age 65 benefit
Spousal Benefit at age 65: 50.0% of the age 65 benefit

For estimating purposes, it is close enough to assume a wife or husband, age 62, who is drawing against a spouse's benefit at his or her age 62, will receive 50% of that sum.

WHEN TO APPLY FOR SOCIAL SECURITY

In the year you are planning to retire, apply three months before your expected retirement date. In any case, be sure to have your application on file three months before your 65th birthday so your full Medicare coverage will start on time. You will need proof of age (public record of birth certificate or religious record of birth), and proof of marriage, if applicable.

RETIREMENT EARNINGS PENALTY

If part-time work is on your must do list, you will want to be aware of the effect your labor will have on your Social Security check. The maximum dollar amounts you may earn without losing part of your Social Security check is as follows:

Age	1992 Earnings Limitation[1]	Benefit Forfeit
62	$ 7,440	1 for 2
65	$10,200	1 for 3
70+	Unlimited	Zero

1. Earnings limitations are indexed yearly by the Consumer Price Index percent increase.

Clara has decided to work part-time for a few more years even though John is going to fully retire. She expects to make $800 a month or $9,600 annually. She will forfeit some of her Social Security per the following calculations:

Earnings	Limitation	Excess
$9,600	$7,440	$2,160

Her excess is now divided by 2 ($2,160/2) to calculate the amount of her reduced benefit. Her Social Security benefit is reduced by $1,080. For every $2.00 she earned above the limitation, she gave $1.00 back to the government. This would make Clara carefully consider the number of hours she really wants to work. As soon as she exceeds the earnings limitations, she is only earning 50% of her hourly wage. If Clara were 65, working and earning $1,000 a month, the formula would be altered.

Earnings	Limitation	Excess
$12,000	$10,200	$1,800

This excess, $1,800, is divided by 3 to calculate the amount of the Social Security reduction ($1,800/3 = $600). For every three dollars earned, Clara forfeits one. Her excess earnings are now valued at 66% of her hourly wage.

Some methods which work to help alleviate this problem are:

- Establish a consulting firm: Bill your clients every other year rather than yearly.
- Defer your compensation: Establish a contract with your employer which defers your compensation until a specific date in the future when you no longer expect to be working. Typically, an employer would deposit your earnings into a non-qualified deferred compensation plan which would start making payments to you after your termination.
- Incorporate your business as a C corporation: You can now leave earnings above the earnings limitation in the business and pay tax on those earnings at corporate tax rates (15% up to $50,000). Direct the corporation to invest the proceeds in stocks of other corporations' stocks and receive 80% of the dividends tax free inside the corporation. Perhaps it makes sense to borrow from the corporation. In that case, document the loan with a note and make principal plus interest payments to the business. Eventually, you would have to dissolve the corporation and recognize the gains for tax purposes.
- Incorporate as an S corporation. Take a salary from your S corporation up to the amount of the earnings limitation ceiling and have your corporation pay out dividends. Keep in mind that the IRS will scrutinize these types of arrangements very carefully. If it appears that the dividends are really compensation for services, they may be treated as earnings.

SOCIAL SECURITY TAX PITFALLS

Yes, it is true. You can retire and pay taxes on your Social Security benefits — the government's penalty for having spent your way to wealth so successfully. This tax trap is called the Modified Adjusted Gross Income (MAGI) test. The MAGI is a combination of all taxable income, municipal bond interest, work income and one-half of your Social Security. If that combined total exceeds a base amount, then one half the excess or one half of Social Security, whichever is less, is included on your federal 1040 income tax return as taxable income.

Taxable Interest		-$-
IRA Distributions		-$-
Pensions		-$-
Work Income		-$-
1/2 Social Security		-$-
Municipal Bond Interest		-$-
	Total	-$-
	Less	$32,000 if married
	or	$25,000 if single
	Excess	-$-

John and Clara may be part of the growing group of retirees who pay federal income taxes on some portion of their Social Security if they proceed with their present plans. The effect of Clara working and earning only up to the Social Security earnings limitation is shown below:

Pensions		$18,000
1/2 Social Security		7,200
Taxable Interest & Dividends		4,000
Municipal Bond Interest		3,000
Work Income		7,080
	Total	$39,280
	Less	$32,000
	Excess	$ 7,280

Since 1/2 the excess is less than 1/2 of the Social Security, they divide the excess, $7,280, by 2 and add another $3,640 to their real taxable income. Now there is a further disadvantage to Clara's working, not only are her earnings taxed but this activity costs them an extra $546 ($3,640 x 15% tax rate). Is there no relief?

This system also penalizes married couples. For example, two singles who live together have a combined threshold of $50,000 ($25,000 each). John and Clara don't intend to get a divorce to avoid this tax trap, but do wonder if the government is indirectly encouraging older Americans to stay single. Combine this penalty with the loss of one $125,000 residence profit exclusion, and many a widow or widower may consider the price of marriage too great.

Here are some methods which work to reduce the modified adjusted gross income total so that Clara can enjoy work without guilt:

- Exchange the municipal bond which pays interest for a zero coupon municipal bond.
- Review the sources of taxable income to see if one or more of the following investment ideas deferring growth or sheltering income will be practical:

  Series EE bonds
  Growth Stocks
  Tax Deferred Annuities
  Rents from Real Estate (assumes sheltered from taxes by depreciation)
- Continue to shelter before-tax retirement investments in IRAs or qualified plans.

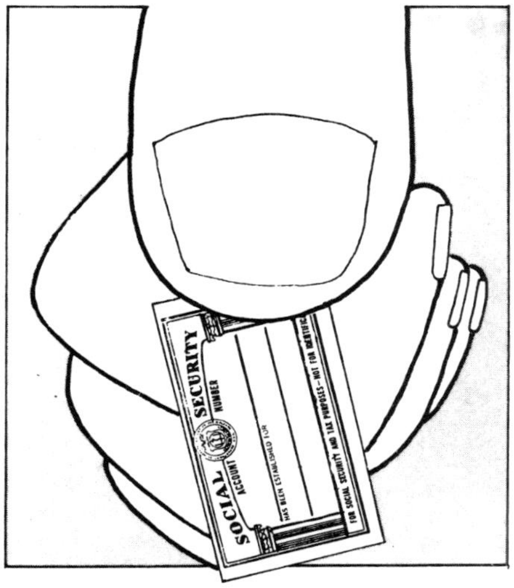

EITHER MY HANDS ARE GETTING LARGER . . . OR ?

RETIREMENT PLAN DISTRIBUTION CHOICES

Many retirees ponder their retirement program distribution choices by endlessly asking the following questions:

Should we take a lump sum pension distribution or opt for the lifetime income payment?

Which pension survivorship option should be selected?

Shall I self insure the survivorship benefit?

Should I leave my money with my ex-employer until forced to take it out (usually age 70-1/2)?

Is it better to roll over a distribution into an IRA or average the tax over 5 or 10 years?

These questions and more make the retirement event a very stressful transition period in anyone's life. Not only do individuals have to make decisions that will impact them financially the rest of their lives, these decisions often must be made within a matter of a few weeks. Recently, a major corporation in the Northwest extended an early retirement offer to certain employees. These employees had all of six weeks to make their decision — not enough time. The emotional impact of disconnecting from a steady paycheck can take the wind out of even the most stalwart.

A visit with a retirement specialist can be a very cost effective experience. This person should be able to analyze the net present after-tax value of a pension annuity and compare it to the after-tax lump sum distribution amount and then recommend which option is better, given your unique circumstances. Additionally, she or he can project your cash flow based on a lump sum averaged net pension versus an IRA rollover. Each of these issues must be examined in detail.

Pension Annuity or Lump Sum

Not everyone has a choice in the matter. Boeing employees, for example, do not. They must take their pension benefits in a series of paychecks in the mailbox rather than as a liquid pool of money. Other corporations give their employees a choice. Here are some of the advantages and disadvantages of both options:

	Advantages	Disadvantages
Pension Annuity:	Predictable Low investment risk	Disappears upon death or is discounted to purchase a survivor pension
Lump Sum:	Liquid Unlimited opportunities for growth	Investment return depends on economic conditions and investment skills

If you believe you can make more money investing than the annuity provides, then perhaps you should choose the lump sum. It has one redeeming feature which is not immediately apparent — estate value. If the retiree dies, the lump sum stays the same. If married and both die, the lump sum passes to other beneficiaries. This is the main difference between the lump sum and the pension annuity. It is impossible to pass any estate value of an annuity beyond your life or your spouse's, if married. In my ten years of consulting, I have witnessed less than five individuals who selected a pension annuity over a lump sum pension.

Pension Annuity Survivorship Option

This is another difficult decision area. For individuals who must take a pension annuity, federal law mandates that unless a joint pension with some provision for a surviving spouse is selected, the spouse must consent in writing to the decision. Those individuals with a dependent spouse who select a single life only pension risk losing that pension for the spouse in the case of their own death. This risk can be alleviated, however, through the purchase of beneficiary life insurance, the cost of which often compares favorably with the cost of survivorship pensions. The strategy of purchasing beneficiary life insurance is known by several names; Pension Maximization and Pension Enhancement are the most common.

John and Clara are faced with this decision. The costs for John to provide Clara a survivor pension through his company are shown below:

	Retiree	Spouse	Cost
Single Life	$1,500	-0-	-0-
Joint / 50%	$1,425	$ 702	$75/month
Joint / 75%	$1,350	$1,075	$150/month
Joint /100%	$1,275	$1,275	$225/month

It is not an easy choice to make. Someone has to be paid to provide Clara a level of security should John predecease her. To share a pension with a spouse, you can have a deduction taken from the pension as shown above. As long as John lives, the expense will continue. In ten years time, if John elects the Joint/100% survivor option for Clara, they will have spent $27,000, none of which can be recovered should Clara predecease John.

Here are the drawbacks to such a plan:

- If Clara predeceases John, the benefit for which they have paid disappears while, often, the cost continues.
- John has zero return on all the dollars paid for a benefit which is now gone. He had a limited term insurance policy — zero cash value and no opportunity to continue the policy after Clara's death.
- There is no remaining value to transfer to a contingent beneficiary such as John and Clara's child(ren).
- John and Clara can never pay up this policy or cancel it as long as John is alive.

There is a better choice. Rather than pay your company to provide the survivor income, develop an alternate plan. This strategy seeks to insure John's life for a lump sum amount adequate to replace the survivor pension in the event of John's death. John elects the single life pension and uses the $225/month increase in his pension to pay for enough life insurance to replace the survivor benefit. In this case, a $100,000 universal life policy could be adequate. There are a variety of benefits to this program:

- Benefits if John lives: The alternate plan could potentially cost less, be paid up earlier, provide a growing cash emergency fund which can be borrowed tax free, and have a premium that is not fixed.
- Benefits if John predeceases Clara: She can take the life insurance as a lump sum or an annuity, the insurance lump sum is received tax free, and the benefit can be left to subsequent heirs should Clara not need all of it.
- Benefits should Clara predecease John: He can stop paying for the protection and have a reduced life insurance face value to pass on to his heirs, or he can cash in the policy and potentially receive a cash refund of as much as, or more, than the cost of the protection.

Pension enhancement can only work if the retiree is healthy enough to pass an insurance physical. This program should be started a few years in advance of retirement to eliminate the later risk of disqualification due to poor health. Be careful that you only deal with a top rated insurance company. Remember, you are trading off one guaranteed benefit for another. Make sure the company is rock solid financially.

Lump Sums Baby-sitters

Many companies allow their retired employees to leave their before-tax savings money in the company until age 70-1/2. Retirees often take advantage of this provision because 1) they do not need extra income from this source at the onset of their retirement, 2) they are familiar with the investment choices, 3) there are no fees associated with the program, and 4) it allows them to delay making a decision regarding an IRA rollover or forward tax averaging until later. If the retiree should die while the money is still in the plan, beneficiaries retain the option to utilize five or ten year tax averaging on the lump sum. Spouses can also roll over these dollars into an IRA.

There are good reasons to take distribution of one's lump sum upon retirement. The most important is the lack of investment control over the funds when you choose to leave the funds inside your former employer's retirement plan. As explained in Chapter 19, 401(k) fund choices are usually limited to four areas: a company stock fund, managed equity fund, bond fund, and guaranteed insurance contract. These may be good investments, but they suffer from lack of diversity. Retirees can do better. You can utilize more than one equity manager, limit your participation in insurance contracts, consider government bonds, and have the ability to make immediate changes on your portfolio.

Lump Sum Forward Tax Averaging

This provision of the tax law allows a retiree to use a favorable tax calculation, one time only, on a qualifying lump sum distribution. Essentially, the tax is treated as if the money had been split into five or ten even portions and received over that number of years. This tax calculation is performed independent of your regular income tax and is payable in the year you average. To be eligible for tax averaging, you must meet the following requirements:

You are at least age 59-1/2 or born before January 1, 1936.
You participated in the plan for at least five years.
The distribution is received in its entirety.
All plans of one type are distributed at the same time.
Distributions of the plan(s) are paid within one calendar year.

There are two types of forward averaging allowed: 1) five-year, using current year single taxpayer rates, and 2) ten-year, based on the single taxpayer rates in effect in 1986. The eligibility regulations, however, are confusing. For instance, if you are eligible for ten-year averaging you can also five-year average. If not, five-year averaging is unavailable to you until after your age 59-1/2. To compute the appropriate tax on your qualified lump sum distribution, refer to the worksheets at the end of the chapter.

Ten-year averaging is on the way out. With the 1987 tax act, the ten-year forward averaging privilege was grandfathered and made available only to those born before 1936. In ten years, this provision will be just about phased out because all the grandfathered individuals will have reached age 65.

Following is the amount of tax due on lump sums which have been calculated with the ten-year method:

Lump Sum Distribution	Tax Using 10-YR Forward Averaging	1986 Effective Tax Rate
$ 25,000	$ 1,800	7.2%
$ 50,000	$ 5,870	11.8%
$100,000	$ 14,470	14.5%
$150,000	$ 24,570	16.4%
$200,000	$ 36,920	18.5%
$250,000	$ 50,770	20.3%
$300,000	$ 66,330	22.1%
$400,000	$102,600	25.6%
$473,000	$132,640	28.0%
$500,000	$143,680	28.7%

Because the five-year tax averaging calculation is based on current tax rates, it is not reproduced. Suffice it to say that those eligible for ten-year averaging will elect to use it until their lump sum is over $500,000 or so. It is difficult to get much more specific than that as the tax rates change from year to year. This is because 1) tax brackets are indexed to the Consumer Price Index and 2) Congress continues to tinker with the brackets, as evidenced recently by the top bracket increase to 31%. This surely won't be the last change. Tax averaging is on the chopping block and, at some point, may be entirely eradicated from tax law by the stroke of one White House pen — maybe even before the ink is dry in this chapter.

Should you tax average or roll over your pension to an IRA? For funds which exceed $100,000, consider an IRA rollover carefully. The power of continuing to earn interest on unpaid taxes is shown below:

Assumptions: $100,000
Age 62 Retiree
Marginal tax bracket 28%
Investment return 10%

	Distribution	Yearly Income After Tax
5-year averaged	$84,605	$6,091.56
Rolled over into IRA	$100,000	$7,200.00

The rollover is capable of producing 18% more yearly after-tax income than the tax averaged sum in the year of retirement. Another lesser known reason for rolling over is to eliminate a 15% penalty assessed on one-time distributions in excess of $750,000, indexed yearly by the CPI.

Lump Sum Rollover

Establishing an IRA rollover account to hold your pension distribution may be your best choice. This choice will allow you to delay all unpaid taxes on the rollover until after your age 59-1/2, when you can withdraw the money without a 10% penalty. You can even choose to let those unpaid taxes continue to earn interest until mandatory distributions are required at your age 70-1/2. Here are the basic rules:

- A sixty-day window from date of receipt is available to you before you must put the funds in a rollover IRA to avoid penalties and federal income taxes.
- Once a pension is rolled over to an IRA account, you forfeit the five- or ten-year averaging option unless you use the strategy explained in the next paragraph.
- A rollover account can be a separate account from contributory IRAs. If you use the account only to hold the rollover from your former employer's pension or your 401(k) plan, these funds can be rolled back later into a qualified pension plan with a couple of caveats: 1) you go back to work either as a self-employed individual or for a corporation, and 2) a pension plan is available which will accept transfers. The advantage to you is that the forward averaging privilege is restored.
- Taxes are delayed until money is withdrawn. You can start withdrawing voluntarily at age 59-1/2 and take as little or as much out of the account as you wish. At age 70-1/2 you must take out the minimum withdrawal of 1/16th. This is mandatory and calculated from life expectancy tables. Don't make a mistake here. If you fail to take out the minimum distribution, the IRS will pin a 50% penalty on the amount you should have drawn, but didn't.
- Qualified distributions can be placed into an IRA if you roll over a minimum of 50% of the pension balances. Distributions, total or partial, must be received in one tax year.
- You may have one self-directed or several IRA rollover accounts. It is generally more convenient to consolidate your rollover dollars into one account. Simplify your life. This point is particularly important as you get older.
- A qualified plan distribution is eligible for rollover treatment if it has been received for one of the following reasons: 1) you reached age 59-1/2, 2) you no longer are employed, 3) you are self-employed and became disabled, or 4) you are the

beneficiary of your spouse's retirement plan.

- You can roll over the earnings on after-tax contributions made to a retirement plan. You cannot, though, roll over any return of after-tax contributions. Just put it in your pocket; it's a tax-free return of money spent long ago to fund your retirement.
- This next provision is not widely known. You can take receipt of securities such as stocks, certificates of deposit, bonds, mutual funds — whatever your employer's portfolio was composed of — and place them in your rollover IRA. Be sure before you do this that your rollover IRA custodian will accept securities rather than cash. Most individuals find it more convenient to ignore this option and take cash. Simplicity has its virtues.

The advantages of an IRA rollover versus 5-year averaging or taxation all at once at full and ordinary rates is pictorially depicted below:

Assumptions:
1) $100,000 qualified distribution.
2) Under 59-1/2 distribution is taxed at 28% plus a 10% pre 59-1/2 penalty.
3) Over 59-1/2 withdrawal is 5-year forward averaged.
4) Future earnings taxed at 28%.
5) Distribution rolled intact into an IRA.
6) Investments average 9%, compounded monthly

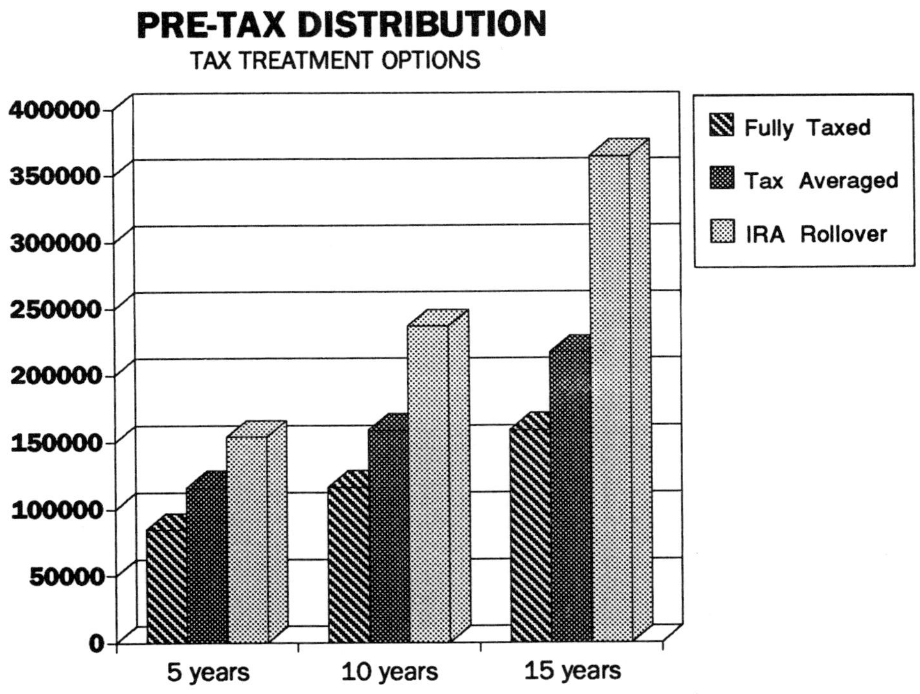

SELF-DIRECTED IRA

The self-directed IRA was discussed briefly in Chapter 18. Refer to page 210 if you need to refresh your memory. This is a good choice for those individuals retiring with lump sum distributions suitable for an IRA rollover. If you've read the investment chapters, you may have a good idea of which type of asset would make the most sense for your IRA(s). This IRA account is just an empty box until you or your financial advisor directs the trustee to purchase the investment of your choice. The benefits are consolidation of IRAs, low administration fees, quarterly account statements, automatic sweep of dividends and interest to money markets, and simplicity.

SELF-DIRECTED IRA

Savings Accounts
Money Market Funds
Certificates of Deposit
Bonds
Stocks
Mutual Funds
Unit Investment Trusts
Collateralized Mortgage Obligations
Fixed and Variable Annuities
Real Estate Investment Trusts
Limited Partnerships
Gold/Silver

SLEEP MORE SECURELY

A thorough analysis of your retirement pension options, investment strategies, and anticipated expenses is highly recommended. Disconnecting from the working world does not need to stack financial stress on top of the unavoidable physical and social stress of separation from familiar routines. If you can start your retirement journey with a feeling of financial security, you will sleep more securely.

WORKSHEET 19A

10-YEAR LUMP SUM TAX AVERAGING CALCULATIONS

1. Total amount of plan ____________

2. Subtract your after-tax contributions ____________

3. Taxable Income ____________
   (If this line is $70,000 or more, skip lines 4 and 5 and enter this amount on line 6)

4. Minimum Distribution Allowance
   A. Divide line 3 by 2 but do not enter more than $10,000 ________
   B. Subtract $20,000 from line 3 Enter result. If line 3 is $20,000 or less, enter zero ________
   C. Multiply line 4.B. by 20% ________

5. Minimum Distribution Allowance
   (Subtract line 4.C. from line 4.A) ____________

6. Net Taxable Income (Subtract line 5 from line 3) ____________

7. Divide line 6 by 10, enter result ____________

8. Add the Single Tax Payer Zero Bracket Amount for 1986 ($2,480) to line 7 ____________

9. Calculate tax on line 8 sum from Worksheet 19B, 1986 Single Tax Table ____________

10. Multiply line 9 by 10. This is your total 10-year averaging tax to be paid in tax year of receipt ____________

WORKSHEET 19B

1986 SINGLE TAX RATE SCHEDULE FOR USE IN 10 YEAR AVERAGING CALCULATION

	TAXABLE INCOME (Line 8 from Worksheet 19A)					TAX COMPUTATIONS (Due in year of receipt)	
	"A" Over	But	"B" Less Than	"C" Flat Tax	OR	On Income Over "A" & Under "B"	Plus Flat Tax "C" On Line
1.	$ -0-		$ 2,480	$ 0.00	0%	$ -0-	
2.	2,480		3,670	130.90	11%	2,480	1
3.	3,670		4,750	260.50	12%	3,670	2
4.	4,750		7,010	576.90	14%	4,750	3
5.	7,010		9,170	900.90	15%	7,010	4
6.	9,170		11,650	1,297.70	16%	9,170	5
7.	11,650		13,920	1,706.30	18%	11,650	6
8.	13,920		16,190	2,160.30	20%	13,920	7
9.	16,190		19,640	2,953.30	23%	16,190	8
10.	19,640		25,360	4,411.00	26%	19,640	9
11.	25,360		31,080	6,157.00	30%	25,360	10
12.	31,080		36,800	8,101.00	34%	31,080	11
13.	36,800		44,780	11,134.20	38%	36,800	12
14.	44,780		59,670	17,388.00	42%	44,780	13
15.	59,670		88,270	31,116.00	48%	59,670	14
16.	Over		88,270	PAY	50%	88,270	15

WORKSHEET 19C

5-YEAR LUMP SUM TAX AVERAGING CALCULATIONS

1. Total amount of plan ____________

2. Subtract your after-tax contributions ____________

3. Taxable Income ____________
   (If this line is $70,000 or more, skip lines 4 and 5 and enter this amount on line 6)

4. Minimum Distribution Allowance
   A. Divide line 3 by 2 but do not enter more than $10,000 ________
   B. Subtract $20,000 from line 3 Enter result. If line 3 is $20,000 or less, enter zero ________
   C. Multiply line 4.B. by 20% ________

5. Minimum Distribution Allowance (Subtract line 4.C. from line 4.A) ____________

6. Net Taxable Income (subtract line 5 from line 3) ____________

7. Divide line 6 by 5, enter result ____________

8. Calculate tax on line 7 sum from current year's single tax payer rates[1] ____________

9. Multiply line 8 by 5. This is your total 5-year averaging tax to be paid in tax year of receipt ____________

---

1. Due to yearly cost of living increases, changing tax laws and the resultant tax rate changes, a tax schedule is not included. To use this table, use the applicable year's single tax rate schedule when completing this worksheet.

CHAPTER 20

LIFETIME FINANCIAL STAGES

"Now is no time to think of what you do not have, think of what you can do with what there is."

Ernest Hemingway

Someone once said, "Dream your dreams, then blueprint your dreams, and finally, contract with yourself to construct them stone by stone."

Everyone has financial dreams which are uniquely different, and it is difficult to predict whether or not they will be realized. You will have a much better chance of achieving your dreams if you follow the pertinent advice sprinkled throughout this book. The degree to which you will embrace any particular strategy depends on your life stage, income resources, knowledge level, and goals. To round out your understanding of this process, this chapter highlights financial tasks which are specific to different life stages.

The older one gets, the easier it is to say, "I remember when I was ___ (you fill in the number); I wish I had known then what I know now." The best way to avoid making this statement is to understand the transitions most people go through in each decade of life. This will aid you in identifying financial tasks that fit within each decade. Then if you get started on your financial tasks early, you won't have to say, "I wish I had..."

While not everyone will fit so neatly in the predictable life stage boxes described, the majority will. The one group you won't see is single heads of households. Singles with dependent resident children are a growing segment of our population base, but most of the tasks relegated to married couples with minor children apply.

Don't forget that goals come first, financial tasks next. "Live in each season as it passes," said Henry David Thoreau. "Breathe the air, drink the drink, taste the fruit, and resign yourself to the influences of each."

STAGE ONE
SINGLE AND WORKING (S&W)

This period of life, the early 20s and 30s, is a time when young people think they'll live forever. It is a great time to start implementing financial actions that will pave the way for a secure future.

With little responsibility and job mobility, the S&W group may be unwilling to make long-term commitments, but they are more likely than other age groups to consider riskier investments.

These youngsters may not identify with the traditional view of financial planning. Without some prodding, they may to fail to spend sufficient capital for an emergency fund and it is difficult to motivate these S&Ws to spend money for goals 20 to 40 years away. Time will be their ally if they harness the power of compound interest early enough.

Tasks	Action Steps
Set goals.	Dream a little. Think forward to when you will be in another life stage. What kind of achievements and financial goals will you have achieved? Develop a plan for where you want to be in 5, 10, or 30 years.
Evaluate your spending.	Plan to create a cash emergency fund reserve at least 3 to 6 times as large as your monthly expenses. This fund is not to be touched but held intact as a rainy day backup.
Establish credit.	Apply for a department store, gas/oil card or collateral loan at a bank. Don't carry a balance, but use the cards or loan to establish your credit. Safeguard your credit. Bad credit can deter many future plans.
Evaluate insurance needs.	Cover your risks! Disability insurance, auto needs, home owners or renters insurance, and maximum liability are starters. This is a good time to spend in this area if you have any concerns about insurability later.
Determine whether to buy a home.	Not everyone is suited or in a high enough tax bracket to make home ownership a good economic decision. Evaluate carefully.
Begin systematic spending on investments.	Slice off 10% of your net income or one-half of your discretionary income, whichever is greater, and divide it between a liquid investment account and long-term retirement program. Have a financial advisor validate your retirement goals.
Plan for disposition of your estate.	However little you feel you have accumulated, you do have an estate. Secure a will and durable power of attorney now.

STAGE TWO
DOUBLE INCOME — NO CHILDREN (DINC)

Most, but not all, married couples who put off having children also benefit from two salaries coming into the household. During this stage many couples will indulge heavily in consumer spending, purchasing homes, furniture, vehicles, and luxury items. High spending prompted by peer pressure takes its toll as dollars which could have been investment-oriented make their way into toys for today's joys.

The stimulation of this way of life may overshadow the motivation to start a financial planning foundation for future security.

For the spender, managing expenses may be an appropriate first step in the financial planning process. Financing a life-style by full use of both incomes also creates a need for life insurance consideration. Personalizing the power of compound interest as it relates to retirement goals will serve to motivate DINCs to start investing now.

Tasks	Action Steps
Same as for prior stage PLUS	
Update insurances.	Increase liability coverages; inventory your assets to make sure your home insurance coverages are adequate. Once both incomes are necessary to maintain a life-style, life insurance and disability should be carried on both parties. It's also necessary if the family is primarily reliant on the income of just one spouse.
Purchase a residence.	If one of the DINCs didn't come into the marriage with a home, now is the time to seriously consider the tax benefits of owning versus renting.
Safeguard income and assets from unnecessary taxes.	Consider tax-deferred retirement accounts, tax-deferred annuities, tax-free municipal bonds, growth stocks, and investment real estate. All of these have some form of a tax benefit.
Create new estate documents.	Now that you're married, you each need a will treating the assets you have brought to the marriage or accumulated since. Revise your durable power of attorney to name your spouse in case of your mental or physical incapacity. These can be drawn up at the same time as your wills.

STAGE THREE
MARRIED WITH MINOR DEPENDENTS (MWMD)

This stage can feel like it goes on forever. Those darling little babies conceived in love have turned into endless garbage disposals, and you wonder if you'll ever have two nickels to rub together again.

If you were a DINC before, your new role as MWMD may force your family to rely on just one income while children are raised. Living costs continue to increase and, at the same time, retirement and children's educational needs become primary goals. Life insurance is more important than ever to protect your dependents' futures. Wills need to be revised to include trusts and guardians for minor children. Controlling cash outgo continues to be important if multiple goals are to be addressed.

<u>Tasks</u>	<u>Action Steps</u>
Same as for prior stage PLUS	
Adjust insurances again.	Consider adding an excess liability policy to cover your growing net worth. Make sure your medical insurance is adequate to care for at least 18 years of runny noses and midnight emergencies. Life insurance coverages may need to be increased to cover the contingency of educational funding.
Increase spending on children's educational needs.	Consider gifting money to children for education. Evaluate tax-free bonds, Series EE bonds, mutual funds, or certificates of deposit as funding choices (see Chapter 16).
Continue retirement investment purchases.	Contribute your share to employer profit-sharing/pension plans, 401(k)s, and IRAs. Don't earmark dollars for retirement without first analyzing the approximate amount necessary to reach retirement goals.
Accumulate assets.	If there's any money left after retirement and education, take full advantage of other investment opportunities. Consult with a financial advisor to determine appropriate asset categories which reflect your defensive, conservative, moderate, or aggressive investment posture.
Update wills and estate plans.	Revise your wills once more to reflect provisions to take care of your children in the event of your early demise. Establish in your wills a testamentary trust for your children as well as a guardian. By now you should be best friends with your attorney.

STAGE FOUR
PRIME TIMER (PT)

This fourth stage of life, after the children have flown the coop, dumps busy parents into an empty nest. This is a major life transition which may include physical and emotional changes along with peak career demands.

The PT stage can range from 15 to 20 years, depending on how old you are when the last child leaves. This is one of the most powerful stages in which to squirrel away sufficient investment resources for the day when retirement is knocking on your door.

As in all previous stages, asset management is important. For a PT, risk aversion becomes more important; conservative growth and tax-sheltered income may seem desirable investment characteristics.

Tasks	Action Steps
Same as for prior stage PLUS	
Management of insurance coverages.	Life insurance may still be appropriate, as well as complete medical coverage, replace ment value on auto and home coverages, and an umbrella liability policy. Remember, insure the big risks but pay for the runny noses. Now is the time to review your assorted insurances to identify their appropriateness.
Increase investing.	Capital accumulation becomes paramount for retirement. Your eye should be on the countdown to retirement. Consulting with a financial advisor who can read your pulse is an option you may wish to employ. When retirement arrives, you want to welcome it with open arms.
Revise wills.	With the children grown, wills can be revised. This is a good time to make sure you are using all available strategies to avoid any potential estate taxation at the first or second death.
Avoid taxes.	As in all other stages, tax avoidance is important. This stage may find your taxes higher than earlier as the dependent count has dropped, incomes are greater, and perhaps the home mortgage is yielding little shelter. Tax-advantaged investments, before-tax spending into retirement programs, and prudent use of residential mortgage interest deductions may be your best bets.
Major family decisions	This is often the time in one's life that the itch to change careers arises. Serious consideration of the pros and cons of such an event can help place in perspective the consequences of such an economic move.

STAGE FIVE
FREE AND INDEPENDENTLY RETIRED (FAIR)

This stage of life can be one of the most rewarding stages. Dreams of activities for which you never had time can come to fruition as a lifetime of working and earning pays off. Successful retirement for most means continuing a life-style similar to that enjoyed during pre-retirement.

Cutting the strings between yourself and your employer can cause mild trauma as empty days must be organized to create fulfilling activities, whether it be expansion of a hobby or the start of another career.

Most FAIRs consider conservative investments and safeguarding their principal a first priority. While receiving monthly income is important, it is also important to understand how fast original capital can be used without running the risk of outliving the assets.

Now is a good time to once again review your estate planning concerns, such as planning for or avoiding probate, making provisions to avoid or reduce estate tax, and checking your beneficiary list twice. Start sorting out and organizing your financial affairs so you can ease the burden of settling your estate for family members.

Tasks	Action Steps
Same as for prior stage PLUS	
Modify insurances.	A Medicare supplement policy will be necessary at age 65. In addition, this is the time to decide whether or not to continue carrying life insurance(s). Spending now on a nursing home policy is your best protection against financial bankruptcy later.
Document monthly income sources.	Listing monthly income sources can help alleviate fears about your future ability to spend. A financial planner can calculate cash flow needs over your lifespan and set up a strategy to help you live within your means.
Allocate assets.	Assets may need to be repositioned to a more defensive posture. Yet some portion of your portfolio should be invested in growth assets to hedge inflation.
Modify estate planning.	Life is getting shorter and immortality is no longer an issue. As some of your peers die prematurely, the issue of your demise becomes more of a reality. See your attorney for, perhaps, the last go-round of modifications in your estate documents.
Financially organize.	If you haven't been good at this, bone up. Document your investment accounts, the location of important papers, who your professional advisors are, sources of income, etc., and leave your survivors a legacy of love.

SUCCESS STORIES

Having been in the financial advisory business over a decade now, I have seen a variety of successes (individuals who mirrored the life stage definitions above). In whatever stage, they took financial planning opportunities seriously.

Here are a few of those success stories:

Single and Working

Mary came to me as a S&W professional. Out of college only a few years, she was dedicated to her emerging career but concerned about her financial needs. As we plotted her course to financial independence, the first item on the agenda was to direct spending to build an emergency fund. Next, we started IRA programs.

AS CONDITIONS CHANGE YOU HAVE TO MAKE ADJUSTMENTS

I see Mary a couple of times a year in order to re-evaluate her investment positions, check on her progress toward retirement goals, and discuss changes in her life. Last year she informed me she was getting married and her financial plans would change. She wanted to discuss the benefits of purchasing a home and the challenge of getting a down payment together for that pending purchase.

Mary has been thorough in her dedication to financial fitness. She's lucky her employer offers the opportunity to purchase disability insurance and provides medical coverage free. She is now eligible for a tax-sheltered annuity at work where the employer will match part of her contributions.

This S&W has started the lifetime pursuit of creating a present and future life-style of her own design. She's taken control and is confident of her success.

Double Income — No Children

Here's a delightful example. Roger and Pat are DINCs in their early 30s who have chosen not to have children. Instead, they continue to pursue their careers and other rewarding activities.

What's unique about them is their incredible conscientiousness in making sure they are doing enough to meet their retirement goals. They're lucky their employers will provide a nice pension for each of them. Since their retirement pensions require them to take a monthly annuity payment for life, they have chosen to provide a survivor benefit to each other. This will be accomplished through the use of life insurance and the employers' 50% survivor option.

Besides protecting their pensions, owning life insurance will also minimize the impact on their somewhat extravagant life-style should one of them die.

Roger and Pat have taken the Financial Wellness Quiz presented in Chapter 4 and can answer the 10 questions with positive answers.

Married with Minor Children

Mark and Marilyn have in their family Sam, Troy, Melanie, and John. They hope that will be all. This MWMD family has many concerns, with paying for the children's college educations at the top of the list. Since they are all in elementary school or younger, Mark and Marilyn have time to gain control of the problem.

When they came to see me, their main concern was to make sure their children's custodial accounts were not going to generate income which would be taxable at their marginal bracket rather than the children's tax bracket. Their second concern was to find out how much more they needed to spend for college funding so the children would have 75% of their educational costs paid.

With this goal taken care of, Mark and Marilyn concentrated their efforts on positioning the rest of their investment assets for maximum growth potential. Mark was a fairly aggressive investor who wanted at least 70% of their investments in growth assets since retirement was about 25 years ahead of them.

Mark and Marilyn worked over a period of months to set up a monitored spending plan so their multiple goals could be met. To their surprise, with just a little adjustment, their pleasure priorities could also be met. Like many couples who have been busy with families, these MWMDs needed to revise their wills to update guardians and establish testamentary trusts for the benefit of the children.

Since Marilyn had ceased working at the birth of the second child, life insurance was of great concern. Mark increased his coverage through his employer with the intent of adding a permanent life insurance policy later. Although Marilyn was not earning money, she was certainly contributing economic value. Mark decided to carry a term policy on her to help pay for childcare expenses should she die during the years the children were young.

This couple has taken action on most of their financial priorities, and they are diligent in periodically undergoing a professional checkup to ensure they stay on track.

Prime Timer

I have numerous clients in this very important wealth-building stage. Most of them, like Tom and Dorothy, are resolved to be ready when retirement arrives.

Tom is a corporate employee who has access to a tax-deferred retirement program, discounted stock purchases, and other valuable employer-provided benefits. He has wisely maximized his use of these options for the last five years.

Dorothy runs their bed and breakfast inn, which besides providing a tax shelter, produces a steady cash flow. Though the cash flow is not enough for Tom to quit his job, it will certainly be a valuable income supplement when they move into the FAIR stage.

At least twice a year these clients need assurance that they are making progress. Tom and Dorothy have another ten years or so before Tom leaves the corporate system. Meanwhile, they've adopted a defensive investment strategy by repositioning some investments into fixed income areas.

Asset monitoring is vital to their peace of mind to assure a continued, steady compounding of their nest egg. I think they'll make their goal on time, but the word retirement may never be totally in their future.

Free and Independently Retired

Leisure living has finally arrived for Sam and Sally. Years of employment as a corporate executive and wise use of all available benefits has set this FAIR couple up in style. Imagine their surprise when I informed them that their after-tax retirement income could potentially provide more spendable income than was available during Sam's working years. What a pleasure to be the bearer of this piece of information.

Sam and Sally's main concern is making good investment decisions about the management of their pension assets. They have several choices: they can choose individual investments by themselves independent of professional advice; rely on a financial advisor for selection information and monitoring; or turn the assets over to a professional money manager. Since neither Sam nor Sally is interested in getting involved with the maintenance of their investment portfolio, they are leaning toward the second choice.

Regardless of what method they use to manage their assets, they've decided to keep 60% of their assets in conservative areas — such as bonds, tax-deferred annuities, certificates of deposit, and government securities. Another 40% will be positioned in assets — such as blue chip, utility, and quality international stocks. Conservative growth and conservation of capital is the goal.

Estate planning has once more become very important to Sam and Sally as their net worth now exceeds the $600,000 exclusion limit from Federal estate taxes allowed every individual. They wisely decided to get legal advice on how to establish a disclaimer testamentary trust to reduce or avoid estate taxes at the second death.

Sam and Sally have also established financial files to organize their important papers and information for the benefit of their survivors.

This couple is delighted to be able to continue their standard of living during retirement years. They are all set to chase the sun and play endless golf. With good health and wise financial management, Sam and Sally can look forward to an enviable future.

ARE YOU ON TRACK?

You are somewhere in those five stages — employee, business owner or retiree, male or female, single or married. Whatever your unique niche in the overall picture, the real question is "Are you on track?" The purpose of sharing these stories is to help you identify and examine your own potential for success. You can do it. By yourself, maybe. With professional guidance, probably. With dedication and determination, absolutely!

CHAPTER 21

DO YOU NEED A FINANCIAL ADVISOR?

"Money is like an arm or leg — use it or lose it."
Henry Ford

Now that you'e arrived at the last chapters, you may wonder whether or not you need professional financial advice. That depends a lot on you. Some will try financial planning on their own and succeed. More will try it, but procrastination will keep them from finishing. A few will try it and quit after deciding it is too complex. And the rest will wisely seek out a knowledgeable financial advisor.

FINANCIAL GURUS

There is no shortage of financial gurus. However, finding one that meet your needs in terms of satisfying your goals and objectives within the confines of your pocketbook may be a challenge. The first step in choosing an advisor is to sort through the alphabet soup of credentials attached to a plethora of advisors available. Here is a partial list of credentialed advisors:

1. Certified Financial Planner (CFP): This certification is awarded to individuals who have passed six half-day tests over a two-year period, satisfied a three-year experience requirement, and provided proof of an undergraduate degree and completion of a financial planning curriculum registered with the International Board of Standards and Practices of Certified Financial Planners (IBCFP). The experience requirement varies according to the degree of education achieved. For example, those planners not holding an undergraduate degree must have five years experience while planners with a masters degree in financial planning can be awarded the CFP designation with just one year of experience. Client references are also required.

   In 1991, for new registrants, the IBCFP implemented a single two-day exam equivalent to that now taken by CPA candidates. Fifteen hours yearly of continuing education is required for CFP registrants by the IBCFP. In addition, the IBCFP is in the process of establishing standards of practice for CFPs. CFPs may also belong to their professional organization, the Institute for Certified Financial Planners.

The CFP designation is the oldest financial planning credential and the one best known by consumers. Recently, the College for Financial Planning began offering an advanced studies program. This program allows the professional to choose an areas of speciality and complete studies leading eventually to a masters degree in financial planning. Consumers may call the IBCFP at 1-800-282-7526 and request a list of qualified planners in their area.

2. Chartered Financial Consultant (ChFC): This is a certification issued by the American College in Bryn Mawr, Pennsylvania. Most consultants carrying the initials ChFC have evolved from the insurance industry and generally still have practice specialities involving insurance. This course of study is comprehensive in nature, is usually accomplished over several years, consists of ten two-hour exams, and is held in high esteem by insurance professionals. The American College also issues a graduate degree in financial services.

3. Accredited Personal Financial Specialist (APFS): This designation, issued by the American Institute of Certified Public Accountants (AICPA), is awarded to CPAs who qualify as follows: Membership in good standing in the AICPA, a valid and unrevoked CPA certificate, successful completion of a one day examination, 750 plus hours of experience in personal financial planning activities in the three preceding years prior to application, six references, and a written statement of intent to comply with reaccrediation requirements. APFS practitioners are required to have 24 hours of continuing professional education annually, directly related to personal financial planning.

These are the major players who have been trained to perform detailed analysis of both personal and business finances. There are other individuals who hold certifications. Some of these certifications are issued as side benefits of memberships in organizations. Some other lesser known certifications are issued by educational institutions granting certificates for completion of specified studies in the field of financial planning. There are a number of colleges and universities with approved financial planning curriculums and subsequent degree programs.

Then there is the Registered Investment Advisor. This sounds impressive, but it is just a registration. Advisors who dispense investment advice must register with both the state and federal security and exchange offices, pay $150 to each, and fill out an enormous pile of paperwork. Upon approval, these advisors are required to disclose to clients detailed information about themselves, their mode of operation, methods of receiving compensation, and so forth. Make sure the advisor you choose does provide disclosure documents but, remember, these are no proof of knowledge or skill.

How do you know who to select? First, it is wise to inquire further about the extent of education required in order to attain a particular title before accepting the competency it implies. The real test for financial advisors is whether or not they are knowledgeable about comprehensive financial planning. If not, they can't be equated to professionals who are practicing financial planning. In other words, you may have a very good stockbroker, accountant, banker, attorney, or insurance representative, but you don't have a comprehensive financial advisor. You have what I call five-finger planning: each finger does something different from the others and not one knows what the other fingers are doing. You still lack a professional who can pull it all together and simplify your finances — an advisor with sufficient breadth of knowledge to help you integrate separate financial elements into a cohesive plan.

COMPENSATION SYSTEMS

Perhaps more confusing than which credential to place your faith in is the variety of ways financial advisors receive payment from their clients. There are three basic modes by which you can expect to pay your advisor:

1. Product commissions: Free financial plans and advice are profferred by advisors who make their living solely by either compensation from insurance companies or commissions from investment sales. If you choose this type of advisor, be sure he or she is eminently qualified and the products offered fit your objectives.
2. Fee based: This is a common way planners make their living — charging hourly fees. Commissions are another source of revenue for this advisor which may be on top of fees or offset against fees. Fee offset is becoming increasingly popular. The advisor who operates under this method charges a flat fee for investment and planning advice. If commissions are received, they are offset against a flat fee.

3. Fee only: This mode is becoming more and more popular. Certified Financial Planners, investment advisors, accountants and attorneys comprise the majority of planners operating in this fashion. Hourly fees range upwards from $100 per hour. Many of these individuals also charge a percent of assets for monitoring and managing investments.

You, the consumer, must sort out which method of compensation suits you best and choose accordingly. The important issues to focus on are what type of planning is needed and how you wish to pay. Remember, financial planning is not a sales approach for marketing products, nor is it an academic exercise with recommendations that never get put into practice. Financial planning is a combination of analysis and applications tailored to fit your needs and financial circumstances, which in turn provides you with sufficient motivation to make the necessary financial improvements.

TWENTY QUESTIONS FOR BETTER ADVICE

The following questions will help you choose an advisor who is trained in areas relating to your needs. While you may not use all the suggested questions, you will be well prepared for your initial interview.

1. How long have you been giving financial advice to clients and where did you attain your training for this field?
2. What specific types of advice do you most often disburse?
3. Do you perform comprehensive financial planning or piecemeal planning?
4. What type of planning documentation do you provide?
5. Do you have any special expertise?
6. How large is your practice and what type of client comprises the majority of your clientele?
7. Who is your ideal client?
8. How frequently do you communicate with your clients?
9. What are your favorite investments and what was the worst investment you recommended?
10. How do you get compensated for investment recommendations; if I become a client, how do I pay for investment advice and for planning advice?
11. Do you monitor your investment recommendations?
12. How large is your staff and who would run your practice if you could not?
13. How do you keep current on new strategies?
14. Do you consult with my other advisors?

15. Can you provide client referrals?
16. Who are some other professionals (accountants, attorneys, bankers, stockbrokers) with whom you have worked?
17. Are you a Registered Investment Advisor?
18. If so, may I have a copy of your disclosure documents?
19. What did you do before you became a financial advisor?
20. Do you belong to trade or professional organizations? If so, which ones?

A comprehensive financial advisor will sit at the hub of other advisors, coordinating, explaining, and tidying up all your loose financial ends. They should have at the very least a talking knowledge of each element of planning — taxation, estate, goal setting, retirement planning and benefit programs, cashflow planning, investment choices, debt management — and an in-depth knowledge of those areas in which they profess specialization. Choose your advisor well as they may have a significant impact on your ability to "spendsibly" accumulate wealth.

CHAPTER 22

THE LAST WORD

"Do it today; don't count on tomorrow."

Horace, 65 - 8 B.C.

Is this really the last word? No. If you have read this book from the front to the back, you have gained a global perspective on your finances. But, there is still a lot of information available you might find useful. Basic information such as how to determine which home loan offers the best deal or how to find the crash course in living frugally and enjoying it. More exotic fare would be understanding how to trade stock options or make use of charitable trusts. There is no shortage of publications or gurus to provide further input into your financial development.

My intent in writing this book was to raise all the significant personal financial issues which, if ignored, could have a detrimental impact on wealth or wealth accumulation. Issues such as harnessing spending power, making life-styles safer today, planning for major future expenses as college funding for children or early retirement for the motivated, and managing investments by design rather than luck.

I have suggested that you rethink the way you play the money game and promoted the idea of "spendsible" money management as the means to a growing net worth. Money is only spent in three areas — life-style, taxes, and investments (unless you give it away). "Spendsible" usages of money can lead to fattening your pocketbook rather than 1) the government or 2) shopkeepers. It is up to you.

Moving from where you are to where you want to be is usually not achieved overnight. It takes time. But, it can be speeded up by utilizing certain tools and preparing diligently just as in other activities of life. Think about the results, for instance, if you were to build a house without saws, hammers, measuring tapes, materials, **knowledge, a blueprint, labor, and desire**. It would be a haphazard, tedious, slow activity. What if you tried to develop a garden without hoes, rakes, shovels, seeds or plants, water, fertilizer, **knowledge, a diagram, labor, and desire**. Nothing would grow. Developing a successful career or business without **knowledge, a plan, labor, and desire** would be a miracle. Why should planning your finances be any different?

FINANCIAL TOOL KIT

Several years back, I heard a marketing and motivational consultant, Mr. Ralph Palmen share some tools to tune up motivation motors. As I listened to him, I realized that the concepts he was sharing were just as applicable to financial planning and investing as to other areas of achievement. Here are some of those tools for building your financial future:

- A mirror: Each morning after you awaken, take your mirror and stare eyeball to eyeball with the one person who can change your life — the only person responsible for achieving your desired life-style.
- Education: Knowledge is necessary — enough knowledge to know when you have a problem and to start seeking solutions. Maybe this book will be enough or maybe you will need further education in the form of self-study or classes.
- A blueprint: You must make a plan. Lay out a diagram. Draw a map. Regardless of how you describe determining where you are, where you want to go, and how to detour obstacles and stumbling blocks to select the right solutions, the process is the same. You must define what it is you want (define your future) and describe the actions required in order to accomplish your goals (diagram the construction of it). What does it take to get from where you are to where you want to be? Then, once your plan is set in motion, you must check your progress against your stated objectives on a periodic basis. Your plan is a dynamic tool which will be modified over time to match changing life circumstances or new objectives you form.
- Labor: Did you ever see a farmer carrying a red and white bandanna in his hip pocket? During the day as he worked in the fields, he may have stopped, looked back at what he had done and rubbed the bandanna over his forehead. Then it would be back to work. After a while, the process would be repeated. Was it the act of rubbing the bandanna over his forehead that got his mind in gear to get his work done? Of course not. It was the process of getting sweaty in the first place; of doing the work. It was the labor itself.
- Desire: You can accomplish anything you want in life if you have the right tools and a strong desire. It may mean giving up other activities, but it can be done. It reminds me of this saying, "When it comes to money, there are just three kinds of people: 1) those who make things happen, 2) those who watch things happen, and 3) those who wake up and say what happened."

With that, let me share one last story. A long time ago, there were three horsemen (or perhaps they were women) riding across a very arid plain (a'la Lawrence of Arabia). They were in a hurry to make it to the next oasis as dusk was approaching. As they rode, they heard a voice speak to them, "Halt and get off your horses." None of the three really believed they had heard a voice nor did they acknowledge it to the others. So they continued riding. Again, they heard the voice, "Stop your horses and dismount." This time they instantly looked at each other and knew they had really heard the voice. Obeying the command, they dismounted, stood there, and heard the voice speak for the third time. "Reach down, pick up some pebbles and put them in your pockets." This they did. Not hearing anything further, they mounted and rode off. And, then they heard the voice for a fourth time, "As a result of obeying my commend, tomorrow morning you will be both happy and sad." These riders did not know what to make of this event so they continued on, reached their camp, and bedded down for the night. In the morning, as they arose and pulled on their trousers, they thrust their hands in their pockets where they touched pebbles, now feeling round, smooth, and shiny. As they pulled out their hands and opened them, they saw diamonds, rubies and pearls. Now they remembered the voice which said, "...tomorrow morning you will be both happy and sad." And, they were. They were extremely happy they had picked up as many pebbles as they did and very sad that they did not scoop up more.

This is my last, not so subtle, message. I hope that five years from now, you'll be able to say, "I am glad I took advantage of all my financial options," and won't have to say, "I wish I had acted on more."

START NOW!

APPENDIX

TABLE I
COMPOUND SUM OF $1.00

EXAMPLE: You invest $100 in a savings account that pays 7% a year compounded annually. At the end of the tenth year you will have $196.70 in your account ($100 x 1.967).

Year	4%	5%	6%	7%	8%	9%	10%	11%	12%	13%	14%
1	1.040	1.050	1.060	1.070	1.080	1.090	1.100	1.110	1.120	1.130	1.140
2	1.082	1.103	1.124	1.145	1.166	1.188	1.210	1.232	1.254	1.277	1.300
3	1.125	1.158	1.191	1.225	1.260	1.295	1.331	1.368	1.405	1.443	1.482
4	1.170	1.216	1.262	1.311	1.360	1.412	1.464	1.518	1.574	1.630	1.689
5	1.217	1.276	1.338	1.403	1.469	1.539	1.611	1.685	1.762	1.842	1.925
6	1.265	1.340	1.419	1.501	1.587	1.677	1.772	1.870	1.974	2.082	2.195
7	1.316	1.407	1.504	1.606	1.714	1.828	1.949	2.076	2.211	2.353	2.502
8	1.369	1.477	1.594	1.718	1.851	1.993	2.144	2.305	2.476	2.658	2.853
9	1.423	1.551	1.689	1.838	1.999	2.172	2.358	2.558	2.773	3.004	3.252
10	1.480	1.629	1.791	1.967	2.159	2.367	2.594	2.839	3.106	3.395	3.707
11	1.539	1.710	1.898	2.105	2.332	2.580	2.853	3.152	3.479	3.836	4.226
12	1.601	1.796	2.012	2.252	2.518	2.813	3.138	3.498	3.896	4.335	4.818
13	1.665	1.886	2.133	2.410	2.720	3.066	3.452	3.883	4.363	4.898	5.492
14	1.732	1.980	2.261	2.579	2.937	3.342	3.797	4.310	4.887	5.535	6.261
15	1.801	2.079	2.397	2.759	3.172	3.642	4.177	4.785	5.474	6.254	7.138
16	1.873	2.183	2.540	2.952	3.426	3.970	4.595	5.311	6.130	7.067	8.137
17	1.948	2.292	2.693	3.159	3.700	4.328	5.054	5.895	6.866	7.986	9.276
18	2.206	2.407	2.854	3.380	3.996	4.717	5.560	6.544	7.690	9.024	10.575
19	2.107	2.527	3.026	3.617	4.316	5.142	6.116	7.263	8.613	10.197	12.056
20	2.191	2.653	3.207	3.870	4.661	5.604	6.727	8.062	9.646	11.523	13.743
25	2.666	3.386	4.292	5.427	6.848	8.623	10.835	13.585	17.000	21.231	26.462
30	3.243	4.322	5.743	7.612	10.063	13.268	17.449	22.892	29.960	39.116	50.950

TABLE II
COMPOUND SUM OF AN ANNUITY OF $1.00

EXAMPLE: You invest $2,000 a year in a retirement plan paying 9% a year compounded annually. At the end of the twentieth year, you will have spent your way to $102,320 ($2,000 x 51.60).

Year	4%	5%	6%	7%	8%	9%	10%	11%	12%	13%	14%
1	1.000	1.000	1.000	1.000	1.000	1.000	1.000	1.000	1.000	1.000	1.000
2	2.040	2.050	2.060	2.070	2.080	2.090	2.100	2.110	2.120	2.130	2.140
3	3.122	3.153	3.184	3.215	3.246	3.278	3.310	3.342	3.374	3.407	3.440
4	4.246	4.310	4.375	4.440	4.506	4.573	4.641	4.710	4.779	4.850	4.921
5	5.416	5.526	5.637	5.751	5.867	5.985	6.105	6.228	6.353	6.480	6.610
6	6.633	6.802	6.975	7.153	7.336	7.523	7.716	7.913	8.115	8.323	8.536
7	7.898	8.142	8.394	8.654	8.923	9.200	9.487	9.873	10.089	10.405	10.730
8	9.214	9.549	9.897	10.260	10.637	11.028	11.436	11.859	12.300	12.757	13.233
9	10.583	11.027	11.491	11.978	12.488	13.021	13.579	14.164	14.776	15.416	16.085
10	12.006	12.578	13.181	13.816	14.487	15.193	15.937	16.722	17.549	18.420	19.337
11	13.486	14.207	14.972	15.784	16.645	17.560	18.531	19.561	20.655	21.814	23.045
12	15.026	15.917	16.870	17.888	18.977	20.141	21.384	22.713	24.133	25.650	27.271
13	16.627	17.713	18.882	20.141	21.495	22.953	24.523	26.212	28.029	29.985	32.089
14	18.292	19.599	21.015	22.550	24.215	26.019	27.975	30.095	32.393	34.883	37.581
15	20.024	21.579	23.276	25.129	27.152	29.361	31.772	34.405	37.280	40.417	43.842
16	21.825	23.657	25.673	27.888	30.324	33.003	35.950	39.190	42.753	46.672	50.980
17	23.698	25.840	28.213	30.840	33.750	36.974	40.545	44.501	48.884	53.739	59.118
18	25.645	28.132	30.906	33.999	37.450	41.301	45.599	50.396	55.750	61.725	68.394
19	27.671	30.539	33.760	37.379	41.446	46.018	51.159	56.939	63.440	70.749	78.969
20	29.778	33.066	36.786	40.995	45.762	51.160	57.275	64.203	72.052	80.947	91.025
25	41.646	47.727	54.865	63.249	73.106	84.701	98.347	114.410	133.330	155.620	181.870
30	56.085	66.439	79.058	94.461	113.280	136.310	164.490	199.020	241.330	293.200	356.790

TABLE III
PRESENT VALUE OF AN ANNUITY OF $1.00

EXAMPLE: You receive a note that promises to pay you $500 a year for 7 years. How much is it worth today if a loan of similar risk pays a 12% a year rate compounded annually? The note is worth $2,282.00 ($500 x 4.564) today.

Year	2%	3%	4%	5%	6%	7%	8%	9%	10%	11%	12%
1	0.980	0.971	0.962	0.952	0.943	0.935	0.926	0.917	0.909	0.901	0.893
2	1.942	1.913	1.886	1.859	1.833	1.808	1.783	1.759	1.736	1.713	1.690
3	2.884	2.829	2.775	2.723	2.673	2.624	2.577	2.531	2.487	2.444	2.402
4	3.808	3.717	3.630	3.546	3.465	3.387	3.312	3.240	3.170	3.102	3.037
5	4.713	4.580	4.452	4.329	4.212	4.100	3.993	3.890	3.791	3.696	3.605
6	5.601	5.417	5.242	5.076	4.917	4.767	4.623	4.486	4.355	4.231	4.111
7	6.472	6.230	6.002	5.786	5.582	5.389	5.206	5.033	4.868	4.712	4.564
8	7.325	7.020	6.733	6.463	6.210	5.971	5.747	5.535	5.335	5.146	4.968
9	8.162	7.786	7.435	7.108	6.802	6.515	6.247	5.995	5.759	5.537	5.328
10	8.983	8.530	8.111	7.722	7.360	7.024	6.710	6.418	6.145	5.889	5.650
11	9.787	9.253	8.760	8.306	7.887	7.499	7.139	6.805	6.495	6.207	5.938
12	10.575	9.954	9.385	8.863	8.384	7.943	7.536	7.161	6.814	6.492	6.194
13	11.348	10.635	9.986	9.394	8.853	8.358	7.904	7.487	7.103	6.750	6.424
14	12.106	11.296	10.563	9.899	9.295	8.745	8.244	7.786	7.367	6.982	6.628
15	12.849	11.938	11.118	10.380	9.712	9.108	8.559	8.061	7.606	7.191	6.811
16	13.578	12.561	11.652	10.838	10.106	9.447	8.851	8.313	7.824	7.379	6.974
17	14.292	13.166	12.166	11.274	10.477	9.763	9.122	8.544	8.022	7.549	7.102
18	14.992	13.754	12.659	11.690	10.828	10.059	9.372	8.756	8.201	7.702	7.250
19	15.678	14.324	13.134	12.085	11.158	10.336	9.604	8.950	8.365	7.839	7.366
20	16.351	14.877	13.590	12.462	11.470	10.594	9.818	9.129	8.514	7.963	7.469
25	19.523	17.413	15.622	14.094	12.783	11.654	10.675	9.823	9.077	8.422	7.843
30	22.396	19.600	17.292	15.372	13.765	12.409	11.258	10.274	9.427	8.694	8.055

RESOURCE DIRECTORY

BOOKS

Practicing Financial Planning, Mittra, Sid. Prentice Hall, 1990

Personal Financial Fitness, Klosowski, Allen. Crisp Publications, 1987.

Personal Financial Planning, Hallman, G. Victor & Jerry S. Rosenbloom. McGraw-Hill Book Co., 1985

Sleep Tight Money: A Guide to Managing Your Money Safely and Achieving Financial Peace of Mind, Krause, Lawrence E. Simon and Schuster, 1987

William E. Donoghue's Lifetime Financial Planner, Donoghue, William E. Harper & Row, 1987

Asset Allocation: Balancing Financial Risk, Gibson, Roger. Dow Jones-Irwin, Inc., 1990

How to be a Successful Investor, Bailard, Biehl & Kaiser, Inc. Dow Jones-Irwin, Inc., 1989

How to Buy Stocks, Engel, Louis & Brendan Boyd. Bantam Books, 1982.

Dun & Bradstreet Guide to $Your Investments$, Dunman, Nancy. Harper & Row, updated annually.

Safe Investing: How to Make Money without Losing Your Shirt, Slatter, John. New York Institute of Finance, 1991

Dividends Don't Lie: Finding Value in Blue Chip Stocks, Weiss, Geraldine & Janet Lowe. Longman Financial Services Publishing, 1988

Value Investing Today, Brandes, Charles H. Dow Jones-Irwin, 1989

The Only Other Investment Guide You'll Ever Need, Tobias, Andrew. Simon and Schuster, 1987

The Mutual Fund Wealth Builder, Hirsch, Michael D. Harper Business, 1991

New Strategies for Mutual Fund Investing, Rugg, Donald D. Dow Jones-Irwin, 1988

The Dow-Jones-Irwin Guide to Retirement Planning, Vicker, Ray. Dow Jones-Irwin, 1986

Retiring in Style: The Keys to Prosperity, Harris, Lynda. KCI Communications, Inc., 1988

Retiring Right: Planning for Your Successful Retirement, Kaplan, Lawrence J. Avery Publishing Group, Inc., 1987

Finances After 50: Financial Planning for the Rest of Your Life, Shane, Dorlene V. and the United Seniors Health Cooperative. Harper & Row, 1989

How to Retire Young, Tauber, Edward M. Dow Jones-Irwin, 1989

Planning Your Estate: Wills, Probate, Trusts & Taxes, Clifford, Dennis. Nolo Press, updated annually

Estate Planning After the Reagan Tax Cut, Lippett, Peter E. Reston Publishing Company, Inc., 1982

American Couples: Money Work Sex, Blumstein, Philip Ph.D., and Pepper Schwartz, Ph.D. William Morrow & Co., 1983

How to Stop Fighting About Money & Make Some: A Couple's Guide to Financial Success, Berg, Adriane G. Newmarket Press, 1988

Stop Fighting About Money and Start Making it Work for You, Kyrsty, Kaycee W. and Kristianne Blake. Boston Books, 1989.

Couples & Money: Why Money Interferes With Love & What To Do About It, Felton-Collins, Victoria with Suzanne Blair Brown. Bantam Books, 1990

The Dollars and Sense of Divorce, Briles, Judith. Master Media Limited, 1988

Prospering Woman, Ross, Ruth Ph.D. Whatever Publishing, 1982

Lifegain: The Exciting Program that Will Change Your Health and Your Life, Allen, Robert, Ph.D., & Shirley Linde. Human Resources Institute, 1985

Widow, Caine, Lynn. Bantam Books, Inc.

Lifelines, Caine, Lynn. Doubleday & Company, Inc. Garden City, New York.

The Joy of Money, Nelson, Paula. Bantam Books, Inc.

You and Your Money: A Guide to Financial Self-Confidence for the Suddenly Single, Ungar, Alan B. Calabasas Press, 1989

Alone - Not Lonely: Independent Living for Women over Fifty, Seskin, Jane. An AARP book, Scott, Foresman & Co., 1985

Rich is Better: How Women Can Bridge the Gap Between Wanting and Having It All - Financially, Emotionally, Professionally, Warschaw, Tessa Albert. Doubleday & Company, 1985

The Women's Investment Handbook, Perkins, Gail and Judith Rhoades. New American Library, 1983.

Don't Miss Out: The Ambitious Student's Guide to Financial Aid, Octameron Press, P.O. Box 2748, Alexandria, VA 22301

PAMPHLETS AND NEWSLETTERS

The Kiplinger Washington Letter, 1729 H. Street N.W., Washington, D.C. 20006, weekly, $48 per year.

Free booklet, *Evaluating Investment Performance*, Neuberger & Berman, 605 Third Avenue, 2nd Floor, New York 10158.

Free from Charles Schwab: *Guide to Maximizing Your Retirement Plan Distribution, Retirement Planning, Selecting Investments for Safety and High Return, and Investing for Your Children's Future*, Charles Schwab, 101 Montgomery Street, San Francisco, CA 94104

What I Wish Someone Had Told Me About Retirement: The realities of retirement living as seen by 50 American men and women. 65 Mistakes to Avoid in Retirement: Personal accounts from retirees about the perils and pitfalls they encountered. Money and Your Successful Retirement: A guide to financial success in your retirement. Inexpensive booklets available from 50 Plus Pre-Retirement Services, 28 W. 23rd Street, New York, N.Y. 10010 (212-366-8850)

AAII Journal, American Association of Individual Investors, 625 N. Michigan Ave., Chicago, IL 60611, monthly $48 per year.

U.S. Department of Labor, Bureau of Labor Statistics, *Three Budgets for a Retired Couple.* Washington, D.C. Periodic.

Institute of Lifetime Learning, *Second Career Opportunities for Older Persons,* NRTA and AARP, 1909 K. Street N.W., Washington, D.C. 20049.

Retirement bibliography. SB-285 Federal Publication, Superintendent of Documents, U.S. Government Printing Office, Washington, D.C. 20402

Your Home, Your Choice: A workbook for Older People and their Families. AARP, 1909 K. St. N.W., Washington, D.C., 20049

Free copy of Consumer Information Catalogue, send postcard to Consumers Information Center, Pueblo, CO 81009

Free listing of booklets on aging, Publications, Administration on Aging, OHDS/HEW, Washington, D.C., 20201

AARP, *Modern Maturity,* $5.00 for bi-monthly magazine. Membership Processing Center. P.O. Box 199, Long Beach, CA 90801-9989

Consumers Guide to Long Term Care, Health Insurance Association of America, 1025 Connecticut N.W., Washington D.C. 20036-3998

Guide to Health Insurance for People with Medicare, Thinking about Retiring, Your Social Security, and A Woman's Guide to Social Security - all free from Social Security Offices.

Free from AARP, *The Right Place at the Right Time - A Guide to Long-Term Care Choices for the Elderly; A Handbook about Care in the Home,* 1090 K. Street, Washington, D.C. 200249

Home Equity News, sample sale/leaseback documents and several publications relating to home equity conversion, National Center for Home Equity Conversion, 110 E. Main St., Room 1010, Madison, WI 53703.

Worksheet: Auto Insurance Cost Comparison. Washington State Insurance Commissioners Office, P.O. Box 40255, Olympia, WA 98504-0255

U.S. Savings Bonds: Now Tax Free for Education, $.50 from Consumer Information Center, Dept. 474 W. Pueblo, CO 81009

Planning Now for College Costs: A Guide for Families, $3.00 from Early Planning, P.O. Box 2155, Washington D.C. 20013

Student's Guide to Scholarships and Loans, free booklet from The College Life Insurance Company of America, 3500 West DePaul Boulevard, P.O. Box 68899, Indianapolis, Indiana 46268 (800-624-9990)

INFORMATION BY TELEPHONE

Institute of Certified Financial Planners (800-238-7526), referrals

Individual Investor's Guide to Low Load Insurance Products, International Publishing Corp., Chicago (312-943-7534)

Veribanc, Inc., a bank rating service, (800-442-2657) $10 first report, $3 for each additional.

Directory of free tax publications, IRS Publications Office, (800-241-3860)

Request for Earnings and Benefit Estimate Statement, free from Social Security (800-234-5772)

Information on student loans, Student Loan Marketing Association, (800-831-5626)

Paying for College: A Step by Step College Planning Guide; Planning for Retirement (a kit designed to help you calculate retirement income needs), both free from T.R. Price Mutual Funds (800-638-5660)

Meeting College Costs, The College Board (408-288-6800)

INDEX